Elizabeth Cady Stanton

Elizabeth Cady Stanton

Volume 2

Edited by
THEODORE STANTON and
HARRIOT STANTON BLATCH

ARNO & THE NEW YORK TIMES
New York · 1969

ELIZABETH CADY STANTON

ELIZABETH CADY STANTON
Portrait by Anna E. Klumpke, 1889

ELIZABETH CADY STANTON

As Revealed in Her Letters
Diary *and* Reminiscences
Edited by Theodore Stanton
and Harriot Stanton Blatch

ILLUSTRATED FROM PHOTOGRAPHS

VOLUME TWO

I live . . . .
For the cause that lacks assistance,
For the wrong that needs resistance,
For the future in the distance
And the good that I can do.
LINNÆUS BANKS

HARPER & BROTHERS PUBLISHERS
NEW YORK AND LONDON

ELIZABETH CADY STANTON

Copyright, 1922, by Harper & Brothers
Printed in the United States of America
B-W

ILLUSTRATIONS

Volume II

LETTERS
1839–1850

ELIZABETH CADY STANTON

To Elizabeth Smith.

JOHNSTOWN, *June 4, 1839.*

MY DEAR COUSIN,—I learn from your letter that your philosophy has not yet enabled you to combat that hydra-headed monster, "the blues." But I prophesy that his overthrow is at hand. Have your weapons in order. I too will make mine ready, and when I visit Peterboro, which will be soon, by our united efforts we will compel him to depart from the breast of an unsophisticated country girl and seek companionship with the heartless deceiver, the gay coquette, the *roué*, the *blasé*. I felt relieved to hear that you had received the guitar and liked it so well. When I visit Peterboro, I will give you all the instructions I have received. I play very little—that is, not well. I have taken lessons only six weeks, and in New York I did not find much time to practice. However, I know about half a dozen songs and four waltzes.

To Elizabeth Smith.

JOHNSTOWN, *July 20, 1839.*

MY DEAR LIBBY,—I have determined to depart for Peterboro the first of August. This week I shall probably go to Schenectady to attend the Union College commencement. You need not fear, dear Lib, that I shall be lonely. You do not know me if you think that I am happy only in gay company. A ride on horseback, a long walk with you, or a race with Mag would give me more pleasure than a promenade in Broadway or a party of all the fashionables of that great city. I hear that others too are to spend August with you. We will have a happy time. But what will your mother say to so many wild ones? But here come the children,[1] and now for a regular romp with them.

From Henry B. Stanton.[2]

NEW YORK, *January 4, 1840.*

DEAR ELIZABETH,—Since I was thirteen years old I have been thrown entirely upon my own resources, especially as to money. I have never received a dollar's gratuitous aid from anyone, though it has been frequently pressed upon me. I always declined it, because I knew it would relax my perseverance and detract from my self-reliance, and because I was aware that if I would be a man, I must build on my own foundation with my own hands. Since I was thirteen, I have spent about eight years in study, and during this time defrayed all my expenses; have assisted two brothers in acquiring a liberal education; have expended something for a library, etc., and too much perhaps for mere gratification; have been rather liberal in

---

[1] Harriet and Cady Eaton.
[2] A letter undoubtedly meant for Judge Cady's eye.

my contributions, giving freely to the missionary, Bible, temperance, and antislavery causes; have sustained some pecuniary losses; been the victim of ill health one entire year; and, though I never made the getting of money for its own sake an object, I have saved from these expenditures about $3,000 in cash. During this time I have met and surmounted obstacles before which many would have quailed. You may ask by what means I obtained the necessary funds to do this. I answer, by the hands, the tongue, the pen, and the ingenuity of a New Englander, trained up by a mother who is the great-great-great-grand-daughter of a man[1] who set his foot on Plymouth Rock in 1620.

Lovingly,

HENRY.

To John Greenleaf Whittier.

LONDON, *July 11, 1840.*

DEAR MR. WHITTIER,—Your letter to Henry about your struggles with a poem which we will read so pleasantly and easily by and by reminds me of what Mr. Dyce told me of Samuel Rogers. I have met Dyce several times and caught a glimpse of the poet at a reception. Take heart, for Dyce assured me his idol spent "years" on a poem—I think he mentioned sixteen as required for one poetic flight! "As a rule" he writes only four or five lines a day. This beats you, does it not? And now that I am thinking of Rogers' Boswell—as Henry names Dyce—I recall that

---

[1] Elder Brewster, from whom Mr. Stanton's mother was a direct descendant.

he said that Rogers held the opinion [1] that when there is but one daughter and several sons in a family, the daughter is always of a masculine disposition; but when the contrary is the case, the only son is sure to be more or less effeminate. This was not so with my brother, an only boy among five sisters, all decidedly strong characters. My brother died just after graduating at Union College; I was about eleven years old, but can remember him as a fine, manly fellow, the very apple of my father's eye. He never ceased to mourn his loss. Very truly thine, with Henry's best regards.

To Daniel C. Eaton.

LONDON, *August 18, 1840.*

DEAR BROTHER,—This morning, Henry left me here in London to be absent a fortnight in the northern counties of England. I am so tired of moving that I really prize a little rest, though I must confess I feel sad at the idea of being friendless in this great Babel. We got up quite a scene at our first parting. I never loved my country, my home, my friends, as I do now. Verily, "the heart from love to one grows bountiful to all." You will see from the newspapers that Europe has a "rebellious stomach" too—that is, things here are not going on more quietly than with us. The religiose are combating the Established Church, the Chartists are denouncing the government, the Queen is slighting the French, etc., etc. So the world seems

---

[1] There is probably an error of memory here, as in *Table-Talk* (p. 60) this opinion is attributed to Dr. John Hunter (1728-93), a celebrated Scottish anatomist and surgeon.

to be in a general hubbub, and we need not hope for quietness until the bile of sin all flows back to its great source and centers in its originator, Satan.

To Elizabeth Smith.

JOHNSTOWN, *March 7, 1841.*

DEAR LIB,—I am greatly distressed that Cousin Gerrit should be suffering so much amidst learned homeopathists without once applying to them for relief. Strange that you who are so famous for new measures should be so obstinate on medical points. I do hope that you and Cousin Nancy will use your influence to prevent Cousin Gerrit from submitting to a scientific death by those allopathic quacks. During my recent visit to Tryphena at Seneca Falls, I saw wonders in homeopathy and animal magnetism, enough to make me wonder that all our learned, though not wise, physicians do not at least examine into the principles. Near Seneca Falls there lives a man who has had rheumatism for twenty years and who was under the care of a "regular physician" all that time. During four months every year he has been laid upon his back unable to move either to the right or to the left without suffering exquisite pain. The poor fellow heard of the angel Homeopathy and placed himself under her guardian care. Now he is not only a convert to the doctrines of the great Hahnemann, but is in comfortable circumstances and has the prospect of at least living the remainder of his days without enduring half the time the torments of the rack.

Good night.

To Henry B. Stanton.

JOHNSTOWN, *March 16, 1842.*

DEAR HENRY,—The baby's shoulder was bandaged both by Dr. Childs and Dr. Clark. But I thought their bandages were too severe and made the child uncomfortable; so, with my usual conceit, I removed both successfully and turned surgeon myself. I first rubbed the arm and shoulder well with arnica, then put a wet compress on the collar bone, some cotton batting rolled in linen under the arm, and over the shoulder two bands of linen, like suspenders, pinned to the belly band. This we removed night and morning, washed the shoulder with cold water and arnica and wet the compress anew. The surgeons pronounced my work all very good, and this morning the child is dressed for the first time in ten days. I did not write you about the bandaging until I felt sure I had done well. You know it is a great thing to impress husbands, as Susan Nipper did the devoted Toots, with the belief that their wives are indeed wonderful women!

To Elizabeth Smith.

ALBANY, *February 15, 1843.*

DEAR LIZZIE,—I intended to start for Boston this morning, but I received a letter from Henry yesterday postponing the journey. But this will give me opportunity for further talk[1] with Seward, Joshua Spencer, and Judge Hurlburt. Thank Cousin Nancy for Neil's

---

[1] About the married woman property bill which was before the legislature. It finally passed in 1848.

stockings. Mama is still on the first one. I am sure
Cousin Nancy would laugh to see Mama's stripes
and shape, tho' she knows something of Mama's skill
in shaping. Of this I am sure, Neil grows faster than
the stocking. However it will do for his brother!!
Farewell.

To John Greenleaf Whittier.

NEW YORK, *October 10, 1843.*

DEAR MR. WHITTIER,—Yes, we have Elizur Wright's
La Fontaine, but the volumes are in our library at
home, and I am far from there at this moment, as
you will see by the date of my letter. But you
know that our friend's translation is in verse and so
is not very close, naturally. Here is a translation of
the lines you want, exact enough for your purpose:
"Nothing weighs so like a secret. To bear the burden
for any time is very hard for women. But in this
matter I know many men who are women."[1] I hope
this information will aid you and that you will soon
be in a condition so that you can consult your books
again. I hope too that in what you write, you will
preserve this skit at the expense of your sex! In this
connection, perhaps I ought to call your attention to
what you may not know—*viz.*, that some years ago
Tom Moore—whom I saw twice and chatted with a
few minutes once, one of the reasons why I like to sing
his songs (I only wish I could do it as well as he does!)—

---

[1] *Rien ne pèse tant qu'un secret;*
Le porter loin est difficile aux dames;
Et je sais même sure ce fait
Bon nombre d'hommes qui sont femmes.
                              —*Fables*, VIII, 6.

wrote a witty rhyme entitled "Proposals for a Gynæcocracy," from which I take these lines:

> As Whig Reform has had its range,
> And none of us are yet content,
> Suppose, my friends, by way of change,
> We try a Female Parliament;
> And since, of late, with *he* M. P.'s
> We've fared so badly, take to she's.

The following fact, too, may be of use to you. Henry says that he has read somewhere that an old Scotch philosopher once said to a troublesome lady that "idea is the feminine of idiot." And now I am as ever thine, dear friend of us both.

To John Greenleaf Whittier.

BOSTON, *November 28, 1843.*

DEAR MR. WHITTIER,—What you say about the excessive delicacy of that lady friend of yours reminds me of a very pious relative of mine who thought she had a gift for acquiring the modern languages, and decided to try first the German. One day at the very beginning of her studies she came to me in a perturbed state of mind and pointing to the title on the back of a thin German book which she held in her hand, told me the teacher had forgotten it after his last visit, and then she asked me seriously whether I thought she ought to continue to take lessons "from a man who could read such books." I glanced at the title and this is what I read: *Dichter Grusse von Hell,* which we managed to translate as *Poetic Greetings from Hell!* I must confess that even I was a little startled at this title, for it took me right back to my dark Scotch Presbyterian days, which are not very far off. But when the teacher came next time, our minds were soon set at rest, for he explained that this was a little collection from the poetry of some German writer whose pseudonym was "Theodor Hell." He added rather wittily: "Oh, Fräulein, we Germans have nothing to do with the Lower Regions, for one of them has said, 'Providence has given to the French the empire of the land, to the English that of the sea, and to the Germans that of . . . the air!'" Then we all laughed, gave him back the compromising book and the lessons went on swimmingly again.

To Lydia Maria Child.

ALBANY, *March 24, 1844.*

DEAR MRS. CHILD,—The question of reforming our female attire is not new to me. When, for instance, I was in London three or four years ago, I saw much of a person who had known intimately Lady Stanhope,[1] who had died only the year before I was there. She lived for some twenty years in Syria, and used to go about dressed in the costume of an Arabian chieftain. But just what this costume was like, I could not learn. I was further told that she got many of her radical ideas from her father—another instance of a favorite belief of mine that daughters take after their father, mentally. This father, so I learned in London, advocated throughout his long career a

---

[1] Lady Hester Stanhope (1776-1839), an eccentric but talented niece of William Pitt, the celebrated Prime Minister.

number of important reforms, most of which failed of adoption during his life because both he and his isms were pronounced visionary by a narrow public opinion. But since his death, which occurred some years ago, one after another of his pet schemes have been put on the English statute book. So the example of Earl Stanhope should be an encouragement to you and the younger generation of us in our dream for the amelioration of the condition of mankind and womankind.

FACSIMILE OF HANDWRITING OF ELIZABETH CADY STANTON, 1845[1]

---

[1] This is part of a reduced facsimile letter from Mrs. Stanton to her cousin Charles Dudley Miller. It was written in February, 1845.

To Margaret Livingston Cady.

CHELSEA, NEAR BOSTON, *July 17, 1845.*

MY DEAR MOTHER,—Cousin Gerrit and Nancy have been spending a few days with us, and I have just given them a little dinner party, our guests being, besides them, the Rev. John Pierpont[1] and wife, Mr. Sumner, the Rev. Mr. Leavitt, and Whittier. Sumner is exceedingly well read but rather reserved. We all complimented him, as he deserved to be, on his oration[2] delivered a few days ago. I did not hear it, but Henry did, and he says it was a striking performance. All sorts of new ideas are seething in Mr. Leavitt's head; but I haven't either time or place even to enumerate them, and if I did you and my good father would probably balk at most of them. Mr. Pierpont resigned a few weeks ago from his church here. "Many of my parishioners couldn't stand my temperance ideas," he said to us by way of explaining his course. You know he is a teetotaler who will not even drink tea. But what will be Boston's loss by his going— and it will be a real one, for Pierpont is no ordinary divine—will be your gain, for he tells us he is going to accept a call to a Unitarian church at Troy. So the next time you are in Albany, go and hear him, for he is a superior man in every respect. You know he is a poet of no mean parts. He read us at the dinner table the other night a ballad which he wrote last week, and which has never been published. It was very

---

[1] Rev. John Pierpont (1785-1866), poet and abolitionist, the maternal grandfather of John Pierpont Morgan, American financier.

[2] "The True Grandeur of Nations," given on July 4th, before the civil authorities of Boston; a plea for peace and a vehement denunciation of war.

tender and noble in sentiment. While listening to it, Whittier's eyes filled with tears and Cousin Gerrit was so deeply touched that he kissed Pierpont when he had finished the reading.

To John Greenleaf Whittier.

BOSTON, *April 11, 1846.*

DEAR MR. WHITTIER,—When I was in Edinburgh I bought one day a little volume because of its title, *Records of Woman.* It was by Mrs. Hemans. I took it up by chance this morning and read it for the first time. It is a charming series of poems all in honor of our sex. Mrs. Hemans—so I was told by some of her friends in her native city, Liverpool, whom I met the day before I sailed, and by other friends in Dublin, where she lived the last years of her short life—had a great liking for our country. So I am not surprised to find in this volume many references to the United States. "Edith," which is described by its author as "A Tale of the Woods," is founded on incidents related in an American work, *Sketches of Connecticut*, written by I do not know whom. Henry, who, you remember, was born in Griswold in that state, would like to find out something about this book. Can you aid us, you who browse so much among dusty volumes? "Edith," by the way, contains a pretty song that ought to be set to music. "The Indian Woman's Death Song," which is not the one I refer to in the preceding sentence, has also an American setting, being based on

---

[1] *Sketch of Connecticut Forty Years Since* (1824), by Lydia Howard Sigourney (1791-1865), educator and author,

facts found in Keating's "Narrative of an Expedition to the Source of St. Peter's River." But I confess I do not know just where this river is, though, judging from the name, it may be somewhere in the celestial regions. Speaking of this volume, Mrs. Hemans says: "I have put my heart and individual feelings into it more than in anything else I have written." However this may be, this little collection is a worthy contribution to high-minded womanhood from the pen of a brilliant poetess. How proud I am when I see one of my sex doing anything well; and I know you are too, which is the reason why I have called your attention to this book. Henry's best wishes with this, and mine too.

To Rebecca R. Eyster.

SENECA FALLS, *May 1, 1847.*

MY DEAR FRIEND,—Last evening we spoke of the propriety of women being called by the names which are used to designate their sex, and not by those assigned to males. You differed with me on the ground that custom had established the rule that a woman must take the whole of her husband's name, particularly when public mention is made of her. But you are mistaken about this. It is the custom now, since women have commenced forming themselves into independent societies, to use names of the feminine gender. I have looked over several newspapers and asked several persons, and all agree that the tyrant custom does allow every woman to have a name. If you will glance through the public prints containing accounts of the formation of female societies, you will find no titles such as Miss and Mrs., and no Joseph, or Ichabod, but Elizabeth and Rebecca; therefore, if you follow custom, let us all appear in the Report as women, or else mention no names at all. I have very serious objections, dear Rebecca, to being called Henry. There is a great deal in a name. It often signifies much, and may involve a great principle. Ask our colored brethren if there is nothing in a name. Why are the slaves nameless unless they take that of their master? Simply because they have no independent existence. They are mere chattels, with no civil or social rights. Our colored friends in this country who have education and family ties take to themselves names. Even so with women. The custom of calling women Mrs. John This and Mrs. Tom That, and colored men Sambo and Zip Coon, is founded on the principle that white men are lords of all. I cannot acknowledge this principle as just; therefore, I cannot bear the name of another. But I must stop lest I weary your patience.

To John Pierpont.

SENECA FALLS, *September 2, 1847.*

DEAR MR. PIERPONT,—I am sending you a London newspaper which I received a few days ago from Amelia Opie. In it you will find an article, marked by her, on your poems. I rather think she is the author of the review, though she does not say so in her letter accompanying the journal. She only writes: "Please send the paper to your friend and tell him how much I have enjoyed his little volume, which I saw for the first time only last month. In fact I have copied a stanza or two of one of the poems into my commonplace book." You know Mrs. Opie was originally a Unitarian, as you are still, unless that ardent Albany Catholic has brought you over to *his* unitarianism, that is the Papacy. But when I saw Mrs. Opie in England, she had become a Quaker, wearing the costume, but not, I think, adopting all their peculiar views. Like you too, she indulges in poetry with success. So she knows a good gift from Mount Parnassus when it comes; consequently, you should feel that her praise is worth having. Here is the stanza which she selected from your admirable collection:

> A weapon that comes down as still
>   As snowflakes fall upon the sod;
> But executes a freeman's will,
>   As lightning does the will of God;
> And from its force nor door nor locks
> Can shield you—'tis the ballot-box.

It seems to me odd that a Quaker woman in conservative old England, where only the upper classes vote, and even then not in a ballot-box, if I remember rightly, should have made such a selection from your sheaf. But perhaps this portends the coming of a new day in the political life of Great Britain.

From Lucretia Mott.

AUBURN, NEW YORK, *7 mo. 16, 1848.*

DEAR ELIZABETH,—My husband is very poorly, and it is not likely I shall be able to go to Seneca Falls before the morning of the convention.[1]   I hope, however, that he will be able to be present the second day. My sister Martha will accompany me, and we will with pleasure accept thy kind invite to your house that night if you should not be too much crowded with company. James says thy *great* speech [2] thou must reserve for the second day, so that he and others may be able to hear it. The convention will not be so large as it otherwise might be, owing to the busy time with the farmers, harvest, etc. But it will be a beginning, and we may hope it will be followed in due time by one of a more general character. [3]

Lovingly thine,   LUCRETIA MOTT.

To George G. Cooper,
Editor of the *National Reformer*,
Rochester, New York.

SENECA FALLS, *September 14, 1848.*

DEAR SIR,—There is no danger of the Woman Question dying for want of notice.   Every paper you take up

---

[1] The first woman's rights convention ever held took place at Seneca Falls, New York, July 19 and 20, 1848.

[2] In support of the ninth resolution, the first formal and public demand made in the United States for woman suffrage.   It was from Mrs. Stanton's pen.

[3] In a letter of much later date, March 16, 1855, Mrs. Mott, in writing to Mrs. Stanton in regard to a proposed book, says: "In thy coming work thou must do thyself justice.   Remember, the first convention originated with thee.   When we were walking the streets of Boston together in 1841, to find Elizabeth Moore's daughter, thou asked if we could not have a convention for Woman's Rights.   Then when James and self were attending the Yearly Meeting at Waterloo, in 1848 was it? thou again proposed the convention which was afterward held at Seneca Falls.   I have never liked the undeserved praise in the Report of that meeting's proceedings, of being 'the moving spirit of that occasion,' when to thyself belongs the honor, aided so efficiently by the M'Clintocks."

has something to say about it, and just in proportion to the refinement and intelligence of the editor has this movement been favorably noticed. But one might suppose from the articles that you find in some papers, that there are editors so ignorant as to believe that the chief object of these recent conventions was to seat every lord at the foot of a cradle, and to clothe every woman in her lord's attire. Now neither of these points, however important they be considered by humble minds, was touched upon in the conventions. We did not meet to discuss fashions, customs, or dress, the rights of man or the propriety of the sexes changing positions, but simply our own inalienable rights, our duties, our true sphere. If God has assigned a sphere to man and one to woman, we claim the right ourselves to judge of His design in reference to us, and we accord to man the same privilege. We think that a man has quite enough to do to find out his own individual calling, without being taxed to find out also where every woman belongs. The fact that so many men fail in the business they undertake, calls loudly for their concentrating more thought on their own faculties, capabilities, and sphere of action. We have all seen a man making a failure in the pulpit, at the bar, or in our legislative halls, when he might have shone as a general in our Mexican war, as a captain of a canal boat or as a tailor on the bench. Now, is it to be wondered at that woman has doubts about the present position assigned her being the true one, when everyday experience shows us that man makes such fatal mistakes in regard to himself? There is no such thing as a sphere for sex. Every man has a different sphere, in which he may or may not shine, and it is the same with every woman, and the same woman may have a different sphere at different times. For example, the highly gifted Quakeress, Lucretia Mott, married early in life and brought up a large family of children. All who have seen her at home agree that she was a pattern as a wife, mother, and housekeeper. No one ever fulfilled all the duties of that sphere more perfectly than did she. Her children settled in their own homes, Lucretia Mott has now no domestic cares. She has a talent for public speaking. Her mind is of a high order, her moral perceptions remarkably clear, her religious fervor deep and intense; and who shall tell us that this divinely inspired woman is out of her sphere in her public endeavors to rouse this wicked nation to a sense of its awful guilt, to its great sins of war, slavery, injustice to woman, and to the laboring poor?[1]

To Lucretia Mott.

SENECA FALLS, *September 30, 1848.*

MY DEAR FRIEND,—Thanks for the copy of the Philadelphia *Public Ledger* of the 26th inst., containing a leading editorial article devoted to our recent convention. I see that the editor is especially agitated over my ninth resolution, for he says: "The New York girls desire to mount the rostrum—*to do all the voting.*" No; not all, but our part; and that we will

---

[1] The text of this letter is taken from a copy found in Mrs. Stanton's papers, and is not exactly the same as that which appeared in the *National Reformer.*

do some day, mark my word, though probably after
our death and that of the editor of the *Public Ledger*,
unless he is "going in for the hundred." On the
whole, the Philadelphia editorial is better written than
that of the New York *Herald*, which you ask to see,
though both show men of brains holding the pens,
brains in rather narrow heads. The *Herald* writer,
whom I am told is Bennett himself, devotes special
attention to you, who are mentioned by name three
or four times as "Miss (*sic*) Lucretia Mott." My
humble village is also made famous in the columns of
this metropolitan daily. Seneca Falls is printed in
full at least twice along with such world-known cities
as Paris, Philadelphia, and Baltimore. Buffalo and
Utica will be jealous of our little berg. I learn from
the editorial that Bennett published *in extenso*, in a
previous issue, our "Declaration." That is just what
I wanted. Imagine the publicity given to our ideas
by thus appearing in a widely circulated sheet like
the *Herald*. It will start women thinking, and men
too; and when men and women think about a new
question, the first step in progress is taken. The great
fault of mankind is that it will not think. In this
editorial too my "elective franchise" claim seems
particularly "to stick in the crop" of this conservative
editor. The very fact that this happens shows con-
clusively that I hit the nail on the head when I made
that claim. I fully agree with Mr. Bennett's closing
lines, even if you may not. Here they are: "We are
much mistaken if Lucretia would not make a better
President than some of those who have lately tenanted

the White House." Of course you would. Sincerely as ever, Author of the Ninth Resolution.[1]

To John Pierpont.

SENECA FALLS, *September 30, 1849.*

DEAR MR. PIERPONT,—In a letter just received from my Dublin friends, the Webbs, is a clipping from a newspaper that might be made the starting point of a good sermon. It is an account of a man summoned before the police court in London for deserting his wife. When the prisoner was asked by the judge why he had taken up his residence in a certain little hotel, he answered, because of his wife's "nagging" him. Then the warrant officer spoke up and said: "Your Honor, I have arrested several husbands at this same hotel and they all offered as an excuse that they had more comfort there than in their own homes." And don't overlook the reply of the culprit, when the judge asked him if he meant to return to his wife— "As Ovid has well said, '*Nec sine te nec tecum vivere possum,*'" which I take to mean, "Whether I am with

---

[1] To this letter Mrs. Mott replied under date, "Philadelphia, 10 mo. 3, 1848. I am now trying to awaken sufficient interest to hold a woman's rights meeting in this city. It is far more difficult than we found out West. Still, there are numbers here who feel a deep interest in the cause. Few, however, are accustomed to public speaking. Why can't thou come on here to attend such a meeting? Thou art so wedded to this cause that thou must expect to act as pioneer in the work. Richard Hunt speaks very favorably of thy speech at Waterloo. He says some of their respectable inhabitants were well pleased. I rejoiced that thou wast willing to deliver that lecture, and hope thy talents in that way will be well 'exercised by reason of use,' and 'speak to thy people that they go forward.' Do write to Rochester and stir up those women to their duties. We must not depend upon any who have been apostles before us, but be ready for 'those things which shall hereafter appear unto us.' With the dearest love to all."

thee or absent from thee, I cannot live,"—a rather noncommittal and even somewhat cryptic answer. I do not know what was done with the forlorn husband; the item and the Webbs are all silent on this point, important to him, though not so interesting to us. But if I had been the judge, I should have been very lenient, for there is no doubt of it that too many wives worry their husbands in petty ways. My chief explanation of this fact is that most women the world over have no really absorbing interest in life, nothing to take their minds off of the little domestic troubles, real or imaginary, generally the latter. If women took part in public affairs, I am sure that there would be far less nagging at the family hearth. I sometimes wish I were a clergyman for this very reason, for then I could easily reach the ear of slumbering womanhood.[1] So do give us one of your good strong sermons, perhaps from the text, "She that is married careth for the things of the world." (I Cor. 7: 34.) If you do, please send on the sermon and I will have it published in the *Lily*, the reform paper we started here in Seneca Falls at the beginning of the present year. Your anti-nagging friend.

[1] The germ, perhaps, of a custom which became, in later years, one of the peculiar features of Mrs. Stanton's life as a public lecturer. "I never let an occasion slip to storm a pulpit, though the storm generally breaks after I have taken a back seat!" she once wrote to Mrs. Bagley, wife of John Bagley, Governor of Michigan.

1850–1860

To Elizabeth Smith Miller.

SENECA FALLS, *April 20, 1850.*

DEAR LIZ,—Have you any flower seeds for a body, especially mignonette? I as yet have never succeeded in raising that flower. My children have all been through the mumps dispensation. How do yours manage whooping cough? The spirits seem to be making some new manifestations![1] I am convinced that it is all humbug. How strange, is it not, that these very minds which reject Christ and his miracles and all the mysteries of the Bible, because these things are opposed to reason and the truth as we see it in other revelations of God's laws, should be deluded by this miserable piece of chicanery! I believe this is all done by some human means. There is nothing more wonderful about it than the performances of a necromancer. Have sent my letter to Salem.[2]

To Amy Post.[3]

SENECA FALLS, *December 4, 1850.*

DEAR AMY,—It was decided at the Worcester convention[4] that eight states of the Union would petition

---

[1] This was the period of "The Rochester rappings," when the Fox sisters were attracting much attention.

[2] Ohio woman's rights convention, April 19 and 20. Letter on amending constitution. (*History of Woman Suffrage*, vol. i, p. 810.)

[3] Miss Amy Post (1801-89), one of the early abolitionists, took part in the Seneca Falls convention, and was the chief spirit at the Rochester convention, remaining an ardent advocate of woman's rights to the end of her long life.

[4] Held at Worcester, Massachusetts, in October, 1850, was the first

for woman's right to exercise the elective franchise. The western part of this state is left to me to organize. I must ask each district to see that its senator carries with him a petition to the coming session at Albany. Will you attend to your district? A hundred and fifty names are sufficient to make a petition very respectable.

To Henry B. Stanton.[1]

SENECA FALLS, *December 9, 1850.*

DEAR HENRY,—It is now over four weeks that I have watched our dear Neil [2] through weary, anxious days and nights, and seen him steadily decline. A day or two since, I thought him better. Now I think, I know not what—no better, no worse. It is the first time I have ever seen a child grow pale and thin. The doctors say there is nothing dangerous in his case, and I suppose there is not; but I am anxious beyond endurance. He has a fearful cough, particularly at night. I have no faith in any of the pathys, and now I intend to try my own skill for a few days, and if he is no better the last of this week, you had better come and see him. I shall go the whole round of the simple remedies, and if they do no good, I shall get my sister to take him next week to the water-cure at Clifton. Under my "quack" system, Neil is now sleeping more quietly than for a week past. He has not coughed

woman's rights convention of a national character, with delegates from several states. Mrs. Stanton signed the call for New York. (*History of Woman Suffrage,* vol. i, pp. 217, 821.)

[1] Mr. Stanton was in Albany attending the session of the Senate.

[2] Daniel Cady Stanton, the oldest child of the family.

in two hours. I feel guilty when I have a sick child.
Write soon. Good night.

To Elizabeth Smith Miller.

Seneca Falls,
Monday morning, February 11, 1851.

Dear Liz,—Laugh in your turn. I have actually
got my fourth son! Yes, Theodore Stanton bounded
upon the stage of life with great ease—comparatively!!
He weighs ten and one-half pounds. I was sick but a
few hours, and did not lie down until half an hour before he was born, but worked round as hard as I could
all night to do up the last things. At seven o'clock
Sunday morning he was born. This morning I got
up, bathed myself in cold water, and have sat by the
table writing several letters.

To Henry B. Stanton.

Seneca Falls, *February 13, 1851.*

Dear Henry,—I received this morning the public
documents and shall inform myself on this free school
question. As the legislators at the Capitol are undoubtedly trembling in their shoes at the prospect of
an encounter with me, do relieve your particular
friends from their state of suspense. Tell them they
have one more year to live, as I shall not be there to
annihilate them this season. We are all well. No
less than eight gentlemen have penetrated the privacy
of my bedroom and made me long calls. As to the
ladies who have been here, they are without number.
I am regarded as a perfect wonder. Many people

THE CADY-STANTON FAMILY, 1848

Mrs. Stanton and sons from daguerreotypes. Mr. Stanton from painting of World's Anti-Slavery Convention, National Portrait Gallery, London

are actually impatiently waiting for me to die in order to make their theories good. But I am getting better and stronger every day. Good night.

To Henry B. Stanton.

PETERBORO, *April 11, 1851.*[1]

DEAR HENRY,—I have sent greetings to the Convention at Akron.[2] There is some uncertainty about my going to Johnstown, for Cousin Gerrit says that papa is so distressed about my dress.[3] However, I have written to them that if my friends cannot see me in the short dress, they cannot see me at all, and it may be they will send me an urgent invitation to come. In that case, I shall go there next Saturday. But if they should not do this, I shall return home and I should be very glad to have you escort me. I hear nothing from the New Yorkers. I fear the short dress will cost me the loss of my kin. We weighed the baby to-day. He weighs fifteen pounds, a gain of five since his birth. Good night.

To Daniel and Henry Stanton.[4]

SENECA FALLS, *May 4, 1851.*

Spring has come in lazily, dear boys, but our grass is now green and our trees leafing out. We are through

---

[1] On the back of a letter forwarded to Mrs. Stanton at this time, Mrs. Amelia Bloomer, assistant postmistress at Seneca Falls, wrote: "Dear Mrs. Stanton: This is the first letter since you left for Peterboro. After a few days we shall be looking for your return home. Shorten your visit as much as possible, for people have nothing to talk about while you are gone."

[2] National Woman's Rights Convention, May, 1851. Letter given in full, *History of Woman Suffrage,* vol. i, p. 815.

[3] The Bloomer costume, called at the time the "short dress," and by certain newspapers in ridicule, the "shorts."

[4] Who were at boarding school.

II.—3

housecleaning, and the grounds are all in fine order. We have all turned out and worked during the last week—Father, Amelia, Bridget, Gattie and I. Theodore, in his carriage, calmly looked at the laborers. The sun shines bright to-day, hosts of little birds are singing sweetly on all sides, and the wind is so soft and warm that one would not think it could ever be cold, dark, and dreary again. We shall meet, dear boys, while the flowers are blooming and all nature is happy and joyous. Good night.

MOTHER.

To Elizabeth Smith Miller.

SENECA FALLS, June 4, 1851.

DEAR LIZZIE,—I have just received a letter from your father rejoicing over the supposed defeat of my husband last week Tuesday.[1] We have had a crowing letter from Papa also. But he and Cousin Gerrit have "gone off" too soon. The first reached me whilst the guns are firing, crackers popping and bonfires burning in honor of Henry's triumph over the foul lies and cruel machinations of his Whig enemies. I rejoice in the victory with my whole soul, for in spite of all my

---

[1] Mr. Stanton was elected to the New York State Senate in 1849, taking his seat in January, 1850. In the session of 1851, the Whigs introduced a bill appropriating many millions of dollars to enlarge the Erie canal. It passed the Lower House, but to prevent the presence of the three-fifths quorum necessary to carry it in the Senate, twelve senators resigned office and the bill fell. Elections to fill the vacancies were ordered. Six senators, whose districts were far away from the canal, were successful, but of the other six, whose constituencies lay in the canal regions, only one, Mr. Stanton, was rechosen, and he by a majority of five votes. At first it was reported that he was defeated. The twelve stump speakers in the field against him were marshaled by Gerrit Smith.

seeming liberality towards his opposers, I would sooner see every relative and friend I have on the face of the earth blown into thin air, and that old ditch running from Buffalo to Albany filled in with mud, than have had Henry mortified by a defeat in this election. The severest trial of my life, dear Lizzy, I have just passed through. Your father's tour through this district turned out a more bitter pill for me than for the one for whom it was intended. My going to hear Cousin Gerrit speak and walking out with him flew like wildfire, and all the Whigs had it that Mr. Stanton's family and friends were against him, even his wife disapproving of his course. My name was hawked about the streets and in all the public meetings. Two men had a fight in one meeting about my hat. My dress was a subject of the severest animadversions. Some good Democrats said they would not vote for a man whose wife wore the Bloomers. Then the Whigs and pro-canal Democrats—you know the party was not united on the question—got up all kinds of stories about me. Some said I was bribed by Cousin Gerrit to go against Henry. The truth is I felt no interest whatever in the canal question *per se*, but desired Henry's re-election. But as no one seemed satisfied with my neutral position, after posting myself on the subject, and the Constitution's bearing thereon, I came out an unterrified Democrat, defending resignation and abhorring debt. This seemed to increase the activity of the street urchins, who hissed and sung and screamed "breeches" with the greatest vim throughout the whole campaign. The night after the election—just a week ago this evening—when it

was reported that Henry was defeated, they shouted
in chorus all through the streets:

> Heigh! ho! the carrion crow,
> Mrs. Stanton's all the go;
> Twenty tailors take the stitches,
> Mrs. Stanton wears the breeches.

But to-night, no dog dares wag his jaw! My boys
have shared in the family experiences. Kit came
home from school one day and asked: "Is father
beaten down in Albany and has had to run?" Of
course "beaten" and "run" were not taken by him
in the political sense. I told him the Whigs wanted
his father to borrow nine millions of dollars and he
would not. "Oh," said Gat, "I wish he had bor-
rowed it, and then we could have a horse." Gat
knows who is a Whig and who a Democrat all through
the town, and whenever a strange man appears at the
house, he always comes and whispers: "Is he on
father's side?" A few mornings since, when I was
washing the baby, he asked me with all seriousness
and with a real touch of anxiety in his voice, "Is the
baby a Democrat?" So you see, dear Lizzie, I have
had my battle to fight here, whilst you outraged the
metropolitans. When I heard of the cold looks you
had to encounter, my bruised heart did pity you.
Well, we have lived through it—I through this campaign and you through this New York visit—and
are stronger for the trial. But had I counted the
cost of the short dress, I would never have put it on;
on, however, I'll never take it off, for now it involves
a principle of freedom. Your hostess [1] has not written

---

[1] Harriot Cady Eaton, Mrs. Stanton's sister.

me a line since she saw you, and the only communication I have had with the New Yorkers has been one merciless letter from my brother-in-law when you were at his house. He expressed disapproval of the dress and of my friendly relations with your father. On the other hand, I have had a pleasant visit from Lizzie Fitz, who put on the short dress and went all over town with me. Then I went up to Geneva with her and spent the day with Aunt Bell,[1] and oh, what a peaceful time I had. They all liked the dress. Hortense Swift even put on my suit and made several calls. Everybody admired the costume very much. General Swift approved of it highly. Now do not scold. I gave the hat you sent me to Lizzie Fitz to make her costume complete. It just suited her, but I thought it too severely plain for me. I feel that in introducing a new dress, we ought to use the richest materials, not gaudy, but everything as tasteful as possible. But to go back to the beginning of this paragraph, I am often tired of this fight. How wearisome to be forever warding off attacks. To-night I am ready to lay down my life, but oh! to-morrow the sun will shine and my blessed baby will open his sweet blue eyes, crow and look so lovingly on me that I shall live again joyfully. Thursday morning. The sun is up, the baby has crowed and his mother feels happy. Your own Johnson.[2]

---

[1] Sister of Mrs. Gerrit Smith and wife of Joseph Gardner Swift (1783-1865), brigadier-general, U. S. A., the first graduate of West Point, and later superintendent of the academy.

[2] In the family circle Mrs. Miller and Mrs. Stanton were often referred to as "Julius" and "Johnson." These names originated in this way: When the Christy minstrels first appeared, they went one evening to hear the per-

To Elizabeth Smith Miller.

SENECA FALLS, *July 2, 1851.*

DEAR JULIUS,—You will have read the *Lily* before you get this, and seen your claims set up for the glory of having been the first American woman to wear "the shorts" as a constant dress. The article signed J. V. N. is by your beloved Massa Johnson. But do not mention it, or Mrs. Bloomer would tear my eyes out. In this number, by the way, are six editorials written by me. The whole column where your name is mentioned is mine, and the "Detroit Tribune," the "Lowell Girls" and the "Man in Petticoats" are also from my pen. My baby is very good and grows finely. I continue to be his wet as well as his dry nurse. It is easier to look after him myself than to train an ignorant girl to do so. I have invented a variety of ways to keep him quiet—that is, ways for him to keep himself quiet.

To Elizabeth Smith Miller.

SENECA FALLS, *August 5, 1851.*

DEAR JULIUS,—Now I have something to tell poor Julius that will cheer his sad heart. Well, you heard of the proposed festival at Glen Haven. I went to it and had a most pleasant time. I took Amelia,[1]

formance. The wit and philosopher of the occasion were called, respectively, Julius and Johnson. On returning home they amused their seniors with a rehearsal. They took their parts and reproduced all the remarks they made. The next morning as they appeared at the breakfast table, Gerrit Smith said: "Good morning, Julius and Johnson." One after another relatives adopted the pseudonyms.

[1] Amelia Willard, who was throughout her life Mrs. Stanton's faithful aid at home, filling every role from that of maid, cook, and nurse, to that

who was in "shorts," and Theodore. There I saw
ten ladies in costume—three from Syracuse, four in
our party, and the rest residents of Glen Haven. Theo-
dosia Gilbert's get-up pleased me very much. She
was dressed in a short green tunic not reaching to the
knee, and white linen drilling trousers made *à la
masculine*. They all wore white trousers with dresses
of various colors. In a word, the "shorts" were the
theme of conversation, tracts and addresses. Oh,
that you had been there! We dined in the open air and
had a great many agreeable people at table, so that
the conversation was quite brilliant and interesting.
At dessert, William Burleigh spoke in high praise of
the "shorts" and with great disgust of the "longs."
"The long dress is now an offense to my eyes," he
said; "and I cannot help exclaiming to myself whenever I see a woman trailing bedraggled petticoats
through the dust, 'Oh, the dirty creature!'" Warm
applause from the delighted listeners. But Mr.
Burleigh had with him a Miss B., whom he treated
with too great attention. I like fun and frolic, romps
and jokes, but sentimental pawings are excessively
disgusting to me. Returning from Glen Haven, we
reached Skeneateles at seven, and lo and behold, all
the town had come out to see us! We had left our
carriage and coachman there, and the news had spread

of sewing woman, housekeeper, and confidante. In a letter dated "Indianap-
olis, March 1, 1879," Mrs. Stanton, when on one of her lecture tours, writes:
"Dear Amelia: Take things as easily as you can, and be assured I appreciate your faithful service and all the self-sacrifice you have made for me.
My life work, if worth anything to the race, is due in large measure to the
leisure your executive ability has secured to me; and thus by each one
filling some niche, the wheels of progress move on. Gratefully."

through the village that four ladies in "shorts" were
to come down in the evening boat; so there the multitude stood—men, women, and children. Ossian
Dodge with his guitar in a green baize bag and I with
my baby in a blue merino cloak took the lead, the
three other ladies and two or three odd-looking gentlemen in long hair following. What a spectacle for
men and angels as we solemnly proceeded from the
boat to our carriages. What would the venerable
judge [1] have said could he have witnessed the scene!!
I expected to be insulted, but not one word was said.
The people had evidently been impelled by an honest
curiosity to see—nothing more. But I was glad
enough to find myself shut up in a carriage in brisk
motion with my blessed baby safe in my lap. Julius,
how long will the heathen rage? I have received
another awful shot about the short dress, and seven
vials of wrath have been poured on my devoted head.
I think they were bottled by one of my New York
sisters. They have a metropolitan odor. We are
very much like the poor fox in the fable, who having
cut off his tail and not being able to restore it, found
that nothing remained for him to do but to persuade
the other foxes to do likewise that he might not be a
by-word among his kind. As we have performed
this surgical operation on our entire wardrobe, nothing
remains for us to do but to induce as many as possible
to follow our example. We can have no peace in
traveling until we cut off the great national petticoat. God grant that we may be more successful
than the fox.

---

[1] Mrs. Stanton's father.

To Henry B. Stanton.

SENECA FALLS, *September 2, 1851.*

DEAR HENRY,—I think I will shut up the house for a week or two and take a trip to Johnstown and on to Worcester.[1] The Whigs here are now all very gracious and attentive to me. The boys speak about you every day, asking if you are in your seat. They continue to talk about the wicked Whigs, and were much distressed to learn that their grandfather was a Whig. But I told them it was only the Whigs of this district who abused father. Whereupon Kit said: "Yes, you must not think, Gat Stanton, that the Whigs are the same all over the world." George Thompson is to be here soon, and I trust you can manage to be home when he is our guest. Chauncy Burr has been lecturing here and proving "rappings" to be the merest humbug. He called on me this morning, and we had a long conversation on all the topics of the day. He talks well, possibly better than he thinks. But this is a common failing. Let us know what day and hour you will be here that we may kill the fatted calf. Good night.

To Daniel C. Stanton.

SENECA FALLS, *October 14, 1851.*

DEAR NEIL,—You do not wish me to visit you in a short dress! Why, my dear child, I have no other.

[1] Massachusetts, where a National Woman's Rights Convention was to be held October 15 and 16, 1851. At the first Worcester Convention a Central Committee had been appointed representing all the states. Mrs. Stanton was on this Central Committee. She had also been appointed to the Educational Committee and to the Committee of Civil and Political Functions,

Now, suppose you and I were taking a long walk in the fields and I had on three long petticoats. Then suppose a bull should take after us. Why, you, with your legs and arms free, could run like a shot; but I, alas! should fall a victim to my graceful flowing drapery. Like the deer, you remember, in the fable, my glory would be my destruction. My petticoats would be caught by the stumps and the briars, and what could I do at the fences? Then you in your agony, when you saw the bull gaining on me, would say: "Oh! how I wish mother could use her legs as I can." Now why do you wish me to wear what is uncomfortable, inconvenient, and many times dangerous? I'll tell you why. You want me to be like other people. You do not like to have me laughed at. You must learn not to care for what foolish people say. Such good men as cousin Gerrit and Mr. Weld [1] will tell you that a short dress is the right kind. So no matter if ignorant silly persons do laugh. Good night to both of my dear boys.

YOUR MOTHER.

To Elizabeth Smith Miller.

SENECA FALLS, October 18, 1851.

DEAR JULIUS,—Only see how they are all coming round.[2] Mama and sister Mag, who are now making

---

[1] Theodore D. Weld, the head of the school the boys were attending.

[2] This letter was written on the back of the following one from Mrs. Stanton's brother-in-law: "Dear Sister: Mr. and Mrs. Charley Miller are to make us a visit next week or the week after, and we all of us greatly desire that you would accompany them, bringing with you your two youngest children, so that we may once more have a good old-fashioned visit. You and Mrs. Miller can keep each other in countenance whenever

me a visit, do not seem to dislike the short dress. Mama even says that when Papa returned from here, he was quite pleased with his visit and his daughter, and declared that he never would have noticed the "shorts" if he had not heard so much about them. He thought them "well enough." I suppose he expected to see me looking just like a man. Well, the ball went off finely. Henry and I danced until four o'clock. Massa Johnson dressed in white, as the black satin waist was tight and I could not sacrifice the most glorious part of our reform—a loose waist— to the becoming. Everybody said I looked well, and I thought I did.

To Daniel and Henry Stanton.

JOHNSTOWN, *New Year's Day, 1852.*

DEAR BOYS,—How much longer it takes children to learn to walk and talk than it does little kittens and puppies to run about and express their ideas in their way. But I dare say if children had four legs, they would stand alone much sooner. Which would you rather be, a boy or a puppy? If you were a puppy, you would not be obliged to study any lessons, to wash your teeth, or bathe and dress yourself; you could run faster than any boy in school; you could sit up all night and bark at the moon; you could run about in heat and cold, in rain and shine, without hat or

---

you wish to promenade Broadway in 'shorts.' The novelty of seeing a Bloomer in New York is so effectually worn off that I hear of no more insult or annoyance being offered to such as choose to wear the costume. So please pack up your coats and trousers and come along. Affectionately, your Brother, D. C. Eaton."

coat; you could travel all over the world without trunk or money; you would be in no danger of vices; you would never chew tobacco, smoke, drink whiskey, steal, lie, or use vulgar language. Now tell me in your next letter why, in spite of all these advantages, it is better to be a boy. Think it all out yourselves and let me know just what your idea is. A thousand kisses from the end of my pen, dear boys.

YOUR MOTHER.

To Susan B. Anthony.[1]

SENECA FALLS, April 2, 1852.

MY DEAR FRIEND,—I think you are doing up the temperance business just right. But do not let the conservative element control. For instance, you must

---

[1] This letter is the earliest extant of the voluminous correspondence carried on for over fifty years between Mrs. Stanton and Susan B. Anthony. They first met in May, 1851, at an antislavery convention in Seneca Falls. At this time Miss Anthony was curious about, rather than sympathetic with, Mrs. Stanton's ideas on woman's enfranchisement, and for some years gave her best efforts to the temperance and antislavery reforms, but was finally converted to the importance of the woman question. The following letter as bearing on this point is interesting. It is from Matilda Joslyn Gage, who was co-editor with Mrs. Stanton and Miss Anthony of the *History of Woman Suffrage*, to Lydia Becker of England, and reads: "Syracuse, New York, August 30, 1878. Dear Miss Becker: Thanks for sending me the *Englishwoman's Review*. Yes, the article which you have marked contains not only *a* mistake, as you guess, but several. The first woman's rights convention was *not* held at Akron, Ohio; it was *not* called by Mrs. Frances Dana Gage, and it did *not* take place in 1847. The first woman's rights convention the world ever knew was called by Elizabeth Cady Stanton and Lucretia Mott, though the latter always insists that she only 'supported' Mrs. Stanton, whose idea it was and who took the initiative; and, too, it was held in Mrs. Stanton's own village in July, 1848. Miss Anthony had nothing to do with this Seneca Falls convention. At that time she was entirely ignorant of the movement, and although the Seneca Falls meeting adjourned to Rochester, where Miss Anthony lived, she was not only not present at it, but was rather inclined to deride its principles, as she has

take Mrs. Bloomer's suggestions with great caution, for she has not the spirit of the true reformer. At the first woman's rights convention, but four years ago, she stood aloof and laughed at us. It was only with great effort and patience that she has been brought up to her present position. In her paper, she will not speak against the fugitive slave law, nor in her work to put down intemperance will she criticize the equivocal position of the Church. She trusts to numbers to build up a cause rather than to principles, to the truth and the right. Fatal error! The history of the antislavery agitation is, on this point, a lesson to thinking minds. Among the abolitionists, the discussion began by some insisting on compromises in order to draw in numbers and bring over to them a large and respectable body of priests and rabbis. They also decided to turn the cold shoulder on woman's co-operation, as well as let the Church go unrebuked. Where now is that brilliant host in panoply so sacred and so respected? Gone back to learn anew the a, b, c, of the reformer. All this I say to you and to no one else, and you will understand why. I would not speak aught to injure Mrs Bloomer. Yes, I repeat, beware of her conservative suggestions. We

---

more than once told with her own lips. In September, 1853, the third national convention was held in this town where I am now writing you. But it had been preceded by perhaps half a dozen state or national gatherings, and in none of these did Miss Anthony take part, though Mrs. Stanton attended in person or sent letters to all or most of them. It was at this convention of 1853 that Miss Anthony made her debut in our movement, and even here she came as a temperance delegate, which was her favorite reform work at this time. But when she once got fairly started in the woman's rights agitation, she made up for lost time. Very truly yours, M. J. Gage."

shall test the church people at our next annual meeting by getting up some strong resolutions touching
upon this "brotherhood of thieves"—the slave-holding
oligarchy of the South. The Church is a terrible
engine of oppression, especially as concerns woman.
I shall keep my Appeal in this connection as a text
for my next speech. Oh, what a dose it will be at the
end of the year! I shall elaborate it and double distill
it. Lord have mercy on those who gag in swallowing!
By the way, you know many temperance advocates
are prepared to carry this question into the churches.
Shall our society lead or follow? I say, lead. Have
you read Emerson's speech? If not, read it and note
what he says of majorities. I will gladly do all in
my power to aid you in getting up such a lecture as
you desire. In due time I, as an individual, will
speak to the women of the state. If my speech as it
stands would serve you as a kind of skeleton for a
lecture I will send it to you and you can fill out the
heads more fully. In reference to "thinking on one's
feet," I have no doubt that a little practice will render
you an admirable lecturer. But you must dress
loosely, take a great deal of exercise, be particular
about your diet, and sleep enough. The body has
great influence on the mind. If you are attacked in
your meetings, be good-natured and keep cool; and
if you are simple and truth-loving no sophistry can
confound you. I have been re-reading the report of
the London convention of 1840. How thoroughly
humiliating it was to us! How I could have sat there
quietly and listened to all that was said and done, I do
not now understand. It is amazing that man can be so

ELIZABETH CADY STANTON, 1851

[See p. 171, vol. I

ELIZABETH CADY STANTON, 1901

utterly unconscious of his brutality to woman. In the good time coming, what a cause of wonder it will be to recall the fact that the champions of freedom, the most progressive men of the nineteenth century, denied women the right of free speech in an anti-slavery convention, when, at the same time, they would have received with the greatest *éclat* the most degraded man from a rice plantation. If Sambo had been cast out of the convention for any reason, I wonder if Wendell Phillips and George Thompson would have coolly remarked on his discomfiture, "Well, he is as happy outside as in!" Men and angels give me patience! I am at the boiling point! If I do not find some day the use of my tongue on this question, I shall die of an intellectual repression, a woman's rights convulsion! Oh, Susan! Susan! Susan! You must manage to spend a week with me before the Rochester convention,[1] for I am afraid that I cannot attend it; I have so much care with all these boys on my hands. But I will write a letter. How much I do long to be free from housekeeping and

---

[1] The women delegates to the Temperance Convention held in Albany in the winter of 1852 had been refused the right to speak. They consequently withdrew, formed a separate organization and arranged for a Woman's State Temperance Convention, which met at Rochester on April 20th, and which Mrs. Stanton did attend. In fact, she was elected president, and made a powerful speech of acceptance, two points of which caused endless comment in press and pulpit. "1st: Let no woman remain in the marriage relation with a confirmed drunkard; let no drunkard be the father of her children. Let us petition our state government so to modify the laws affecting marriage and the custody of children that the drunkard shall have no claims on wife or child. 2d: Inasmuch as charity begins at home, let us withdraw our mite from all associations for sending the Gospel to the heathen across the ocean, for the building up of a theological atistocracy and gorgeous temples to the unknown God, and devote ourselves to the poor and suffering around us."

children, so as to have some time to read, and think, and write. But it may be well for me to understand all the trials of woman's lot, that I may more eloquently proclaim them when the time comes. Good night.

To Daniel Cady Stanton.

SENECA FALLS, *May 2, 1852.*

DEAR SON,—The boys [1] are upstairs in bed and asleep. I sit in the dining-room alone. Father has gone down town to see if the mail brings any letters for us, and Amelia is in the kitchen mixing bread. We have had our garden partly made. But the weather here is very cold, so that it will be some time before the little seeds peep their heads out of the ground. I take all the care of the baby myself. Amelia and I live so nicely together that we thought we should try and get on without any additional help. I hope you will do everything you can to aid those around you. I should love to see you, dear Neil, very much, but it is a long journey to take with little Theodore, and I fear I shall not see you before you come home. I should love to hug and kiss you to-night, to give you a drink of water and put you in bed. I wonder, Neil, if you love me as I do you? Do you often think of me? Father was pleased with your letter. He thinks it is such a good idea to send us your letters just as you write them, without any corrections. Do you think what to write yourself or does some one tell you? I shall send your last letter

_____

[1] The third son, Gerrit, and Theodore, the fourth.

to your grandmother Cady, to let her see that you can write a letter. Write again soon. A thousand kisses. Good night.

Your Mother.

To Gerrit Smith.

Seneca Falls, *May 25, 1852.*

Dear Cousin Gerrit,—I am glad you are to be at the state temperance meeting.[1] I send you for this convention four resolutions,[2] which I wish you would present to the assemblage as coming from our Woman's State Temperance Society. I do wish you would also speak there on divorce, people have such false, low views on what constitutes true marriage. If women knew their duty on this point, it would tell in the temperance cause. Man has never begun to appreciate the wrongs of woman.

---

[1] The Men's State Temperance Society, which met at Syracuse in June.

[2] The resolutions read as follows: "Resolved, That inasmuch as man claims to represent woman in all our national councils, we have a right to demand of him laws that shall protect us and our children in our homes, persons and property; and laws that shall remove temptation from the paths of our sires and sons. Resolved, That drunkenness is a just ground of divorce, yea more, that it is a sin for any woman to consent to entail on innocent beings the curse and degradation that are the certain heritage of the drunkard's offspring. Resolved, That it is the duty of our temperance host to dissolve all connection with churches which wink at the hideous crimes of the distiller, rumseller, and drunkard. Let that priest, who, for his personal interest, fails to rebuke any such in his congregation or tolerates these monsters in Christian communion, be denounced as unworthy of his office, unfit to teach spiritual truths, himself ignorant of the first great principles of Christianity. Resolved, That it is your duty if you find yourselves wanting in the high moral courage and holy self-sacrifice necessary faithfully to represent woman in this cause, that you so change your discipline and laws that she may speak for herself in church and state. If you cannot protect her, then stand aside and let her protect herself, and so deliver us from a government which has neither the justice nor the power to defend the weak against the strong."

From M. S. Grove Nichols.

STAMFORD, CONN., *August 21, 1852.*

MY DEAR FRIEND,—I am very thankful to you for all you are doing. Every article you write hits the nail on the head. I like you vastly. I was complimented by being asked several times, and by my own husband, if I wrote that article of yours in the *Tribune.* You are winning golden opinions. Bless you. I mean to have a paper, and I will pay you more to write for it than anyone I know. Pray write me when you can. I am very thankful for your letters, and my husband rejoices in their strength and spirit. I received your "call."[1]

Truly yours,

M. S. GROVE NICHOLS.

To Lucretia Mott.

SENECA FALLS, *October 22, 1852.*

DEAR LUCRETIA,—I am at length the happy mother of a daughter.[2] I never felt such sacredness in carrying a child as I have in the case of this one. She is the largest and most vigorous baby I have ever had, weighing twelve pounds. And yet my labor was short and easy. I laid down about fifteen minutes, and alone with my nurse and one female friend brought forth this big girl. I sat up immediately, changed

[1] To the National Woman's Rights Convention which met in Syracuse, New York, September 8, 9, 10, 1852. The call (*History of Woman Suffrage,* vol. i, p. 518) was signed by the following names: Elizabeth Cady Stanton, Paulina Wright Davis, William Henry Channing, Lucy Stone, Samuel J. May.

[2] Margaret Livingston, Mrs. Stanton's fifth child.

my own clothes, put on a wet bandage, and, after a few hours' repose, sat up again. Am I not almost a savage? For what refined, delicate, genteel, civilized woman would get well in so indecently short a time? Dear me, how much cruel bondage of mind and suffering of body poor woman will escape when she takes the liberty of being her own physician of both body and soul! I have been wishing to write you ever since the convention [1] to say how pleased I was with the whole proceedings. As to the presidency, it is a matter of congratulation, and argues a great advance in our movement that we now have competitors for the office, when at our first convention no woman could be found with the moral hardihood to take that post of honor. I was greatly pleased too that a bloomer [2] was the pet of the meeting. Depend upon it, Lucretia, that woman can never develop in her present drapery. She is a slave to her rags. But I cannot prove that to you now, for I must write about my daughter to a dozen other friends.

A Happy Mother.

To Elizabeth Smith Miller.

Seneca Falls, November 21, 1852.

Dear Liz,—Yesterday the baby was a month old and weighed fourteen pounds. I have not named her yet. She and I have been in perfect condition all the time. I have no milk leg nor any other legs

---

[1] The Woman's Rights Convention, Syracuse, New York, September, Mrs. Mott being president.

[2] Lucy Stone.

than those I have been accustomed to in my highest
condition. The nurse is still with me, and will remain
until the baby is six weeks old. I stand appalled,
Julius, before the coming winter. I have five children,
two Irish servant girls, a house and many public
duties. With me time does indeed fly. Teaching
the boys regularly is now out of the question, the two
babies and the two daughters of Erin taking all my
time and mind. Just before the baby came I read
Uncle Tom's Cabin. It is the most affecting book I
ever read. I should like to see papa read it. He
would cry all the way through. If you have not
already done so, read it. That book will tell against
slavery; of that you may be sure. Good night.

To Daniel Cady.

NEW YORK, *January 12, 1853.*

MY DEAR FATHER,—The last time we met, we discussed as usual my various "idiosyncrasies," as you
call my favorite theories and beliefs, the isms by which
I differ from the common herd, I am happy to say,
but which give soul and zest to my life. It may be
that there is a tendency in me to resemble the folk of
Lunel, who, to quote an old song I heard in Paris ten
years ago, "go a-fishing for the moon." But you
know I always hold fast to my conviction that "dream-
ers" are as often right in the end as the common-place
conservatives. Among other things you brought up
phrenology, and while I warmly defended Gall, Spurz-
heim, and Combe, you were disposed to consider
them arrant humbugs. Well, I called last week on

Fowler and Wells, at their "Phrenological Cabinet," in Clinton Hall, and the first of these gentlemen, "Professor of Phrenology," as he signs himself, examined my "bumps and hollows." A certain E. D. Stark took down in "phonography" what Mr. Fowler said, and it was remarkable to see how rapidly his hand and pencil moved over the paper. It was the first time I ever saw this system of writing, and it is truly wonderful. I have just received the result of all this feeling of my cranium and this lightning writing, and I enclose my "Phrenological Character." After reading it, I think you will agree with me that it often hits the nail on the head—I really did not mean to make a phrenological comparison—in a rather striking way. Do give me your honest opinion about it and let mother see it too. Tell me what you really think, even if you do have to come down from your high horse a little. But whether, after this demonstration of the evident science of the system, you continue a firm anti-Combist, I shall nevertheless always remain,

Your affectionate but radical daughter.

'Tis strange how like a very dunce,
Man, with his bumps upon his sconce,
Has lived so long; and yet no knowledge he
Has had, till lately, of phrenology—
A science that by simple dint of
Head-combing he should find a hint of,
When scratching o'er those little pole-hills
The faculties throw up like mole-hills.

Tom Hood must have had you in mind, my dear father, when he wrote these lines.

To Susan B. Anthony.

SENECA FALLS, *March 1, 1853.*

DEAR FRIEND,—I do not know whether the world is quite willing or ready to discuss the question of marriage. I feel in my innermost soul that the thoughts I sent the convention are true. It is in vain to look for the elevation of woman so long as she is degraded in marriage. I hold that it is a sin, an outrage on our holiest feelings, to pretend that anything but deep, fervent love and sympathy constitute marriage. The right idea of marriage is at the foundation of all reforms. How strange it is that man will apply all the improvements in the arts and sciences to everything about him, animate or inanimate, but himself. If we properly understood the science of life, it would be far easier to give to the world harmonious, beautiful, noble, virtuous children, than it is to bring grown-up discord into harmony with the great divine soul of all. I ask for no laws on marriage. I say with Father Chipman, remove law and a false public sentiment, and woman will no more live as wife with a cruel, bestial drunkard than a servant, in this free country, will stay with a pettish, unjust mistress. If lawmakers insist upon exercising their prerogative in some way on this question, let them forbid any woman to marry until she is twenty-one; let them fine a woman $50 for every child she conceives by a drunkard. Women have no right to saddle the state with idiots who must be supported by the public. You know that the statistics of our idiot asylums show that nearly all are the offspring of drunkards. Women must be made to feel that the transmitting of immortal life is a solemn, responsible act, and should never be allowed except when the parents are in the highest condition of mind and body. Man in his lust has regulated long enough this whole question of sexual intercourse. Now let the mother of mankind, whose prerogative it is to set bounds to his indulgence, rouse up and give this whole matter a thorough, fearless examination. I am glad that Catholic priest said of my letter what he did. It will call attention to the subject; and if by martyrdom I can advance my race one step, I am ready for it. I feel, as never before, that this whole question of woman's rights turns on the pivot of the marriage relation, and, mark my word, sooner or later it will be the topic for discussion. I would not hurry it on, nor would I avoid it. Good night.

To Elizabeth Smith Miller.

SENECA FALLS, *May 1, 1853.*

DEAR LIZ,—I send you the Rochester *Journal.* Well, doesn't the editor pitch into me without mercy? I would answer him, but he wouldn't publish what I might say; so there is no use. For the present we must let these narrow-minded and unfair critics rage. They cannot put down our ideas, and we will have our day in the end. I have finished Charley's "cracks."[1] I hesitate about sewing on the soles. My boots would furnish a model which is too small, while Henry's would be too large. You ask me what

---

[1] Crackovans, a warm bedroom shoe which Mrs. Stanton knit for friends to the end of her life.

I wear. Just what I wore last winter; all but the brilliant jewel I now bear in my arms—my lovely daughter. You see, by the way, that the Emperor of France has proposed the short dress for court dress. Stand firm a little longer, dear Liz, and we shall be a respectable majority—respectable and respected. I love what I suffer for, and I have suffered a good deal for this dress.[1] The *Home Journal* speaks in high praise of the short dress. It has been such a boon to me this past winter, which has been the hardest of my life. I have two good girls, but still I have been confined to the baby, for I fear to trust her in other hands. But this dress makes it easier to do all these things—running from cradle to writing-desk, from kitchen to drawing-room, singing lullabies at one moment in the nursery and dear old Tom Moore's ditties the next moment on the piano-stool. If I had on long skirts, how could I accomplish all this? God only knows. Good night.

To Susan B. Anthony.

SENECA FALLS, *June 20, 1853.*

DEAR SUSAN,—Say not one word to me about

---

[1] A change, however, was near at hand, as is shown in a letter written the thirteenth of the next month, reading: "I have been out twice in the new style of dress you and I talked of an experiment in. I have a pair of morocco boots about four inches higher than an ordinary gaiter, laced up in front. My dress comes about one inch below the top of the gaiter. Everybody says the costume is far prettier than the bloomer. In fact I have now three dresses within one inch of my boot tops. They are not so convenient as the bloomer, but I shall wear the new style when I travel as it attracts but little attention. Indoors, however, I wear the old style most of the time. How could you ask me if I would not visit in a bloomer? You know I gave up the short dress not because I did not like it, but because others allowed me no peace so long as I wore it. Your Johnson."

another convention.[1] I forbid you to ask me to send one thought or one line to any convention, any paper, or any individual; for I swear by all the saints that whilst I am nursing this baby I will not be tormented with suffering humanity. I am determined to make no effort to do anything beyond my imperative home duties until I can bring about the following conditions: 1st, Relieve myself of housekeeping altogether; 2nd, Secure some capable teacher for my children; 3rd, See my present baby on her feet. My ceaseless cares begin to wear upon my spirit. I feel it in my innermost soul and am resolved to seek some relief. Therefore, I say adieu to the public for a time, for I must give all my moments and my thoughts to my children. But above all this I am so full of dreams of the true associative life that all the reforms of the day beside that seem to me superficial and fragmentary. You ask me if I am not plunged in grief at my defeat at the recent convention for the presidency of our society.[2] Not at all. I am only too happy in the relief I feel from this additional care. I accomplished at Rochester

---

[1] For woman's rights, held the following September in New York City. In regard to this convention Lucy Stone wrote to Mrs. Stanton, August 14: "I shall be glad to get your thoughts on divorce, for there is not another woman in our ranks who thinks or who dares speak what she thinks on this topic, so far as I know. If I make any speech at the convention in New York, it will be on the right of divorce for drunkenness. That plea ought to be heard there, and I was feeling very safe since that subject was in your hands. But if you do not go, your mantle must fall on me. Affectionately and truly yours."

[2] The Woman's State Temperance Society, Rochester, New York, June 1st and 2d. Because of Mrs. Stanton's then radical views in regard to equal rights and divorce for drunkenness she was defeated for re-election as president. Thereupon, she and Miss Anthony resigned from the society which they had founded, and, after a precarious existence of one or two years, it finally broke up,

all I desired by having the divorce question brought up and so eloquently supported by dear little Lucy Stone. How proud I felt of her that night! We have no woman who compares with her. Now, Susan, I do beg of you to let the past be past, and to waste no powder on the Woman's State Temperance Society. We have other and bigger fish to fry.

To Elizabeth Smith Miller.

SENECA FALLS, *June 20, 1853.*

DEAR LIZ,—Having just finished breakfast, I leave house cares, children and everything to announce to you the melancholy fact that I am still in the flesh in this low, circumscribed and much abused sphere. And what is worse, I am coolly informed by physiologists on earth and by disembodied spirits who are supposed to be in heaven, but who come to us through our tables, that I shall probably remain here to suffer and struggle for about half a century longer —barring accidents and God being willing. That is to say, it appears that my machinery is capable of running a long time. Of course I may burst my boiler screaming to boys to come out of the cherry trees and to stop throwing stones, or explode from accumulated steam of a moral kind that I dare not let off, or be hung for breaking the pate of some stupid Hibernian for burning my meat or pudding on some company occasion. My babies, the boys and these Irish girls, as well as the generally unsettled condition of the moral, religious, and political world, are enough to fret to pieces the best constructed machinery.

Some days I feel a general giving away, but I find
that a new sun brings me fresh courage and vigor.
It is a great comfort to know that the children are
now all well. Seated on my front piazza in a big
chair, listening to the birds and all the pleasant summer sounds, alternately thinking and reading, I have
been enjoying Mrs. Child's sketch of Madame de Staël.
What a magnificent creature that mortal was! How
I do love that woman! It is seldom we see the intellectual and affectional natures so harmoniously developed as in her. In the midst of all her triumphs, she
sighed for love. How we mortals cheat ourselves out
of our birthright; how few ever taste the blessedness
of loving, nobly, generously, passionately. In a
word, how little we cultivate love, that sentiment
which is the highest heaven, and can make a paradise
on earth. Have you, dear Liz, lived long enough to
enjoy solitude, to look upon a few hours of uninterrupted quiet as a precious feast for the soul, to look
for it and long for it as an epicure does for his dinner?
If not, you are yet to live. With age comes the inner,
the higher life. Who would be forever young, to
dwell always in externals?

To Elizabeth Smith Miller.

Seneca Falls, *September 30, 1853.*

Dear Julius,—After you left me, if I may go back
so far, I plunged at once into preserving, in which
dispensation I continued until my little closet and every
available bowl and tumbler in the house were filled.
Any time during that season a man might have been

seen wending his way hither with bundles of sugar. The spoons and tables, the knobs of the doors, the children's bibs, the servants' hands, and even your blessed Johnson were all more or less sticky. But oh! how glorious the result! Not the most brilliant of Cæsar's achievements could surpass this campaign. Such jellies, such quinces—a magnificent array of fruits standing in solemn silence, each waiting a summons to appear before the first distinguished guest that may present himself. Would that Julius could be that one. After this, I cleaned house, then fitted up the children and their parents for winter, and it is only now that I am just beginning to breathe freely and to feel like taking a kind of geographical survey of my friends who are ornamenting the various dots on this vast globe. After going to bed last night, I read *Bleak House* for an hour or two. I laughed so hard over Mr. Chadband's sermons that I awoke Maggie, who lay in bed beside me, and that ended my reading for last night.

To Susan B. Anthony.

SENECA FALLS, *Dec. 1, 1853.*

DEAR SUSAN,—Can you get any acute lawyer—perhaps Judge Hay [1] is the man—sufficiently inter-

---

[1] William Hay of Saratoga Springs, New York, jurist and author, was a warm supporter of woman's rights. He wrote to Miss Anthony: "I will most cheerfully prepare notes or memoranda containing points of law that are unjust to woman, and some of her consequent claims. But the person who arranges and condenses our suggestions into an address should, from every consideration, be Mrs. Stanton, because her style is admirably suited to such a subject." And William H. Channing wrote to Mrs. Stanton: "Let me add my word of earnest request to that of Judge Hay that you will draft the Address to the Legislature on the Legal Disabilities of Women.

ested in our movement to look up just eight laws concerning us—the very worst in all the code? I can generalize and philosophize easily enough of myself; but the details of the particular laws I need, I have not time to look up. You see, while I am about the house, surrounded by my children, washing dishes, baking, sewing, etc., I can think up many points, but I cannot search books, for my hands as well as my brains would be necessary for that work. If I can, I shall go to Rochester as soon as I have finished my Address and submit it—and the Appeal too for that matter—to Channing's criticism. But prepare yourself to be disappointed in its merits, for I seldom have one hour undisturbed in which to sit down and write. Men who can, when they wish to write a document, shut themselves up for days with their thoughts and their books, know little of what difficulties a woman must surmount to get off a tolerable production.

To Susan B. Anthony.

SENECA FALLS, *January 20, 1854.*

DEAR SUSAN,—My Address is not nearly finished; but if I sit up nights, it shall be done in time. I fear, however, it may not suit the committee,[1] for it does

On all accounts you are the person to do it. There is not one of us who could tell the story of woman's wrongs as strongly, clearly, tersely, eloquently as yourself."

[1] In a letter dated February 8th, Mr. Channing, in commending the address, said: "This Address will be a good cathartic, I fancy, to the body politic. It will surely cause a sensation, and stir up, if not carry off, the bile of our Legislators. Pardon my metaphors. But verily I cannot but think of that unfortunate Legislature except as a patient about to swallow a very bitter pill—candied on the outside maybe, but candid within." It was

not suit me.   But make no arrangements with reference to my coming to Rochester, for I cannot say
when I can come, if even I may come at all.   Yesterday one of the boys shot an arrow into my baby's
eye.   The eye is safe, but oh! my fright when I saw
the blood come and the organ swell, and witnessed
her suffering! What an escape!   Imagine if I had
been in Rochester when this happened!   Then, to-day,
my nurse has gone home with a felon on her finger.
So you see how I am bound here.   In haste.

Sallie Holley [1] to C. L. Holley.

JOHNSTOWN, *February 4, 1854.*

MY DEAR BROTHER,—From Little Falls, I went to
Johnstown.   I was asked to stop at Mrs. Cady's; so
here I am in an elegant great house.   Mrs. Cady is
a very refined, lady-like, loving, spirited woman; and
you who know how sensitive I am to beautiful
things and tasteful environments, will believe me when
I say that my whole being dilated with bounding
delight when I saw the comfortable surroundings,
the genteel mistress and her cordial smile, and heard
her gentle sweet voice.   I am now writing in a well
arranged front "upper chamber."   Judge Cady is
over eighty years of age.   It is pleasant to look at

delivered twice in Albany, once before the New York State Woman's
Suffrage Convention, over which Mrs. Stanton as president presided,
February 14th and 15th, and again before the Judiciary Committees of
the Legislature sitting in joint session in the Senate Chamber.   This was
the first time a woman had addressed the Legislature.   For a full report
of this address see *History of Woman Suffrage,* vol. i, p. 595.   After it had
been put in pamphlet form Lucretia Mott wrote: "Thy speech we circulate
unsparingly.   It gives great satisfaction."

[1] Miss Holley at this time was an antislavery lecturer,

him. He has a finely moulded head, and is a John
Quincy Adams type of man. He has the appearance
of one who has always been obedient to the laws of
health. Mrs. Cady tells me that he has ever been
an early riser and a great student. Do you remember
that essay of Cameron's on Spiritual Laws? "A man
passes for what he is worth; that has engraved itself
on his face, on his form, on his fortunes in letters of
light. There is confession in the glance of our eyes,
in our smiles, in the grasp of our hands. Concealment avails nothing, boasting nothing." I thought
of this as I looked at Judge Cady. I have just come
upstairs, feeling somewhat amused by Judge Cady
selecting for family worship that chapter in the Bible
about "It is a shame for women to speak in the church."
I suppose it was especially aimed at me. The judge
is not a "woman's rights" man.[1]

Affectionately,

SALLIE.

To Elizabeth Smith Miller.

SENECA FALLS, *June 4, 1854.*

DEAR LIZ,—If you knew how impatient I feel in my
domestic bondage and how aggravating a thing an
invitation is, so far from ever tempting me to step

---

[1] This letter is interesting not only for the picture it gives of the Cady
home, but because of the impression of Judge Cady's point of view. It
was at this very time Mrs. Stanton had one of her severest battles with
her father. On her way to Albany with her two babies and nurse she
stopped off to see her parents. Judge Cady had learned that his daughter
was to speak before the legislature, and the expected welcome turned into
an attack. He tried to change her purpose by the promise of the deeds
of a house she desired. She would not yield, but his pride led him, as is
shown in the Reminiscences, to help perfect her address.

beyond the garden gate, you would point out all the joys, privileges, advantages, and blessings that pertain to the wife, mother, nurse, and cook. If I could visit you in Washington, oh, what pleasure it would give me! The thought of it transports me. Tell Cousin Gerrit I read his speech with great pleasure. I cannot understand the thrusts of the *Tribune*, for it certainly was the most radically true speech that has been made during the session on the Nebraska question. It made me think of Hercules and the giant Antæus. With the strong arms of truth, Cousin Gerrit raised those earth-born souls up into a purer air and more heavenly atmosphere. But alas! they caught no glimpse of the sun; they floundered about in weakness, for all their strength is from the earth. What a stormy time they must have had during those night sessions! What rowdy legislators for this mighty Republic. I can well understand that Cousin Gerrit is hesitating about standing at his post another session—in fact that he really intends to resign. Everybody declares that he should not resign, and even papa says it must not be. During a recent visit to me here, the latter said: "Gerrit has behaved much better than I expected. He has said but little, but said that little well." He did not tell me what he expected, but I can imagine!

To Susan B. Anthony.

SENECA FALLS, *February 15, 1855.*

DEAR SUSAN,—I have just been engaged to lecture before the Teachers' Association of this county. Two weeks from Wednesday is the appointed time. My fee is to be $10. I am now absorbed in the subject of education, teachers, visiting committees, scholars, school houses, etc., etc. Pray the gods that I may do well. I have my Rochester and Waterloo lectures blocked out. But oh! I ought to read and think so much. But the days are so short, and the nights too; I live by sleep. If with my brain I had a nervous temperament, I could accomplish so much. But then I would die soon. As soon as you all begin to ask too much of me,[1] I shall have a baby! Now, be careful; do not provoke me to that step. An article for the *Tribune* which I sent Henry three weeks ago, he returns to me to-day for revision and correction. I shall send no more to him for criticism; husbands are too critical. Henceforth, they shall go direct to Greeley, fresh from my brain. I am vexed. Good night.

To Susan B. Anthony.

PETERBORO, *September 10, 1855.*

DEAR SUSAN,—I wish that I were as free as you and I would stump the state in a twinkling. But I am not, and what is more, I passed through a terrible scourging when last at my father's. I cannot tell you how deep the iron entered my soul. I never felt more keenly the degradation of my sex. To think that all in me of which my father would have felt a proper pride had I been a man, is deeply mortifying

---

[1] The incessant demand upon her in the development of the woman suffrage movement may be traced in part in the three volumes of the *History of Woman Suffrage*. If she could not attend a convention she always wrote and signed the call, wrote the resolutions, and contributed a stirring letter.

II.—5

to him because I am a woman. That thought has stung me to a fierce decision—to speak as soon as I can do myself credit. But the pressure on me just now is too great. Henry sides with my friends, who oppose me in all that is dearest to my heart. They are not willing that I should write even on the woman question. But I will both write and speak. I wish you to consider this letter strictly confidential. Sometimes, Susan, I struggle in deep waters. I have rewritten my "Indian," and given it into the hands of Oliver Johnson, who has promised to see it safely in the *Tribune*. I have sent him another article on the "Widow's Teaspoons," and I have mailed you one of mine which appeared in the Buffalo *Democracy*. I have sent six articles to the *Tribune*, and three have already appeared. I have promised to write for the *Una*.[1] I read and write a good deal, as you see. But there are grievous interruptions. However, a good time is coming and my future is always bright and beautiful. Good night.

As ever your friend, sincere and steadfast.

To Elizabeth Smith Miller.

SENECA FALLS, *September 20, 1855.*

DEAR JULIUS,—On my way back, I met Wendell Phillips in the cars and talked with him from Syracuse to Auburn. He thinks Sumner is coming out with his view of the Constitution that it is an antislavery document. He said he wished Cousin Gerrit would give them some speeches East this winter, and spoke

[1] A reform paper edited by Paulina Wright Davis.

of him in the most flattering terms. I found awaiting to receive me, Amelia, the children, the dinner, and the house in apple pie order. What a treasure Amelia is! And Maggie is too cunning and lovely to live. I have kissed and hugged her till she went to sleep. The joy a mother feels on seeing her baby after a short absence is a bliss that no man's soul can ever know. There we have something that they have not! But we have purchased the ecstasy in deep sorrow and suffering. Cousin Gerrit would roll up the whites of his eyes if he knew what I am reading just now—*The Life and Writings of Thomas Paine!* Just tell him and see the effect. As the New York *Observer* and the *Presbyterian* have dubbed me "infidel," I thought I would look up my associates. So at the present writing, Tom Paine and Fanny Wright lie on my table!! I am quite surprised to find them such rational and beautiful writers. We had a visit a little while ago from my venerable sire. Just at this time I believe I lie more heavily on his soul than does his erratic nephew. As we sat alone one night, he asked me: "Elizabeth, are you getting ready to lecture before lyceums?" "Yes sir," I answered. "I hope," he continued, "you will never do it during my lifetime, for if you do, be assured of one thing, your first lecture will be a very expensive one."[1] "I intend," I replied, "that it shall be a very profitable one." Whereupon he took a candle and left the parlor by one door, and I took a candle and left by another. Oh, for a lodge in some vast wilderness where unmolested

---

[1] Judge Cady disinherited Mrs. Stanton in his will at this time. But before his death finally relented.

the soul might develop as the leaves of the forest! It would be as wise to hope to prevent by public or statute law the flowers from opening to a summer sun or the stately grain from bending its head to each passing zephyr, as to hold in abeyance the thoughts and feelings of the human soul. This coming winter, we wish to send up to our Legislature a mammoth petition asking for the right of suffrage. Will, Julius, help to swell the list of names? I send you the Appeal to the women of the State. We wish it inserted in every country paper. If you know any women in Morrisville, Hamilton, Cazenovia, or Canistota who would circulate petitions, send them blanks with a request to get names. Susan Anthony has been with me, and we have addressed and sent petitions to every county in the State. I have sent Neil and Gat down to Johnstown. One boy makes less noise than three. Do you know that? Good night.

Your pen-weary

JOHNSON.

To Susan B. Anthony.

SENECA FALLS, *November 4, 1855.*

DEAR SUSAN,—I am rejoiced to say that Henry is heart and soul in the Republican movement and is faithfully stumping the state once more. I have attended all the Republican meetings and have had Senator John P. Hale staying with us. The day he was expected I met a Republican editor in the street. "Well, I suppose we are to hear Hale to-night," I remarked. "*We*," he replied, "we do not wish to spare any room for ladies; we mean to cram the hall with voters." "I have done my best to be a voter," was my response, "and it is no fault of mine if unavailable people occupy your seats. So I for one am determined to go and hear Hale." I went to the meeting with Mr. Hale and Henry, and we found a dozen women already there. I am and have been up to my chin in business and company. Thomas Beecher has also been here again. He gave us a very fine lecture, and I had a very pleasant talk with him.

To Gerrit Smith.

SENECA FALLS, *January 3, 1856.*

MY NOBLE COUSIN,—You said you have but little faith in this reform—the Woman's Rights Movement—because the changes we propose are so great, so radical, so comprehensive; whilst they who have commenced the work are so puny, feeble, and undeveloped. The mass of women are developed at least to the point of discontent, and that, in the dawn of this nation, was considered a most dangerous point in the British Parliament, and is now deemed equally so on a Southern plantation. In the human soul, the steps between discontent and action are few and short indeed. As to the general cause of woman, I see no signs of failure. We already have a property law, which in its legitimate effects must elevate the *femme covert* into a living, breathing woman—a wife into a property holder, who can make contracts, buy and sell. In a few years, we shall see how well it works. It needs but little forethought to perceive that in due time these property holders must be represented in the government; and when the mass of women see that there is some hope of becoming voters and lawmakers, they will take to their rights as naturally as the negro to his heels when he is sure of escape. Their present seeming content is very much like Sambo's on the plantation. If you truly believe that all the burning indignation that fires your soul at the sight of injustice and oppression, if suffered in your own person, would nerve you to a lifelong struggle for liberty and independence, then know that what you feel, the mass of women feel also. We need not wait for one more generation to pass away in order to find a race of women worthy to assert the humanity of women; and that is all we claim to do.

From Susan B. Anthony.

Home-getting, along towards 12 o'clock,

THURSDAY NIGHT, *June 5, 1856.*

And, Mrs. Stanton, not a word on that Address for the Teachers' Convention. This week was to be leisure to me, and the Mercy only knows when I can get a moment; and what is worse, as the Lord knows full well, if I get all the time the world has, I can't get up a decent document. Oh, dear, dear! There is so much to say and I am so without constructive power to put in symmetrical order. So, for the love of me and for the saving of the reputation of womanhood, I beg you, with one baby[1] on your knee and another at your feet, and four boys whistling, buzzing, hallooing "Ma, Ma," set yourself about the work. It is of but

---

[1] Harriot born January 20, 1856.

small moment who writes the Address, but of vast moment that it be well done. Ah! Mrs. Stanton, don't say No, nor don't delay it a moment; for I must have it all done and almost commit to memory. During July, I want to speak certainly twice at Avon, Clifton, Sharon, and Ballston Springs, and at Lake George. Now will you load my gun, leaving me to pull the trigger and let fly the powder and ball? Don't delay one mail to tell me what you will do, for I must not and will not allow these schoolmasters to say: "See, these women can't or won't do anything when we do give them a chance." No, they sha'n't say that, even if I have to get a man to write it! But no man can write from my standpoint, nor no woman but you; for all, all would base their strongest argument on the unlikeness of the sexes. Antoinette Brown wrote me that she should do so were she to make the address. And yet, in the schoolroom more than any other place, does the difference of sex, if there is any, need to be forgotten. Now do, I pray you, give heed to my prayer. Those of you who have the talent to do honor to poor—oh! how poor—womanhood, have all given yourself over to baby-making; and left poor brainless me to do battle alone. It is a shame. Such a body as I might be spared to rock cradles. But it is a crime for you and Lucy Stone and Antoinette Brown to be doing it. I have just engaged to attend a progressive meeting in Erie County, the first of September, just because there is no other woman to be had, but not because I feel in the least competent. Oh, dear, dear! If the spirits would only just make me a trance medium and put the right thing into my mouth. You can't think how earnestly I have prayed to be made a speaking medium for a whole week. If they would only come to me thus, I'd give them a hearty welcome. How I do wish I could step in to see you and make you feel all my infirmities—mental, I mean. Do get all on fire and be as cross as you please. You remember, Mr. Stanton told how cross you always get over a speech.

Good bye,

SUSAN B. ANTHONY.

To Susan B. Anthony.

SENECA FALLS, *June 10, 1856.*

DEAR SUSAN,—Your servant is not dead but liveth. Imagine me, day in and day out, watching, bathing, dressing, nursing, and promenading the precious contents of a little crib in the corner of the room. I pace up and down these two chambers of mine like a caged lioness, longing to bring to a close nursing and housekeeping cares. I have other work on hand too. That you may see what it is, I send you the letters [1] of Oliver

---

[1] Mr. Johnson said: "I wish you could attend the Fourth Annual Convocation of Pennsylvania Progressive Friends and present the question of Woman's Rights. I know no other person who would do it so well. If your household cares won't let you come, I wish you would write two octavo pages putting the question in proper shape for the endorsement of our body. Of course your name will not go with this, though it may be privately known that you are the writer. Besides this, I would like to have you write us a letter in your own name, to be read to the meeting and published in our pamphlet." Across the back of this letter was written: "Both finished and mailed." Mr. May said: "Horace Mann writes me from Antioch College asking me for information concerning the rights of married women in New York state. Please help me to answer fully Mr. Mann's inquiries. Have any important changes gone into operation since you addressed the Legislature in 1854?"

Johnson and Samuel J. May. Is your speech[1] to be exclusively on the point of educating the sexes together, or as to the best manner of educating women? I will do what I can to help you with your lecture. Let Lucy and Antoinette rest awhile in peace and quietness and think great thoughts for the future. It is not well to be in the excitement of public life all the time; do not keep stirring them up or mourning over their repose. You need rest too, Susan. Let the world alone awhile. We cannot bring about a moral revolution in a day or year. Now that I have two daughters, I feel fresh strength to work. It is not in vain that in myself I have experienced all the wearisome cares to which woman in her best estate is subject. Good night. YOURS IN LOVE.

From Lucy Stone.

NEW YORK, *October 22, 1856.*

DEAR MRS. STANTON,—It is just as I expected. All that you consider legitimate for our convention,[2] I do too. I not only think that so much is proper to be discussed, but ought to be. I do so much wish that you could come and speak it all out. Can't you write a letter? It is a great, serious subject that only a few intuitive souls dimly understand, while a thousand aching and uncompanioned hearts and minds, wedded only in name, wait for the first ray of light

---

[1] An address on "Co-education," which Miss Anthony gave before the State Teachers' Association, which met at Troy, New York, in August, 1856.

[2] To this, the Seventh National Woman's Rights Convention, held in New York, November 25th and 26th, Mrs. Stanton did send a letter in which was an able arraignment of the marriage relation, as commonly understood. It is printed in full in the *History of Woman Suffrage,* vol. i, p. 860.

to lead out of their abyss of sorrow. I wish I could see you. I want so much to talk with some one who has thought this matter all over and who dares to speak. I am not one bit afraid of the censure which a discussion of this question will bring. If I were only sure what was the right, I can stand by it through fire and flood. I very much wish that a wife's right to her own body should be pushed at our next convention. It does seem to me that you are the one to do it. Can't you come? I will help all I can. The subject is too broad for a letter and needs to be heard on both sides.   Yours very truly,

LUCY STONE.

To Elizabeth Smith Miller.

SENECA FALLS, *November 15, 1856.*

DEAR JULIUS,—I am spending my leisure moments in reading. After enjoying a memoir of Charlotte Brontë, I re-read all her works. They are wonderful productions. No one before has ever so vividly portrayed the aimless vacuity of woman's life. I have been reading, too, in one of the reviews, an account of Emerson's visit to Carlyle. I like those two men, though I think I prefer the gentleness of the American to the roughness of the Scotchman. I am also in the midst of *Little Dorrit.* It is a sad story thus far, but interesting, as everything of Dickens is. I am so glad now, as I sit away off here in the heart of New York State, that I saw something of this young author, with his fine flowing locks, when I was in London. Did I ever tell you that he said to me that he meant to come to America some day? And while

I have been reading others, I have been writing some myself. I have found time to grind out a few tracts. I send you one. Did you see my "It is so Unladylike"? But writing at Seneca Falls is not like writing at Gadshill. You must not expect me to be a Dickens! So Cousin Gerrit has to hurry home to vote! How queer it will be when we oppressed, down-trodden women shall have to fly to our respective homes to perform the sacred act of devotion to our country. But this annual duty will be much more easy and pleasant than the biennial one to which we are now subject in supplying soldiers and legislators for this model Republic, with its gag laws and fugitive slaves. By the way, what does Cousin Gerrit think of the present course of the government? My own opinion is that the "staving off" policy has been fairly tried, and I am becoming more and more convinced that we shall be in the midst of violence, blood, and civil war before we look for it. Our fair republic must be the victim of the monster, slavery, unless we speedily rise in our might and boldly shout freedom. I am sure Cousin Gerrit holds this view. I know old John Brown does, for a letter from him passed through my hands the other day. Perhaps I may see him after all, for he is expected at Rochester next month, on a visit to Frederick Douglass. Good night.

To Susan B. Anthony.

SENECA FALLS, *July 20, 1857.*

DEAR SUSAN,—I was glad to hear of Lucy Stone. I think a vast deal of her and Antoinette Brown. I regret so much that you and Lucy should have had even the slightest interruption to your friendship. I was much interested in the extract from her letter; although I agree with her that man, too, suffers in a false marriage relation, yet what can his suffering be compared with what every woman experiences whether happy or unhappy? I do not know that the laws and religion of our country even now are behind the public sentiment which makes woman the mere tool of man. He has made the laws and proclaimed the religion; so we have his exact idea of the niche he thinks God intended woman to fill. A man in marrying gives up no right; but a woman, every right, even the most sacred of all—the right to her own person. There will be no response among women to our demands until we have first aroused in them a sense of personal dignity and independence; and so long as our present false marriage relation continues, which in most cases is nothing more nor less than legalized prostitution, woman can have no self-respect, and of course man will have none for her; for the world estimates us according to the value we put upon ourselves. Personal freedom is the first right to be proclaimed, and that does not and cannot now belong to the relation of wife, to the mistress of the isolated home, to the financial dependent.

To Susan B. Anthony.

SENECA FALLS, *August 20, 1857.*

DEAR SUSAN,—I did indeed see by the papers that you had once more stirred that part of intellectual stagnation, the educational convention. The *Times* was really quite complimentary. Henry brought me every item he could see about you. "Well," he would say, "another notice about Susan. You stir up Susan, and she stirs the world." What a set of fools those schoolmarms must be! Well, if in order to please men they wish to live on air, let them. I was glad you went to torment them. I will do anything to help you on. If I do nothing else this fall I am bound to aid you to get up an antislavery address. You must come here for a week or two and we will accomplish wonders. You and I have a prospect of a good long life. We shall not be in our prime before fifty, and after that we shall be good for twenty years at least. If we do not make old Davies [1] shake in his shoes we will make him turn in his grave.

To Susan B. Anthony.

Seneca Falls, *December, 1857.*

Dear Susan,—How do you stand on the Lecompton question? [2] You Garrisonians are such a crochety set that generally, when all other men see cause for rejoicing, you howl the more grievously. How is it now? I desire to know, for as I am one of you, I wish to do what is most becoming to one of the order. Shall I fire off my boys' cannon and a bundle of crackers, or shall I wear sackcloth and ashes? We have had

---

[1] Prof. Charles Davies, the distinguished mathematician, always Miss Anthony's bitterest opponent at these Teachers' Conventions.

[2] A pro-slavery convention, sitting at Lecompton, Kansas, prepared a constitution which was distasteful to the Free-State settlers, and it was defeated by a large majority when submitted to the voters.

Greeley here to-day, who gave us two admirable speeches—one on temperance and one on Nebraska, Know-nothingism, and political economy. A curious jumble, is it not? But he managed it all very well. I had a pleasant talk with him later at the house. He was in a rather sunny mood and addressed me as "one of the staff," a playful reference to my occasional scribblings for the *Tribune*. But little did he dream that he awakened in me a slumbering hope. If I were a man and not pinned here, how I would hie to New York—whither I am going, by the way, to-morrow, to join Henry for a brief season—and become one of the *Tribune* corps of regular writers! What could I not do for our cause if I could contribute to the editorial page of such an organ! What a phantasmagoria!

To Susan B. Anthony.

SENECA FALLS, *July 4, 1858.*

DEAR SUSAN,—I went to Junius and read my address on suffrage, which was pronounced very fine. I feel that two or three such meetings would put me on my feet. But, oh, Susan, my hopes of leisure were soon blasted. The cook's brother was taken sick with fever a few days after you left, and she was obliged to go home. So I have done my work aided by a little girl ever since. But I went to Junius in spite of it all. I see that Mr. Higginson belongs to the Jeremy Bentham school, that law makes right. I am a disciple of the new philosophy that man's wants make his rights. I consider my right to property, to suffrage, etc., as natural and inalienable as my right to life and to liberty. Man is above all law. The province of law is simply to protect me in what is mine.

To T. W. Higginson.

SENECA FALLS, *May 1, 1859.*

DEAR MR. HIGGINSON,—I think our friend's tirades on men are just in some respects and unjust in others. Theodore Parker, Garrison, Phillips, Gerrit Smith, and men of that kidney inspire me with love and respect for the sons of Adam. But alas! when we read the view of the average men, their laws, the literature which they father; when we listen to their every-day talk, to their decisions in the courts, to their sermons in the pulpit, and witness their actions at the fireside, then we feel that they richly deserve all that she says. So if that is her mission, let her attack Mrs. Craik and the door-mat theory.[1] We need some one at that point, while our milder spirited supporters can occupy the middle ground, and go on making tender appeals to man's chivalry and sense of justice, while you and I run up and down the scale, always having a royal encounter on "the door-mat," singing with due asperity in the chorus hallelujas to single women, rebukes for spaniel wives, and reasonable denunciations for all flesh in male form. I may add in closing, that I think if women would indulge more freely in vituperation, they would enjoy ten times the health they do. It seems to me they are

---

[1] Dinah Maria Craik, author of *A Woman's Thoughts About Woman,* where are advocated very conservative views concerning the position of women.

suffering from repression. Yours as ever, and with renewed admiration for your championship of my sex.

To Susan B. Anthony.

SENECA FALLS, *July 15, 1859.*

DEAR SUSAN,—Well, here is the tract.[1] I think it is about right now that the best part is all cut out! I should have sent it long ago, but, as I have had to change servants, I had little time to give to writing. Mary went into the factory, as she was tired revolving round the cook stove—I couldn't blame her—and Susan got sick and went home. So imagine me with strange servants, my boys home on their vacation, and excuse my seeming neglect of all your epistles. But when you come, I will try and find time to grind out what you say must be done. In the past, we have issued all kinds of bulls under all kinds of circumstances, and I think we can still do more in that line, even if you must make the puddings and carry the baby [2] while I ply the pen.

To Susan B. Anthony.

SENECA FALLS, *December 23, 1859.*

DEAR SUSAN,—Where are you? Since a week ago last Monday, I have looked for you every day. I

---

[1] During the summer and autumn of this year there was a vigorous campaign in New York State in favor of woman's rights. The usual appeal was the work of Mrs. Stanton, who here, as always, laid stress on the importance of the ballot. The closing paragraph brings this out: "Before another Constitutional Convention shall be called, see to it that the public sentiment of this state shall demand suffrage for women." This appeal, signed by Mrs. Stanton as chairman of the Central Committee, is given complete in the *History of Woman Suffrage,* vol. i, p. 676.

[2] Robert Livingston, the seventh and last child, born March 14, 1859.

had the washing put off, we cooked a turkey, I made a pie in the morning, sent my first-born to the depot and put clean aprons on the children, but lo! you did not come. Nor did you soften the rough angles of our disappointment by one solitary line of excuse. And it would do me such great good to see some reformers just now. The death of my father,[1] the worse than death of my dear Cousin Gerrit,[2] the martyrdom of that grand and glorious John Brown —all this conspires to make me regret more than ever my dwarfed womanhood. In times like these, every-one should do the work of a full-grown man. When I pass the gate of the celestial city and good Peter asks me where I would sit, I shall say, "Anywhere, so that I am neither a negro nor a woman. Confer on me, good angel, the glory of white manhood so that henceforth, sitting or standing, rising up or lying down, I may enjoy the most unlimited freedom." Good night.

---

[1] Judge Cady became suddenly blind in April, 1859, and died on October 31st.

[2] In October John Brown made his famous raid on Harper's Ferry. On November 2 he was found guilty and condemned to be hung. This tragedy unsettled for a time the mind of his friend and supporter Gerrit Smith.

1860–1870

To Susan B. Anthony.

SENECA FALLS, *January 25, 1860.*

DEAR SUSAN,—I am ready, willing, and happy to do next month the appointed work at Albany.[1] However, I cannot, my dear friend, move heaven and earth; but I will do what I can with pen and brain. By the way, do you know that the Auburn resolutions were read on the floor of Congress? This pleased me greatly, and I am very proud to stand maternal sponsor for the whole string.

To Susan B. Anthony.

SENECA FALLS, *April 24, 1860.*

DEAR SUSAN,—My address for the New York convention [2] is finished. It is just forty minutes long.

[1] On March 19th Mrs. Stanton addressed the Judiciary Committee of the New York Legislature on the bill then pending for the enlargement of women's property rights. A magnificent audience was present, and Mrs. Stanton spoke from the speaker's desk. The bill had passed the Senate in February, was concurred in by the Assembly the day after Mrs. Stanton's address, and was signed shortly afterwards by Governor Morgan. This address is given in the *History of Woman Suffrage*, vol. i, p. 679. The Rev. Amory Dwight Mayo, the Unitarian clergyman, who had asked Mrs. Stanton to repeat the address in his church, left at her hotel the following note: "I regret not finding you in, and so must briefly announce our decision on the repetition of the address. We feel strongly that nothing should be done in any way to mar the beautiful impression made this morning. The whole gathering, the day, the character of the audience, the general impression, could not be reproduced. It is the first time I have listened to you, and you will not accuse me of flattery when I say that the hearing has confirmed my previous suspicion that you are the head and front of this offense against the oppressors of womanhood."

[2] The Tenth National Woman's Rights Convention, which met in New York on May 10th. The proceedings of the opening day were pleasant

The remaining part of my time I shall devote to divorce. In a letter from Lucy Stone a month ago she said: "I wish you would call a convention to discuss divorce, marriage, infanticide, and their kindred subjects."[1] I have written to Lucy asking her to sustain me if any discussion grows out of the address. I may add that I am well, and full of steam, that the house is all cleaned for the summer; that every spare moment I seize my pen, and that, in a word, I am now ready to do what is to be done. By the way, I have just written to Stephen Foster to ask him not to forget the woman element in the new political party which some of the radicals are bent on forming. Again, by the way, Henry[2] has just returned from Washington. Susan, there is a dreadful state of things at our national capital. Is there no way you and I can get an oar in there? I think after you finish up the educational interests and old Davies, we must take up the nation and its President! What say you?

and harmonious, but the next morning the whole atmosphere was changed by Mrs. Stanton introducing a set of resolutions declaring that, under certain circumstances, divorce was justifiable. She supported her resolutions by a strong speech, and a long and bitter discussion followed, which was continued in the press for many days throughout the United States. Wendell Phillips was her chief opponent in the convention, a majority of which, however, supported Mrs. Stanton. The resolutions and address may be found in the *History of Woman Suffrage*, vol. i, p. 716.

[1] And in a letter dated "North Orange, April 16, 1860," Mrs. Stone wrote: "I am glad you will speak on the divorce question, provided you are yourself clear on the subject. It is a great, grave topic, that one shudders to grapple. But its hour is coming, and will have fully come when we are ready. God touch your lips if you speak on it!"

[2] Mr. Stanton was Washington correspondent of the New York *Tribune* at this time,

From William Lloyd Garrison.

BOSTON, *March 23, 1860.*

MY DEAR FRIEND,—It is the unanimous desire of the Executive Committee of the American Antislavery Society that you will be one of the speakers at its anniversary in the city of New York in May. I write at their request. We earnestly hope it will be in your power to comply with this invitation.

> When woman's heart is bleeding,
> Shall woman's voice be hushed?

Yours sincerely,

W^{M.} LLOYD GARRISON.

---

[1] Mrs. Stanton accepted the invitation, and was one of the chief speakers at the opening session on May 8th. "It was a capital speech," says Francis Jackson Garrison, who was present on that occasion. Mrs. Stanton began by proposing discreetly the following resolution, which well illustrates her invariable custom of seizing every occasion to advance the cause of woman: "Resolved, That the crowning excellence and glory of antislavery enterprise is that, while its first design is the redemption of the Ethiopian of the South from chattel bondage, it is also, through the genius and power of Eternal Truth, liberating and elevating universal humanity above all the behests of custom, creed, conventionalism or constitutions, wherever they usurp authority over the individual soul; and thus, while our first care is the emancipation of the Southern slave, we women are, under the Divine economy, at the same time working out our own salvation, and hastening the triumph of Love and Liberty over all forms of oppression and cruelty throughout the earth." But this intrusion did not pass without protest in some quarters. Thus, a correspondent of the *Liberator*—see the number for May 18th—writing of the proceedings, says: "I have heard no word of complaint from any genuine antislavery person except in reference to the address of Mrs. Stanton. Those who agreed with her in reference to the degraded condition of the women of our land thought the remarks very much out of place, while those who could not think with her that woman was so shockingly oppressed, could not but have felt grieved to see the cause of the slave burdened with a topic so entirely foreign to the call that brought us together." The editor, in the text of the above letter, adds this comment: "Mrs. Stanton's reference to the condition of her own sex (white) was merely incidental, and, on the whole, very natural."

To Susan B. Anthony.

SENECA FALLS, *May 28, 1860.*

DEAR SUSAN,—I was immensely complimented by the literati of Geneva during my recent visit to that pretty town. Doctor Reed spoke to me especially of the New York divorce resolutions and speech as "showing the most wonderful power of language," and General Swift declared my antislavery speech the best ever made. Cousin Gerrit thought that a grand compliment as the General "had often listened to him." So you see all the world does not look through Phillips's spectacles. Alvah Worden's letter to me is also everything which you and I in our greediness could desire, and Mrs. Seward invites me to come over and spend a day with them at Auburn expressly to discuss this question of divorce. But we must be careful in our conversations not to commit them, as these are their private opinions. Apropos of this whole question, I note what you say about the effect on you of *Adam Bede.* It affected me more deeply; and *The Mill on the Floss* is another agony. If Phillips would read *Adam Bede* he would know why the marriage problem is to me so all-absorbing.

To Amy Post.

SENECA FALLS, *June 1, 1860.*

DEAR AMY,—Every expression of approval from noble women is most grateful to me. I feel so perfectly sure that the last blow struck was a good one that I am truly sorry to have any one turn away. My life has been one long struggle to do and say what I know to be right and true. I would not take back one brave word or deed. My only regret is that I have not been braver and bolder and truer in uttering the honest conviction of my own soul. I am thankful that I did not know how Phillips felt, for I fear the knowledge of his disapproval might have held me back. The desire to please those we admire and respect often cripples conscience.

To Martha C. Wright.

SENECA FALLS, *June 2, 1860.*

DEAR MARTHA,—Is it not amazing what a spirit Phillips manifests? My opinion is that he thinks we slyly sprung the discussion upon the convention. But the fact is that I wrote to Lucy Stone at least six weeks before the convention met, telling her that I should speak on divorce, and urging her to do the same in the way I had once heard her at Rochester. Not a word of disapproval, or the least hint that divorce was not a proper subject for our platform.[1] I asked Susan half a dozen times where Garrison and Phillips would be, and she felt confident they would be with us. To show you how little idea I had of

---

[1] At this point the reader is "behind the scenes" in the suffrage drama. A few years later came the once famous split in the movement, when the Boston "wing," having failed to dominate the National Woman Suffrage Association, broke away and formed the American Woman Suffrage Association. The first excuse given was that Miss Anthony was dishonest in money matters. This attack brought little response. Next Mrs. Stanton's views on divorce were exploited as the cause of division.

any such thing, I may cite the fact that, as soon as I finished speaking, Mr. Longfellow came and introduced himself to me, and when we had talked a while, I said to him: "I wish you would ask Mr. Garrison and Phillips to fill up all the time after Mrs. Rose finishes, so that no free lovers get the platform." The truth is that we have thrown our bombshell into the center of woman's degradation, and of course we have raised a rumpus. The sad women who struggled up to press my hand and who were speechless with emotion, know better than our noble Phillips or politic editors who has struck for them the blow in the right place. Lucretia may trust my "instinct." I shall trust my instinct and reason until some masculine logic meets mine better than it has yet done on the point at issue. I have read with amusement what you say about that dear conservative friend of ours who retires from our movement on account of the "erratic people who sometimes occupy the platform." If her hands are as badly stained with woman's rights as mine are at this present writing with cherries, raspberries, and currants, she must have had a hard time washing them clean. I am glad the little woman has got them and her soul clear of this odious question. But nothing, nobody, can abate the whole-souled, all-absorbing, agonizing interest I feel for the redemption of woman. I could not wash my hands clean of woman's rights, for they are dyed clear down to the marrow of the bone; and even though the most erratic of our co-workers should locate themselves on our platform for all time, I should stay there too. There!

To Susan B. Anthony.

SENECA FALLS, *June 14, 1860.*

DEAR SUSAN,—I am not surprised at the tone of Phillips's note.[1] It harmonizes with his spirit, which I thought very bad. I spoke as an individual, and Phillips as an individual tried to sweep the platform clear of me and my marriage and divorce question. But the convention sustained me, and now he has no more right to whine than I would have if I had been defeated. The fact is he over-rated his personal power, and was mortified to find it so little. With all his excellence and nobility, Wendell Phillips is a man. His words, tone, and manner came down on me like a clap of thunder. We are right, however. My reason, my experience, my soul proclaim it. Woman's degradation is in man's idea of his sexual rights. Our religion, laws, customs, are all founded on the belief that woman was made for man. Come what will, my whole soul rejoices in the truth that I have uttered. One word of thanks from a suffering woman outweighs with me the howls of all Christendom. How this marriage question grows on me. It lies at the very foundation of all progress. I never read a thing on this subject until I had arrived at my present opinion. My own life, observation, thought,

---

[1] Lydia Mott, whose home in Albany up to the time of her death in 1875 was a social center for reformers, wrote to Mrs. Stanton on April 16th: "I hope neither Susan nor yourself will be turned aside by Phillips's course, whatever it may be. I am sure he will be no barrier to the truth. It seems to me that he has been used in this matter by those who are not very high on the ladder of reform as regards woman. One good thing you have done, if nothing more, that is, driven the New York *Tribune* to that very absurd position that divorce is wrong in *any case.*"

feeling, reason, brought me to the conclusion. So fear not that I shall falter. I shall not grow conservative with age. I feel a growing indifference to the praise and blame of my race, and an increasing interest in their weal and woe. In fact, I am good to fire another bomb into the heart of the metropolis. With powder and brains, I am willing Boston should have all the milk. Do not read me off your books because I cannot do all that to you seems feasible. I am of course willing, however, to aid in distributing the report of our last convention; and, too, if you do not succeed in raising enough money to defray the expense of its printing, I will help you out. Perhaps Mrs. Seward will give something too. A peaceful good night.

To Martha C. Wright.

SENECA FALLS, *June 17, 1860.*

DEAR MARTHA,—I think your friend is wise in deciding to leave a position where she must ever find so much discord and antagonism. Such is the nature of the marriage relation that a breach once made cannot be healed, and it is the height of folly to waste one's life in vain efforts to make a binary compound of two diverse elements. What would we think of the chemist who should sit twenty years trying to mix oil and water, and insist upon it that his happiness depended upon the result of the experiment? I have just finished reading the religious services in Music Hall in memory of Theodore Parker. What a life was Parker's, what a testimony against hypocrisy! What a blessing he has been to his genera-

tion, and yet how reviled!   To him my personal debt
of gratitude is profound.

To Wendell Phillips.[1]

SENECA FALLS, *August 18, 1860.*

DEAR FRIEND,—I hold in my hand abundant evidence that you are still a subject for missionary effort.
Only think of it—one of the champions of freedom
denying to woman, at this late day, her own name.
Your letter to Susan B. Anthony is directed to the

---

[1] This letter brought the following response: "Boston, August 21, 1860.
Mrs Cady: Thank you for your pleasant letter, my dear friend. I'm
afraid my excuse will not bring you to the old saint's state of mind—'such
an excuse almost makes me glad you offended'—but will rather banish me
still nearer the North Pole of your dislike.   The truth is, I've no memory
for *first* names and especially girls' names.   Lizzie and Hattie, Sarah and
Susan, Abby and Eliza, mingle and melt in utter confusion.   I'm not quite
so bad as old President Quincy and Sydney Smith, who confess to have
forgotten their own names; but I live next door, so far as women's *first*
names are concerned.   I could not for the life of me be sure whether you
were Lizzie Cady or Susie, or whatnot; and the more I thought, the more
I did not know.   I thought I covered it up nicely by H. B-ing it, for I
always remember by the eye better than by the ear, and H. B. S. lived in
that point of time, 'the memory of man runneth not to the contrary.'
But hereafter you shall be Mrs. Cady, and I've hit on an excellent way
never again to be in doubt.   Queen Elizabeth, you know, red-headed and
so jealous of her looks that she forbade (by proclamation) all but two painters
to attempt painting her likeness—she will exactly bring you to my mind.
As to lectures.   Yes, I'll accept all I can near you and count on the break-
fasts, if Ann's health allows me to plan going so far from home.   But provided, and it being fully understood and agreed—(as the dying man said:
'If I die, I forgive you, otherwise, look out, you scoundrel!')—that this
breaking of eggs and eating of hot cakes does in no wise make up our quarrel
about your lugging on to our platform that noisy, alien Marriage and
Divorce, which dispute I no wise abate, pretermit or smother even in toast
dipped in the richest cream in central New York.   Yes, verily, the matter
is of great moment and deserveth discussion; nathless, it hath no right in
our house.   Let it go now and build for itself a lodging place and summon
thereto the good men and honorable women not a few who take note thereof;
and let there be light shed all about.   But meanwhile, let the interloping

"Care of Mrs. H. B. Stanton," if I do not do your chirography injustice. Now, my dear friend, did you pen that, or was it done by your private secretary, a perfumed young man who never heard that women and negroes are beginning to repudiate the name of their masters and claiming a right to a life-long name of their own? If you are guilty, I shall feel it my duty to make a special effort to convince you of the heinousness and criminality of your offence. But how shall I preach to you the new gospel of individual sovereignty? Not by pen. Your benighted condition would require folios of paper. I cannot go to that part of the land where you dwell, for I am anchored here, surrounded by small craft which I am struggling to tug up life's stream. May I hope that during the coming winter you will stay a few days in central New York? Do accept all the lyceum invitations you may get from this part of the state, that you may thereby place yourself in the way of being hopefully converted, and at the same time refresh us with your presence at many a breakfast and dinner too. You little know how sadly disappointed we all were, nor how many pairs of blue eyes and rosy cheeks watched in vain last spring at the gate to herald your coming. With much love and admiration for Mrs. Phillips and yourself.

---

and unnaturalised alien avoid our Jerusalem, or she shall be, not privily, thrust out of the gates thereof. Selah. And so farewell, Mistress Elizabeth Cady.

> With regards both to thee and H. B.
> And the 'blue eyes and rosy cheeks'
> I hope to see,
> Thine W. P."

To Martha C. Wright.

JOHNSTOWN, *February 10, 1861.*

DEAR MARTHA,—Do you fully appreciate our triumph at our recent convention[1] in taking your dear sister Lucretia before the Judiciary Committee of the Empire State on Divorce? And do you grasp the full force of the radical sentiments which she expressed on that occasion? "All your legislation on that whole subject should be swept away!" And in this connection, I wish you would read in the *Tribune* of the 9th inst. an article headed, "The Latest Criminal Trial." But instead of the authorities turning the women out of the courtroom to prevent them from hearing improper testimony *in regard to women,*

---

[1] This last convention before the Civil War was held at Albany on February 7th and 8th. Lucretia Mott, Mrs. Stanton, and others appeared before the Judiciary Committee of the State Senate, where was pending the Ramsay bill granting divorce for various causes. The text of this bill may be found in the *History of Woman Suffrage*, vol. i, p. 745. The Appeal (see *History of Woman Suffrage*, vol. i, p. 742) for this convention was written by Mrs. Stanton the previous November. In referring to it in a letter of November 26, 1860, Miss Anthony says: "What a grand advertisement the Albany *Argus* and New York *Express* have given 'Mrs. E. Cady Stanton's Appeal.' Parker Pillsbury, who is with me, has taken the papers on to Wendell Phillips. By the way, what think you of Mrs. Child's 'Appeal'? It is good, but so long as to repel the common mind. Parker wished yours were 'more argumentative.' I told him it was not intended for an argument, but precisely what it is. As Lydia Mott insists, we need appeals to the heart more than to the intellect. I am sure yours will have a powerful effect on our people. Lydia Mott is mailing them to every member of Congress and to every member of our Legislature. Parker said to me: 'Tell Mrs. Stanton I think she has power to shake the world, and if she only is true to the light within, I am sure she'll do it.' He read your *Liberator* letter to a parlor full of women in Michigan, and they all rejoiced in your call for 'outspoken rebellion'; and he read it to a number of us in Albany, with power and holy unction. Does Henry feel compromised by your Appeal? How shamefully weak and trembling the Republicans are—even more than the Abolitionists foreshadowed."

would it not have been better to put women on the bench and exclude the men? This sounds like a very radical proposition now, but be sure that some day in the future Americans will ask how these things could ever have been done otherwise.

Henry B. Stanton to D. C. Stanton.[1]

WASHINGTON, *February 22, 1861.*

My DEAR SON,—You will doubtless be glad to hear from this City of Commotion. The Secessionists are wearing their cockades in their hats and strutting about the streets as grand as a canal boatman with the stump of a cigar in his mouth. Toombs of Georgia, Davis of Mississippi, Hunter of Virginia, Trumbull of Illinois, and Seward of our State, made speeches last month in the Senate on slavery, secession, etc. Great numbers of the people think that the Secessionists intend to seize the Capitol, where Congress holds its sessions, and also the treasury, war, navy, post-office, and other public buildings, and prevent the inauguration of Lincoln, and so break up the government. But General Scott says he will not permit this; and therefore he has ordered into this city and its vicinity several companies of United States troops, among which are four companies of flying artillery. These flying artillery are terrible fellows. They can fire their cannons a good many times a minute. The four companies have about twenty pieces in all, and it is said that they can all fire eighty to ninety times in a minute. When loaded with

---

[1] The eldest son. He was eighteen years old.

grape and canister, they would soon sweep Pennsylvania Avenue and the Capitol grounds of Secessionists and traitors.   The governors of several states have offered to send troops here to help defend the capital.   The brave Zouaves of Seneca Falls may volunteer their services; so you may find use for your red shirt and musket hereabouts.   I feel sure that when these Secessionists come to see our brave fellow villagers marching in here, with the gallant Captain Ashcroft at their head, and you, Neal, bearing aloft the star-spangled banner, they will take to their heels and run.   Honest Abraham arrives in this city tomorrow.   There will be a great turnout.   He is determined to put down the Secessionists.   He will set the army and navy to capturing the forts, collecting the revenues and enforcing the laws.   What will come out of it remains to be seen.

Your affectionate father,

H. B. STANTON.

To the Secretary of State.

NEW YORK, *September 19, 1861.*

DEAR MR. SEWARD,—Would it be transcending the limits of our friendship for me to ask, as a personal favor, that you place the name of my son, Henry B. Stanton, Jr.,[1] among the many recommended to you as a candidate for West Point?   As all his proclivities are to the army, I desire that he should have a scientific military education.   I feel that our present struggle

---

[1] He was seventeen years old.   A little later he ran away from home and enlisted.

for liberty is to be a long and hard one, and that for years to come we shall need brave, true men to assert the idea of human equality, and to defend it with the sword against the aggressions of brute force. I have endeavored to fire his soul with a holy love for freedom. Will you help to place him in a position where, to his mind, he can best defend the sacred rights of future generations? The age of bullets has come again; and a rotten aristocracy must be subdued by the only weapons they can feel. I have an unwavering faith in the endurance of the Republic. The turmoil and confusion that now surround us are but "the noise and dust of the wagon bringing the harvest home." This war is music in my ears.[1] It is a simultaneous chorus for freedom; for every nation that has ever fought for liberty on her own soil is now represented in our army. Therefore, to you as a statesman in confidence I come, as one of the mothers of the Republic, asking that her son may be placed in the best possible position to defend those institutions I know you so truly venerate and love.

To Elizabeth Smith Miller.

SENECA FALLS, *November 14, 1861.*

DEAR LIZ,—I was quite interested to hear from Giles Stebbins a report of Cousin Gerrit's conversa-

---

[1] Most of the reformers of the time were in favor of the prosecution of the war, only they wished it made a war for freedom and not merely against secession. Miss Anthony back in March, 1860, had written: "Old Abe talks up. What anxious watching by the millions to catch his every utterance. Parker Pillsbury says: 'Tell Mrs. Stanton I am rejoicing over Old Abe; but my voice is still for war.'"

tion with Simon Cameron. Really, the much abused
Cameron seems to be the radical element in the cabinet. I spent the other evening with Mrs. Worden.
She feels perfectly discouraged about the country and
the war. They all say there will be no fighting on
the Potomac this winter. She moaned over the
treatment of General Fremont. I did not dare say
it was probably due to the policy of Thurlow Weed
and the Secretary of State. The retailing of this
political chit-chat leads me to ask whether Cousin
Gerrit would come and speak here if I would get up a
grand country gathering? The people are willing to
listen to anything on the crisis, and as I hear that my
distinguished relative orates with a new inspiration
I should like to have him stir up this Democratic
county. We have a great many Secessionists here.

To Elizabeth Smith Miller.

NEW YORK,[1] *September 11, 1862.*

DEAR JULIUS,—It needs great faith to be calm now
in this sea of trouble. Henry fears we are going to
flinders; but it does not seem so to me. Out of this
struggle we must come with higher ideas of liberty,
the masses quickened with thought, and a rotten aristocracy crushed forever. I have no misgivings as
to the result. But I do hope the rebels will sack
Washington, take Lincoln, Seward, and McClellan
and keep them safe in some Southern fort until we

---

[1] In 1861 Mrs. Stanton moved from Seneca Falls, and for the rest of her
life resided in or near New York City.

man the ship of state with those who know whither they are steering and for what purpose. Not wholly foreign to this subject is the article in the last *Atlantic* entitled "Cerebral Dynamics." It shows so clearly that children are the victims of the vices and excesses of their ancestors, that I feel more than ever a holy pity and patience with the weak and erring. Each soul lives out the law of its being, and cannot escape it. You will readily see how this same law applies to the present state of mind and the conduct of those south of Mason and Dixon's line. The war spirit has a certain indirect, perhaps direct, influence on my domestic system just now. While my boys are growing in grace, they are all drilling every evening in the gymnasium. I believe in the religious influence of exercise, especially at this time. I place the gymnasium above the "meeting house" for boys on the threshold of manhood. The girls skate, dance, and play much of the time in the open air, taking school in homeopathic doses. Like your Charles, I have great respect for saints with good strong bodies. I may add that my boy Bob is at present unfortunately in the throwing-stone dispensation. I pay for many more broken glasses than is at all desirable considering my resources. I have reasoned with the child, prayed for him and spanked him. Sad to say, the last appeal seemed most potent. To the first, he remarked that he thought the glass was strong; to the second, he replied that God was not looking at him; to the last, he promised to throw no more missiles.

II.—7

From Mrs. William H. Seward.[1]

WASHINGTON, *February 22, 1863.*

MY DEAR MRS. STANTON,—I see a slow approxima-
tion towards justice, and with that I try to be contented. My heart bleeds for the suffering, for the
soldiers and for the slave. I try not to be impatient
for the end, which lies in obscurity. I know it must
come, though the path is now so dark. I would prefer
never to hear of another battle, yet I would have all
men attain their birthright—freedom. How glad I
shall be to talk with you; one can say so little in a
letter. Mr. Seward sends regards.

Very truly yours,

FRANCES A. SEWARD.

_____

[1] This letter from the wife of the Secretary of State was a cautious reply
to the draft of the Appeal to the Women of the Republic (*History of Woman
Suffrage*, vol. ii, p. 51), which Mrs. Stanton had just sent out to a few
friends for comment. Northern women had been accused of remaining
indifferent to the Civil War. Mrs. Stanton points out the reason, and
summons women to change the contest from a mere battle against secession into a conflict to attain fundamental human rights. In response to
this Appeal, Mrs. Lydia Maria Child wrote to Mrs. Stanton on March 24,
1863: "You are interesting to me for your husband's sake, who came
boldly and frankly to the aid of the slave in all the freshness and strength
of his early manhood. How I used to delight in his spontaneous eloquence,
in those dear old days when our little band of moral enthusiasts paid the
American people the compliment of believing that the accursed system of
slavery could be upheaved and overthrown by moral influence! Then
you are especially interesting to me by reason of the tone and earnest
utterances of your soul. Your last reached me to-day. I said to my
husband: 'There is a woman after my own heart!' And he responded:
'Amen!' I respond to John Bright's sentiment that 'God is carrying on
the revolution in America very *slowly*, that He may make emancipation
sure.' Certainly, if the Lord wanted *slow* work to be done, He could not
have employed a better hand than Old Abe." The response to this Appeal
was so widespread and enthusiastic that the call (given in the Reminiscences,
page ooo) was issued for a convention to be held May 14, 1863. The
Woman's Loyal National League was then formed, with Mrs. Stanton as
president.

From Mrs. Maria Weston Chapman.

STATEN ISLAND, N. Y., *June 2, 1863.*

DEAR MRS. STANTON,—Be of good cheer about the country—the cause, whether the petition [1] be numerously signed or not. If not, it will be merely because of a general doubt whether the *thing* being done when the proslavery bubble was burst by the gun-fire of Sumter—the *form* be of moment enough to require special effort. The people engaged in supplying provender are apt to set little by prayers. But I signed the first antislavery petition as I shall my last with the assurance to them that think it of no use, that it can't do any harm.

Always very gratefully yours for the Cause,

M. W. CHAPMAN.

---

[1] Circulated by the Woman's Loyal National League. The heading to the petition read: "To the Senate and House of Representatives of the United States in Congress assembled: The undersigned citizens of ———— believing slavery the great cause of the present rebellion, and an institution fatal to the life of Republican Government, earnestly pray your Honorable Bodies to immediately abolish it throughout the United States, and to adopt measures for so amending the Constitution as forever to prohibit its existence in any portion of our common country." (*History of Woman Suffrage,* vol. ii, p. 897.) It was felt by such leaders among men as Senator Sumner, and among women as Mrs. Stanton, that the Proclamation of Emancipation was not sufficient to secure the United States against slavery. This point is emphasized in a letter from Mrs. Stanton to Martha Wright, January 20, 1864: "Dear Martha: We have 100,000 signatures, but we want a million before Congress adjourns. Remember the President's Proclamation reaches only the slaves of rebels. The jails of loyal Kentucky are crammed with slaves from secession states and advertised to be sold for their jail fees 'according to law' precisely as before the war. There must be a law abolishing slavery. Do pour in petitions. Yours for freedom,"

To Mrs. Gerrit Smith.

JOHNSTOWN, *July 20, 1863.*

DEAR COUSIN NANCY,—Last Thursday I escaped from the horrors of the most brutal mob[1] I ever witnessed, and brought my children here for safety. The riot raged in our neighborhood through the first two days of the trouble largely because the colored orphan asylum on Fifth Avenue was only two blocks away from us. I saw all those little children marched off two by two. A double portion of martyrdom has been meted out to our poor blacks, and I am led to ask if there is no justice in heaven or on earth that this should be permitted through the centuries. But it was not only the negroes who feared for their lives. Greeley was at Doctor Bayard's a day and night for safety, and we all stayed there also a night, thinking that, as Henry, Susan, and I were so identified with reforms and reformers, we might at any moment be subjects of vengeance. We were led to take this precaution because as Neil was standing in front of our house[2] a gang of rioters seized him, shouting: "Here's one of those three-hundred-dollar fellows!" I expected he would be torn limb from limb. But with great presence of mind he said to the leaders as they passed a saloon: "Let's go in, fellows, and take a drink." So he treated the whole band. They then demanded that he join them in three cheers for "Jeff Davis," which he led with apparent enthusiasm. "Oh," they said, "he seems to be a good fellow; let

---

[1] Caused by the army draft.
[2] No. 75 W. 45th Street. The house is still standing (1921).

him go." Thus he undoubtedly saved his life by
deception, though it would have been far nobler to
have died in defiance of the tyranny of mob law.
You may imagine what I suffered in seeing him dragged
off. I was alone with the children, expecting every
moment to hear the wretches thundering at the front
door. What did I do? I sent the servants and the
children to the fourth story, opened the skylight and
told them, in case of attack, to run out on the roof
into some neighboring house. I then prepared a
speech, determined, if necessary, to go down at once,
open the door and make an appeal to them as Americans and citizens of a republic. But a squad of
police and two companies of soldiers soon came up
and a bloody fray took place near us which quieted
the neighborhood.

To Elizabeth Smith Miller.

New York, *September 1, 1863.*

Dear Lizzie,—Our badge is done.[1] Artists pro-
nounce the design and execution to be very fine. It
represents a negro, half risen, breaking his own chains.
We have had the negro in every variety of posture—
hopeless, imploring, crouching at the feet of the Goddess of Liberty. But now, in harmony with our day,
our negro is striking the blow himself with his own
right hand. I wish every loyal woman in the nation
would wear this badge. I wish, too, that you would
magnetize Madison County into activity for this
League work. Do write to some live woman in every
town, so that there may be such a rising up in the

---

[1] Designating membership in the Woman's National Loyal League.

whole region roundabout that not even a dog shall dare to wag his tail until all those whom he watches shall have signed the mammoth petition. Julius must put his shoulder to this enterprise and help us roll up 3,000,000 names. Take a petition, an Appeal, and the Address [1] wherever you go and set some woman agoing. What a good letter that is of your father's addressed to Governor Seymour. Speaking of it the other day, Greeley said to me: "It is capital —so pointed, just and sarcastic." We all felt glad to have Seymour scarified. What license he has inaugurated at Albany! As if we did not have enough trouble on the Potomac, without adding thereto on the Hudson! By the way, has Cousin Gerrit read *Substance and Shadow*, by James? Many down this way think it the great work of the age. To me it seems to finish orthodoxy. Good night.

To Senator Charles Sumner.

New York, *February 1, 1864.*

Sir,—The Woman's Loyal National League has this day forwarded to you the Emancipation Petition [2]

---

[1] This address (*History of Woman Suffrage*, vol. ii, p. 67), drawn up by Mrs. Stanton and signed by her as president of the Woman's Loyal National League, was sent May 15, 1863, by "The Loyal Women of the Country to Abraham Lincoln, President of the United States." It states: "We come not to criticise or complain. We come to thank you for your Proclamation, in which the nineteenth century seems to echo back the Declaration of 'Seventy-six." The address declares "Our special thanks are due to you that by your Proclamation two millions of women are freed from the foulest bondage humanity ever suffered." The President is asked "to finish the work"—"slave creeds, codes and constitutions must now all pass away." The chief fear of the suffrage and abolition hosts was that guarantees of freedom would not be embodied in the Constitution of the United States.

[2] Presented by Senator Sumner, in an appropriate speech, on February 9, 1864. "I offer a petition which is now lying on the desk before me. It

signed by one hundred thousand citizens of the United States. This is the first installment of the million we propose to roll up during the present session of Congress. The petitioners are loyal men and women of the free and slave states unitedly asking their representatives in Congress that all persons of African descent held to involuntary labor or service in the United States be set free at the earliest practicable moment. The mothers, wives, and daughters of the brave men who have fallen in many a bloody battle now pray you to end the war by ending the cause of it, which is slavery. Inasmuch as the "right of petition" is the only political right woman has under the Constitution, it is the duty of her representatives to give her prayer an earnest and serious consideration. We desire that you, ever true to freedom, may have the honor of presenting this petition. It is our wish that the petition be sacredly kept in some enduring form in the national archives, as a part of the history of our second revolution.

To Jessie Benton Fremont.[1]

NEW YORK, *May 4, 1864.*

DEAR MRS. FREMONT,—Miss Anthony and I had a long talk last night in reference to her conversation with you. Alone this morning, two points strike my mind. 1st. The necessity that the call for "the

---

is too bulky for me to take up. I need not add that it is too bulky for any of the pages of this body to carry. . . . I ask the reference of it to the Select Committee on Slavery and Freedmen." It was referred, after earnest discussion, as Mr. Sumner proposed.

[1] Wife of General Fremont.

people's mass meeting" at Cleveland [1] be issued at once, in order that the vacillating—always a large class—may be assured that there is to be a liberal movement, and that Gen. John C. Fremont is its chosen representative. 2d. That the call embody the idea, the right of the people to lay down a presidential platform, and choose a man who has proved himself great enough to stand on it. Now is the time, when all are drifting, for the few, who have sublime faith, to man the life-boat, face the storm and pick up all who are not at peace in Abraham's bosom. As to the call, it must come as if from the nation's advance guard; they who stand on the lofty heights intrenched behind eternal principles. The

---

[1] On May 31st, a convention of Republicans, dissatisfied with Lincoln, met at Cleveland, Ohio, and tendered to Fremont a nomination for President, which he accepted. But in September he withdrew from the campaign in the interests of harmony, "to do my part toward preventing the election of the Democratic candidate." In regard to the nomination of Fremont, Wendell Phillips wrote to Mrs. Stanton on August 22d: "I always valued the Cleveland Convention, chiefly as an intimation to the sound portion of the Democratic party that if they'd nominate a true man, they should, as the *Evening Post* last week said, get liberal and earnest support from Republican Radicals. That, and raising the Baltimore platform and possibly untying timid tongues were all the chances I reckoned on. The Baltimore platform matter was a success, on our part. We raised it. If Grant could have had decided success so as to convince Democrats that slavery was dead and the North really ahead, then Chicago would have followed our lead and bid for our antislavery support. As it is, with Grant, to this date, a failure, though I believe in him—give him time—Chicago will nominate McClellan or worse, and where we are I'll guess when September 22d comes. If no convention ever gets to Buffalo, which I incline to believe, then my only hope is in a live Republican party opposing McClellan in the chair. Though I did not take your advice to speak this summer, I've not been idle. I have kept up untiring conference with Fremont, and trust whatever comes of our movement, he will come out right. If he doesn't, it won't be my fault. I wish I had more influence with Fremont, and that some few men had less. But I believe in him."

people must be roused to feel that they have a right to think and act; that they are not meddlers or interlopers when they demand to know the man, by his public words and acts, before they vote for him to execute their will as President of the nation. Party politicians have betrayed the people more than once by springing on them at the last moment some slippery knave or great unknown. It is time to inaugurate an entirely new mode of making Presidents, namely, let the people place men before the nation and in mass convention make known their choice. The Liberals must be made to feel that the responsibility of splitting the Republican party cannot justly be imputed to them, inasmuch as they chose their leader first, so that all who wish to march after their general have simply to fall in. But if they fall out, why, that is their misfortune. Yes, the vacillating and the drifting must be made to understand that this "Fremont movement" is an organized fact; that its champion is neither to be frightened nor bought off the course. Eight years ago when the college of electors assembled at Albany to declare the Presidential vote, my father, as chairman, in reply to a vote of thanks, said: "Gentlemen, before another Presidential campaign comes round I shall probably have passed away. But I hope you may all be in your seats again to vote for John C. Fremont, the successful candidate." In reporting the proceedings, the Albany *Evening Journal* left out, in this speech, your husband's name and substituted for it the words, "the Republican nominee, whoever he may be"!

To Susan B. Anthony.

NEW YORK, *August 22, 1864.*

DEAR SUSAN,—Did you get five dollars from me for tracts, and have you sent them here, where I am still enjoying the heat and quiet! But I am not alone, as my niece is with me. She is a beautiful woman. I wish you and I had been beautiful; then we could have carried all men with us to heights divine, and entrenched them on principle. Well, Susan, the Lincoln stock is running down rapidly. The wise ones here say there is no chance for him. The movement we inaugurated in our little room was the first plainly spoken protest against the present situation. Do you remember with what bated breath our friends deplored our action? A few evenings since I had a long talk with Oliver Johnson concerning the present situation. He is very bitter towards Phillips, and you have seen how he pitches into me and defends the pro-Lincoln letter of Cousin Gerrit.

To Susan B. Anthony.

NEW YORK, *September 25, 1864.*

DEAR SUSAN,—Well, one by one our giants are being swept down with the current. In the cars yesterday, a gentleman had the audacity to tell me that Phillips would take the stump for Lincoln! Do not suppose for a moment that I feared such a somerset [1] on the

---

[1] Her confidence was well founded. In a letter to Mrs. Stanton dated September 27, 1864, Wendell Phillips sends assurance: "You answered correctly. I would cut off both hands before doing anything to aid Abraham Lincoln's election. I wholly distrust his fitness to settle this thing,

part of our idol, for I believe he sees as clearly as man can although Oliver Johnson says Phillips's glasses get smoky sometimes. But all this talk of the Republicans about loyalty and the good of the country requiring the success of their party is the merest twaddle. After they themselves have exposed the incapacity and rottenness of the administration, what impudence to ask the people to accept another four years under the same dynasty. I do not believe that either party can block the wheels of progress, and it is certainly a good thing to clean out thoroughly the political sty once in four years. The family of men are amazingly like one another; Republicans and Democrats, saints and sinners, all act alike and talk each in his turn the same cant. But it is a comfort to know that the devil and all his imps could not put this Union back precisely as it was under Buchanan. Good night.

From Wendell Phillips.

NEW YORK, *November 11, 1864.*

DEAR EMPRESS,—Your slave, hasting too confusedly to answer your order, forgot to inclose your treasure. Far be it from the faithful hound to rob cabinets of their gems. No, let such autographs blaze in world-famous keeping. Fancy me on my knees for mistaking your MSS. I'd send you the

---

and indeed his purpose. De Retz said: 'Feeble men always reluct at the means necessary for their ends.' Lincoln wishes the end; won't consent to the means. Our friends honestly have quitted the old platform. We used to hold 'that it is always safe to do right.' They don't *dare* do what they confess would be absolutely right now. I still reject Lincoln's quarter loaf. Justice is still more to me than Union."

letter itself, which would justify me largely and
enlighten you, but then perhaps you would not send
it back, and so we'd miss it from our casket. That's
a risk not to be run. Now if you'd imitate my clear
copy-book style of careful and painstaking MSS!!!
such mistakes could never occur. I am not tired,
because the times are so good, aren't they? The old
bugles begin to sound! But really, though I never
stay anywhere but at hotels, if you'll forgive and
forget, and ask me to breakfast, dinner, or tea, I will
snap my fingers at audiences and eat as many of your
good things as I did before, and steal for speeches as
many of your good things that can't be eaten. I
will count on breakfasting with you on Thursday
morning, if you please. Tell me whether I may come
and at what hour? Now, am I not bold? Usually
I stalk from a town after speaking, feeling that the
conservatives who have heard me will think me a
fool, and fearing that the radicals will deem me tame.
Yet I dare to plan to meet you face to face! So fully
I trust you. Your humble, offending, but repentant
servant,

Thine,

W. P.

To Susan B. Anthony.

NEW YORK, *December 8, 1864.*

DEAR SUSAN,—When I was at Peterboro, I formed
two leagues, made speeches, distributed all the tracts
and blew up many copperheads. I spoke over half
an hour extemporaneously in a church at Canistota.
Since my return here, I notice in the press articles

about our petitioning. I think we had better get up paragraphs urging on the petitioning, and give a list of how the different states stand in the matter of names signed. If you will send me the list, I will prepare the paragraphs. Senator Sumner has sent me the complete list of all those who have circulated the petitions. My chief recreation just now is going every Sunday evening to hear O. B. Frothingham, who has been preaching some grand sermons since the election. Much that he said was in my mind as I read Lincoln's message to Congress. What a dry, barren document! The Republican papers make much, however, of the closing paragraphs.[1] He can very safely say that if the people require of him, what he knows they never will, that he will not execute their will. That sounds big, but it is all wind.

To Susan B. Anthony.

New York, *December 29, 1864.*

Dearest Susan,—Glorious, good Phillips! Have you read his speech? During its delivery I sat close on his right, and at its close was the first to clasp his hand and catch the currents of his inspiration. His audience felt his magnetism. But Oliver Johnson sat there, surly and unsympathetic. I did not see him speak to Phillips. I cannot tell you how happy

---

[1] "I repeat the declaration made a year ago, that while I remain in my present position I shall not attempt to retract or modify the Emancipation Proclamation, nor shall I return to slavery any person who is free by the terms of that proclamation, or by any of the acts of Congress. If the people should, by whatever mode or means, make it an executive duty to re-enslave such persons, another, and not I, must be their instrument to perform it." Annual Message of December 6, 1864.

I am to find Douglass on the same platform with us. Keep him on the right track. Tell him in this revolution, he, Phillips, and you and I must hold the highest ground and truly represent the best type of the white man, the black man and the woman. Old Martin Luther says, "God needs good men as much as they do God." This is as true in our day as it was in his. Phillips has just returned from Washington. He says the radical men feel that they are powerless and checkmated. Winter Davis told him the game was up—"Lincoln with his immense patronage can do what he pleases; the only hope is an appeal to the people." They turn to such men as Phillips to say what politicians dare not say. Phillips also expresses astonishment, and I share his astonishment, that Cousin Gerrit and Garrison should defend the proposed apprenticeship system for the emancipated negroes. We say now, as ever, Give us immediately unconditional emancipation, and let there be no reconstruction except on the broadest basis of justice and equality. But if all these men are pledged to Lincoln and his policy, come what will, then Phillips and a few others must hold up the pillars of the temple.

To Wendell Phillips.[1]

NEW YORK, *May 25, 1865.*

DEAR FRIEND,—May I ask in reply to your fallacious letter just one question based on the apparent oppo-

---

[1] This letter is in reply to one from Mr. Phillips given in part in this note. In this year began the battle between Mrs. Stanton and many of her old co-workers over the question as to whether the negro should be enfranchised and woman left disenfranchised. In support of his view Mr. Phillips

sition in which you place the negro and woman. My question is this: Do you believe the African race is composed entirely of males?

To Susan B. Anthony.

NEW YORK, *August 11, 1865.*

DEAR SUSAN,—I have argued constantly with Phillips and the whole fraternity, but I fear one and all will favor enfranchising the negro without us. Woman's cause is in deep water. With the League [1] disbanded, there is pressing need of our Woman's Rights Convention.[2] Come back and help. There will be a room for you. I seem to stand alone.

---

said in a letter dated May 10, 1865: "While I could continue, just as heretofore, arguing for woman's rights, just as I do for temperance every day, still I would not mix the movements. That in my view is where, and the only point where, you and I differ, *i. e.*, in a matter of method, of expedient action. I think such mixture would lose for the negro far more than we should gain for the woman. I am now engaged in abolishing slavery in a land where abolition of slavery means conferring or recognizing citizenship, and where citizenship supposes the ballot for all men. Whenever I begin to labor on suffrage as such, be sure I will never stultify myself by claiming it for only half the race."

[1] The Woman's Loyal League had been disbanded on the passage by Congress of the XIII Amendment. When its work was finished, Miss Anthony had gone to Kansas, where she remained about a year with her brother.

[2] The call (*History of Woman Suffrage*, vol. ii, p. 152) for the first woman's rights convention after the war was issued on March 31, 1866, and was signed by Mrs. Stanton as president of the National Woman's Rights Central Committee. The convention opened on May 10, 1866, in the Church of the Puritans, Union Square, New York. In the call occurred these words: "The question now is have we the wisdom and conscience, from the present upheavings of our political system, to reconstruct a government on the one enduring basis that has never yet been tried—Equal Rights to All." At this convention the American Equal Rights Association was formed as the preamble to the constitution explains: "Whereas, by the war, society is once more resolved into its original elements, and

To Elizabeth Smith Miller.

NEW YORK, *August 13, 1865.*

Oh, sweet Julius, I was heartbroken when I found
that the very day I was to start for the quiet shades
of Peterboro, I was compelled to be in this malodorous
city. This week, which was to have been passed in
sentiment with Cousin Nancy, philosophy with Cousin
Gerrit, and heroic life with Julius and Charles—this
week is now to be desecrated with murderous plottings against moths and mice. This week, when I
was to dream, robed in pure white and flowers—this

---

in the reconstruction of our government we again stand face to face with
the broad question of natural rights, all associations based on special claims
for special classes are too narrow and partial for the hour; therefore, from
the baptism of this second revolution—purified and exalted through suffering—seeing with a holier vision that the peace, prosperity, and per-
petuity of the Republic rest on Equal Rights to all, we, to-day assembled
in our Eleventh National Woman's Rights Convention, bury the woman
in the citizen, and our organization in that of the American Equal Rights
Association." Upon receiving this call, Frederick Douglass wrote on
February 16, 1866, to Mrs. Stanton: "Thank you for your account of the
launching of the good ship Equal Rights Association. No vessel like her
has been given to the sea since Noah's Ark. Without the presence of
woman the ark would have been a failure. I have about made up my mind
that if you can forgive me for being a negro, I cannot do less than to forgive
you for being a woman." In response to a request to be present and speak,
William Lloyd Garrison, April 5, 1866, wrote to Mrs. Stanton: "If I should
fail to be in New York for the May anniversary of the National Woman's
Rights Convention, I will at least send you a letter for the occasion, in
which I shall assuredly give my warm approval of your movement for
impartial suffrage, without regard to sex; and record my protest against
the proposed constitutional amendment, limiting the ballot to males. In
this I am with you to the fullest extent." On the back of the above letter
Mrs. Stanton has written: "Bless the good man." Throughout the period
when the XIV and XV amendments were passing through Congress, Mrs.
Stanton's supreme aim was to broaden out these amendments so as to
secure suffrage to women. Her constitutional arguments may be found
in the *History of Woman Suffrage*, vol. ii, p. 168 (1866); pp. 185, 271 (1867);
p. 320 (1868); p. 348 (1869).

ELIZABETH SMITH MILLER, "JULIUS"

LUCRETIA MOTT
Bust by Adelaide Johnson

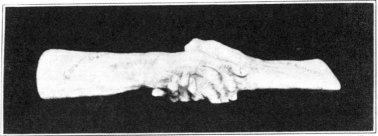

[See chap. X, vol. I

HANDS OF ELIZABETH CADY STANTON AND SUSAN B. ANTHONY, 1895

SUFFRAGE FRIENDSHIPS

week must be confined to hard work, dressed in dark calico and a napkin on my brow. Oh, cruel fate! This week when I was to tune my voice to music and friendship, I have now to school my tongue to stern command, to marshal plumbers, painters, white-washers, and scrubbers up and down four flights of stairs. I try to show a saintly patience, but I really do feel like the very devil! Everybody has something of this evil genius in him that will come out in one way or another. But my devilishness is spasmodic, and though I did feel yesterday ready to curse God and die, to-day, as I sit alone in my sister s parlor— I am staying with Tryphena until my house is in order—reading the Life of Milton, my mountains of trouble have little by little dwindled to sand hills. So write often to your disappointed   JOHNSON.

To Susan B. Anthony.

NEW YORK, *September 10, 1865.*

DEARLY BELOVED,—Of course your critics take no note of all you have been to me, though I have often told them what a stimulus and inspiration you were through years of domestic cares. But while I shall always be happy to write for you whatever document you desire, I am not willing to be bullied when I honestly differ from you in opinion, as I do in the matter you mention. Well, the human family is affording you abundant experience in the degrada-tion of women; their littleness and meanness are the result of their abject dependence, their utter want of self-respect. But this must needs be so until they
II.—8

reach a higher development. Poor things! How can they be frank and magnanimous in view of their education? So let us expect nothing of the present generation of them, and then we shall not be disappointed. The past month's experience has taught me some deep spiritual lessons, and I rejoice more than ever that I have been absorbed in some great question beyond wealth, position, and personal aggrandisement. You cannot imagine how much I miss you.

To Martha C. Wright.

NEW YORK, *December 20, 1865.*

DEAR MARTHA,—I enclose the proof of the memorial.[1] Will you see if you can get the petition published in your city and county papers? I have written to Mr. Garrison asking him to make some mention of us, the only disfranchised class now remaining, in his last *Liberator*. It is fitting that we should be recognized in his valedictory.[2] We have fairly boosted the negro over our own heads, and now we had better begin to remember that self-preservation is the first law of nature. Some say, "Be still, wait, this is the negro's hour." But I believe this is the hour for

---

[1] To Congress (*History of Woman Suffrage*, vol. ii, p. 91). In the XIV Amendment to the United States Constitution, which became law in 1868, political rights were conferred on the emancipated slaves, and the word "male" appears in that instrument for the first time. Mrs. Stanton was the first to see the full significance of this fact, and immediately sounded the alarm. Before the close of the session of 1865-66, ten thousand persons had signed the petitions against the form of the proposed amendment.

[2] The only reference to woman is this: No journal "has vindicated . . . the rights of human nature, without distinction of race, complexion, or sex, more earnestly or more uncompromisingly than the *Liberator*."

everybody to do the best thing for reconstruction. A vote based on intelligence and education for black and white, man and woman—that is what we need. Martha, keep your lamp trimmed and burning, and press in through that constitutional door the moment it is opened for the admission of Sambo.

To Wendell Phillips.[1]

NEW YORK, *December 26, 1865.*

MY DEAR WENDELL PHILLIPS,—By an amendment of the Constitution, ratified by three-fourths of the loyal states, the black man is declared free. The largest and most influential party is demanding suffrage for him throughout the union, which right in many states is already conceded. Although this may remain for five or ten years a question for politicians to wrangle over, the black man is now, from a political point of view, far above the educated women of the country. For the last thirty years the representative women of the nation have done their uttermost to secure freedom for the negro, and so long as he was lowest in the scale of being we were willing to press his claims. We are asking ourselves whether it would not be wiser when the constitutional door is open, to push in by the negro's side, and thus make the gap so wide that no privileged class could ever again close it against the humblest citizen of the Republic. You say, "This is the negro's hour." I

---

[1] In a slightly different form and under the heading "This is the Negro's Hour," the above letter appeared in the *National Antislavery Standard,* of which Mr. Phillips was now editor.

will not insist that there are women of that race, but ask, Is there not danger that he, once intrenched in all his inalienable rights, may be an added power to hold us at bay? Why should the African prove more just and generous than his Saxon compeers? Again, if the two millions of southern black women are not to be secured in their rights of person, property, wages, and children, then their emancipation is but another form of slavery. In fact, it is better to be the slave of an educated white man, than that of a degraded, ignorant black one. We who know what absolute power is given to man, in all his civil, political, and social relations, by the statute laws of most of the states, demand that in changing the status of the four millions of Africans, the women as well as the men shall be secured in all the rights, privileges, and immunities of citizens. If our prayer involved a new set of measures, or a new train of thought, it might be cruel to tax white male citizens with even two simple questions at a time. But the disfranchised all make the same demand, and the same logic and justice which secures suffrage for one class gives it to all. Our fathers, at the end of the first revolution, and in their desire for a speedy readjustment of all their difficulties, in order to present to Great Britain, their common enemy, an united front, accepted the compromise concerning the slave trade urged on them by South Carolina, and a century of wrong, ending in another revolution, has been the result of this action. Now is our opportunity to retrieve the errors of the past and mould anew the elements of democracy. The nation is ready for a long step in the right direction. Party lines are obliterated, and all men are thinking for themselves. If our rulers have the justice to give the black man suffrage, woman should avail herself of this new-born virtue and secure her rights. If not, she should begin with renewed earnestness to educate the people into the idea of true universal suffrage.

To Martha C. Wright.

New York, *January 6, 1866.*

Dear Martha,—I have just read your letter, and it would have been a wet blanket to Susan and me were we not sure that we are right. With three bills before Congress to exclude us from all hope of representation in the future by so amending the United States Constitution as to limit suffrage to "males," I thank God that *two* women of the nation felt the insult and decided to do their uttermost to rouse the rest to avail themselves of the only right we have in the government—the right of petition. If the petition goes with two names only, ours be the glory, and shame to all the rest. We have had a thousand petitions printed, and when they are filled they will be sent to Democratic members who will present them to the House. But if they come back to us empty, Susan and I will sign every one, so that every Democratic member may have one with which to shame those hypocritical Republicans. Martha, what are you all thinking about that you propose to rest on your oars in such a crisis? I conjure you and Lucretia to be a power at this moment in taking the onward step. There is not the slightest hope of settling the negro question now. When Andrew Johnson began the work of reconstruction, the negro's opportunity was lost. Politicians will wrangle over that question for a generation. Our time is now.

To Martha C. Wright.

NEW YORK, *January 20, 1866.*

DEAR MARTHA,—A quick reaction after a cold shower-bath is the best evidence one can give of a healthy condition! Your letter shows you are sound at the core, and proves my skill in making the right application to reveal the fact that your disease was only skin-deep—a lethargy in your surroundings and not in your own soul. I have been out of patience with men, women, and fate. Wendell Phillips Garrison informed Susan that his wife would not sign the petition as "it was out of time." I called on Mrs. Fremont to see if she would head a petition. "Oh, no. I do not believe in suffrage for women. I think women in their present position manage men better." I expressed doubt as to whether it was our business in life to "manage men," and added: "I'll trust men to manage themselves if their wives, mothers, and daughters are true women." I have so scolded with tongue and pen that really the skies begin to clear. See Theodore Tilton's stirring editorial, "A Law Against Women," in the *Independent;* see Martha Wright's last letter, and see Wendell Phillips's last[1]

---

[1] Under date of January 14, 1866, Mr. Phillips had written: "Who told you that Mrs. Wendell Phillips (how you scolded me once for writing to Mrs. Henry B. Stanton!) would not sign a petition for women's voting?

also. These are good signs, and the whole question of "time" is so clear to me that I cannot understand why anyone hesitates. There is now no law favoring slavery,[1] and as it is to the interest of the Republican party to give the black man the suffrage, reformers may as well pass on to some other position a round higher. Good night and yours as ever.

To Robert Dale Owen.

NEW YORK, *April 10, 1866.*

DEAR MR. OWEN,—Yes, the past is full of pleasant memories for me as for you, the present pressed full of work and worship, and the future glorious to those who see a fixed law governing equally mind, morals, and matter. What a grand philosophy of life such men as Herbert Spencer—an English friend has just sent me the program of his "System of Synthetic Philosophy"—are opening to our minds—teaching us to lose sight of ourselves and our burdens in the onward march of the race. The other day I heard Camilla Urso at a rehearsal. She plays exquisitely. Another girl out of her sphere! Just imagine the Academy of Music filled with people and a whole orchestra of men playing soft and low to a maiden's

---

No, no, child; she will sign a petition whenever she hears of one, and your note is the first hint of one. I know of no antislavery 'priesthood' that wishes to prevent it. I'm fully willing to ask for women's vote *now,* and will never *so* ask for negro voting as to put one single obstacle in the way of *her* getting it."

[1] The XIII Amendment to the Constitution forbidding slavery or involuntary servitude within the United States was submitted by the Congress to the several states on February 1, 1865, and was declared in a proclamation by the Secretary of State as ratified on December 18, 1865.

"Fantasia Caprice"—second fiddle to a woman! Where will you poor men stand in another fifty years? You will all be crowded off the horizon. So you had better bespeak in time a foothold on the outer ring of Saturn. If the lady you mention will only sleep all she wants, and make it a rule to rest when she is tired, she will never get ill. If I am going to hear a lecture or deliver one, instead of brushing my hat and coat and doing a score of more or less unnecessary things, I take a nap of fifteen minutes. While others read the litany on Sunday morning and come home tired out and humiliated in confessing themselves "miserable sinners," I sleep and rise in such harmonious conditions with myself, all nature, and the soul of good, that, believing we are as perfect as we can be under the circumstances, in view of ancestors and environment, I am refreshed, invigorated with that feeling of dignity which those who are created in the image of God should feel.

To Elizabeth Smith Miller.

New York, *October 22, 1866.*

Dear Julius,—Oh, thou Tantalus! to hold up to me the delights of Peterboro when you know I am bound here by a conscience that confines me to my duty as mercilessly as the Spanish Inquisition fastened its victims on the rack. Oh, thou tempter! worthy daughter of Eve! After having furnished you that charming little surprise, my Congressional Card,[1]

---

[1] At the November election Mrs. Stanton offered herself as a candidate for Congress in order to impress the public with the fact that constitu-

do you expect the nominee of the eighth district to leave her post when she should be printing tickets and handbills, and, with her political tweezers, holding up her opponents to the criticism of men and angels? Oh, no, Julius; I must buy butter and meat, hear youngsters spell and multiply, coax parted threads in stocking heels and toes to meet again like kindred drops in one, and smooth down the ruffled feathers of imperious men, of cross chambermaids and cook. Then comes Susan, with the nation on her soul, asking for speeches, resolutions, calls, attendance at conventions. So you now see why I cannot accept your invitation. But nevertheless, I am still—
                  Your own   JOHNSON.

To Elizabeth Smith Miller.

NEW YORK, *January 27, 1867.*

DEAR JULIUS,—Your good wishes helped me on the 23rd.[1] Senator Folger introduced me. The Assembly

---

tionally women had a right to run for office. She received only twenty-four votes, but her act caused wide discussion in public and private. In her address to the "Electors of the Eighth Congressional District" she gave as her political creed "free speech, free press, free men, free trade, the cardinal points of democracy," and closed with the assertion: "If the party now in the ascendancy makes its demand for negro suffrage in good faith on the ground of natural right, and because the highest good of the state demands that the republican idea be vindicated, on no principle of justice or safety can the women of the nation be ignored." (See for address in full *History of Woman Suffrage*, vol. ii, p. 180.)

[1] Mrs. Stanton asked to be heard by the Legislature as soon as that body called the Constitutional Convention. Her argument was to the effect that at the time of a Constitutional Convention the state returns to its constituent units, and therefore women as well as men should vote for members of the convention. (*History of Woman Suffrage*, vol. ii, p. 271.) She had been agitating this matter for a year. A letter to her from Rev,

Chamber was crowded with legislators, judges and members of the bar.   Susan was satisfied!!!!

To Martha C. Wright.

ALBANY, *June 27, 1867.*

DEAR MARTHA,—Before going to bed, I must let you know the hearing [1] was a success.   Greeley and other members of the Committee questioned us.   To me he said: "The ballot and bullet go together.   If you vote are you ready to fight?"   "Yes," I replied, "we are ready to fight, sir, just as you did in the late war, by sending our substitutes."   Rather a crushing blow!   And now to bed.   It is two o'clock.

To Emily Howland.

NEW YORK, *September 1, 1867.*

MY DEAR FRIEND,—The other Sunday at Alice Cary's reception, Miss Anthony and I were sitting near a window when we saw Greeley making his way towards us.   We had not seen him since the Consti-

---

Samuel J. May, dated Syracuse, February 27, 1866, reads in part: "I received your letter.   I called on Senator White last evening and left both your letters with him, had some conversation with him on the subject of the Constitutional Convention, and received his assurance that he would give his attention to the matter on his return to Albany."   Andrew Dickson White was state senator from the Syracuse district from 1863 to 1867.

[1] Having failed to persuade the Legislature on January 23d to grant the right to women to vote for delegates to the Constitutional Convention, Mrs. Stanton and her co-workers as soon as the Constitutional Convention convened at Albany on June 4th, asked for a hearing on the question of amending the Constitution so as to secure full suffrage to women.   Accordingly on the evening of June 27th, the Standing Committee on the Right of Suffrage of the Constitutional Convention, Horace Greeley, chairman, held in the Assembly Chamber a public hearing for the advocates of suffrage.

tutional Convention, when by our engineering we got Curtis[1] to present on the floor a petition in favor of woman suffrage, headed by "Mrs. Horace Greeley," just before Greeley presented the adverse report. Well, as he approached us, I said to Miss Anthony, "Prepare for a storm." And sure enough one did burst, and a violent one it was so long as it lasted. To our "Good evening, Mr. Greeley," his reply was rough and curt. Here is about what he said: "You two ladies are about the best maneuverers among the New York politicians. You tried to bother me at the convention, and I confess that you succeeded. The way Curtis presented Mary's petition showed me that you had prepared the plan." Then turning to me, he continued in a more irritated tone of voice: "You are always so desirous in public to appear under your own rather than your husband's name, why did you in this case substitute 'Mrs. Horace Greeley' for 'Mary Cheney Greeley,' which was really on the petition? You know why. Well, I have given strict orders at the *Tribune* office that you and your cause are to be tabooed in the future, and if it is necessary to mention your name, you will be referred to as 'Mrs. Henry B. Stanton!'"[2] And then he abruptly left us. Of course this will not deter me from speaking my mind in the future as in the past, though I am sorry for our cause that the *Tribune* will henceforth be lukewarm. This may do something to retard our final triumph; but it will take more than Horace

[1] George William Curtis.
[2] This custom was persisted in even for several years after the death of Mr. Greeley.

Greeley and the New York *Tribune* to prevent the success of the movement which we both have so much at heart. So, more valiant than ever, I am as always,
Your old friend and co-worker,
"MRS. HENRY B. STANTON!"

To Elizabeth Smith Miller.
"THE REVOLUTION," 37 PARK ROW,
NEW YORK, *December 28, 1867.*

DEAR JULIUS,—It almost broke my heart to pass Canistota without stopping, having just heard that you had returned home. But it was as vain for the cork leg to try to stop as for me, tied as I was to the immortal Train[1] in a series of meetings from Omaha to New York. I told the eccentric George Francis that I felt very much as if I were fastened to the tail of a comet whisking ten thousand miles a minute through the air. During my two months in Kansas[2] I spoke every day, Sunday not excepted, twice or thrice. I enclose my certificate from the Governor.[3]

---

[1] George Francis Train, an eccentric public character, whom Mrs. Stanton met for the first time during the Kansas campaign, became the financial backer of the *Revolution*, the weekly which Mrs. Stanton and Miss Anthony founded in January, 1868.

[2] In the autumn of 1867, a woman suffrage amendment to the state constitution was submitted to the voters of Kansas, and, though lost, received nine thousand and seventy votes out of a total of about thirty thousand. This was the first referendum vote ever cast in the United States for the enfranchisement of women.

[3] Charles Robinson, first Governor of Kansas, took an active part in making it a free state. From Lawrence, Kansas, November 20, 1867, he had written to Mrs. Stanton: "Others may think as they please, but I believe we are indebted for the big vote in Kansas to E. Cady Stanton, Lucy Stone, and Olympia Brown more than to all other instrumentalities, and if we are ever to succeed, it will be by such influences rather than by

You know we stumped the state together. His span of horses took us from point to point. We put up at farmhouses at night. Oh, Julius, the dirt, the food!! Think of Johnson with only sorghum for her coffee!! Lord and Lady Amberley called the other day. I think them rather tame. What did Cousin Gerrit think of them? A recent Peterboro visitor tells me this amusing anecdote of their sojourn with your father. It appears that when Lady Amberley tasted at breakfast, for the first time, hot corn bread, she remarked to her husband, who came down late: "Take some, dear; it is not as nasty as it looks." That is so British that it must be true.

To Martha C. Wright.

NEW YORK, *January 8, 1868.*

DEAR MARTHA,—I hope you have not given my whilom friend the satisfaction of condemning Susan and me unheard. Mr. Train is a pure, high-toned man, without a vice. He has some extravagances and idiosyncrasies, but he is willing to devote energy and money to our cause when no other man is. It seems to me it would be right and wise to accept aid even from the devil himself, provided he did not tempt us to lower our standard. If we can swallow Train, they shouldn't be hypercritical, especially as we are not asking them to participate in this act of deglutition. They might better turn their attention to Wendell Phillips, who by his false philosophy has

the driving and scolding of anyone. I thank you for all you have done for me and Kansas. Now we will all love you as one of the chosen few who are to regenerate the world," paralyzed the very elect. To think of Boston women holding an antislavery festival when their own petitions are ignored in the Senate of the United States! If we love the black man as well as we love ourselves, we shall fulfill the Bible injunction.

To T. W. Higginson.

NEW YORK, *January 13, 1868.*

DEAR FRIEND,—Our "pathway" is straight to the ballot box, with no variableness nor shadow of turning. I know we have shocked our old friends, who were half asleep on the woman question, into new life. Just waking from slumber, they are cross and can't see clearly where we are going. But time will show that Miss Anthony and I are neither idiots nor lunatics. But in starting a paper, the first thing was to advertise it; and that you must admit we have done effectually during the last month. We do care what all good men like you *say;* but just now the men who will *do* something to help us are more important. Garrison, Phillips, and Sumner, in their treatment of our question to-day, prove that we must not trust any of you. All these men, who have pushed us aside for years, saying, "This is the negro's hour," now, when we, dropped by them, find help in other quarters, they turn up the whites of their eyes and cry out their curses. No, my dear friend, we are right in our present position. We demand in the reconstruction, suffrage for all the citizens of the Republic. I would not talk of negroes or women, but of citizens. There is where Wendell

Phillips failed. He should have passed, when slavery was abolished, from the abolitionist to the statesman, instead of falling back to the Republican platform and thus losing, as he did, negro suffrage in all the northern states.[1]

To Elizabeth Smith Miller.

NEW YORK, *January 8, 1869.*

DEAR JULIUS,—In a letter to Susan, your father refuses to sign our petition.[2] I am dissecting him in the next *Revolution.*[3] Tell Charley that as he thinks I sing and dance well, I expect him to *say* I reason well. Are you coming to Washington?[4]

Your lonely MASSA JOHNSON.

To Lucretia Mott.

WASHINGTON, *January 21, 1869.*

DEAR LUCRETIA,—At last we shall have a definite, constructive rallying point. We pass from the sphere of vainly endeavoring to broaden the narrow demands

[1] The XIV Amendment to the United States Constitution was proposed to the legislatures of the several states by the Congress, June 16, 1866. On the 21st of July, 1868, Congress adopted a resolution declaring that thirty of the thirty-six states had ratified the amendment. At the date of Mrs. Stanton's letter to Mr. Higginson the fate of the amendment hung in the balance. Twenty-one states only at this time had ratified the amendment, and a movement in the northern states had started to withdraw the ratification. Ohio, for instance, ratified the amendment January 11, 1867, and withdrew this ratification in January, 1868.

[2] "To the Senate and House of Representatives in Congress assembled: We the undersigned citizens of the State of ———— earnestly but respectfully request that in any change or amendment of the Constitution you may propose to extend or regulate suffrage, there shall be no distinction made between men and women."

[3] January 14, 1869.

[4] For the first time the Suffrage Convention was held at Washington, January 19, 20, 1869.

of men to an amendment wholly our own.[1] Hon.
George W. Julian acceded to our wish, and will propose a XVI Amendment,[2] basing the right of suffrage
on citizenship "without any distinction and discrim-
ination whatever founded on sex." I feel an added
dignity!

To John Stuart Mill.

NEW YORK, *May 11, 1869.*

DEAR MR. MILL,—I wish to thank you for your
noble work on *The Subjection of Women.* To my
mind, no thinker has so calmly, truthfully, and logically revealed the causes and hidden depths of woman's
degradation, and so clearly pointed out the secret
springs of the sycophancy of the more fortunate
women to man. It is my earnest hope that progress
will vouchsafe to all men the power of seeing as clearly
as you do the demoralizing effect on all alike of the
idea that man is to be served and woman to serve.
I lay the book down with a peace and joy I never felt
before, for it is the first response from any man to
show that he is capable of seeing and feeling all the
nice shades and degrees of woman's wrongs, and the
central point of her weakness and degradation.

Believe me, dear Mr. Mill,

Yours in deepest gratitude.

[1] In her opening address (see *History of Woman Suffrage,* vol. ii, p. 348)
Mrs. Stanton urged a Federal suffrage amendment.

[2] Such a resolution was introduced in Congress March 15, 1869, by Mr.
Julian. The amendment proposed in this joint resolution read: "Art. XVI.
The right of suffrage in the United States shall be based on citizenship
and shall be regulated by Congress; and all citizens of the United States,
whether native or naturalized, shall enjoy this right equally without any
distinction whatever founded on sex."

To E. P. Whipple.

NEW YORK, *September 9, 1869.*

DEAR MR. WHIPPLE,—What did you think of our breakfast to Greeley? He was as amiable as he could be, which is not much, however. But I wouldn't let him "get mad." His mind is as odd as his body, which makes him the more interesting. How great he would be, if he were not so little. Both of my coadjutors[1] are away for the moment, and Phœbe Cary is helping me with the *Revolution.* I was sorry not to meet you the last time I was in Boston. I had a nice chat with Lydia Maria Child. I always prefer Mrs. Child's conversation, quiet though it be, to her writings, brilliant though they be. She was present at a reception in the parlors of the Tremont House, where Wendell Phillips, in quite a large circle of my friends, refused to shake hands with me, rebuffing my advance with the rather surly remark, "Mrs. Stanton is no friend of mine." Mrs. Child is very much attached to Phillips, and I could see that this rude action quite upset her for a moment. Poor fellow! After serving up every living man himself, he cannot stand my satire in the *Revolution.* Well, seeing that he feels it, I will give him some more!

To Susan B. Anthony.

ST. LOUIS, *December 28, 1869.*

MY DEAR SUSAN,—As to changing the name of the *Revolution,* I should consider it a great mistake. If

---

[1] Parker Pillsbury, coeditor, and Susan B. Anthony, proprietor, of the *Revolution.*

all these people who for twenty years have been afraid to call their souls their own begin to prune us and the *Revolution*, we shall become the same galvanized mummies they are. There could not be a better name than *Revolution*. The establishing of woman on her rightful throne is the greatest revolution the world has ever known or ever will know. To bring it about is no child's play. You and I have not forgotten the conflict of the last twenty years—the ridicule, persecution, denunciation, detraction, the unmixed bitterness of our cup for the past two years, when even friends crucified us. A journal called the *Rosebud* might answer for those who come with kid gloves and perfumes to lay immortal wreaths on the monuments which in sweat and tears others have hewn and built; but for us and for that great blacksmith of ours[1] who forges such red-hot thunderbolts for Pharisees, hypocrites, and sinners, there is no name like the *Revolution*. It does not seem to me worth while for me to take that long trip to Washington when I have all I can do all winter out here in the West. This field is ripe for the harvest. I am doing more good in stirring up these Western women than in talking to those old Washington politicians. I do not want to manage other people, neither do I want other people to manage me. I stand ready to pay anybody you can get to go to Washington in my stead. But of course I stand by you to the end.[2] I

---

[1] Parker Pillsbury.

[2] This refers to the split in the suffrage movement, which illustrated the bitterness engendered when coadjutors disagree. Private accusations of dishonesty against Miss Anthony, the soul of probity, were widely spread, of "free love" against Mrs. Stanton, who was frankly and conscientiously

would not see you crushed by rivals even if to prevent it required my being cut into inch bits. If you will promise solemnly to let me free in May, I will wear the yoke a few months longer, bravely and patiently. But I do hate conventions, for I dislike to be in a position where any set of people have the right to say, "For the sake of the cause don't do this or that." In fact I had rather give you five hundred dollars than go to Washington. But if your life depends on me, I will be your stay and staff to the end.[1] No power in heaven, hell or earth can separate us, for our hearts are eternally wedded together. Ever yours, and here I mean *ever*.

---

advocating liberal divorce laws, and of disloyalty against both because they steadily, and as time proved, wisely, opposed the introduction of the word "male" in the XIV Amendment, and the omission of the word "sex" in the XV. Their opponents founded the American Woman Suffrage Association in November, 1869. The two societies united again at a convention held in Washington, D. C., in February, 1890. Mrs. Stanton was elected president, and Miss Anthony vice-president-at-large, of the combined societies.

[1] Mrs. Stanton attended the convention, which was held January 19, 1870, in Washington, and as president, presided. She made a strong constitutional argument before the Congressional Committee. (*History of Woman Suffrage*, vol. ii, p. 411.)

1870–1880

To Susan B. Anthony.

TENAFLY, *May 30, 1870.*

DEAR SUSAN,—You and Parker Pillsbury gone and our *Revolution*[1] no more! There is a sadness, though relief, in the fact. I was sorry Parker took out of our farewell editorials all mention of him. It was wrong in him to do so, because it makes us look selfishly forgetful. And think of our sacred columns full of the advertisements of quack remedies! The present owners have asked me and urged me a dozen times to write for them. But I do not feel moved by the spirit. Theodore Tilton told me that in writing for the paper he wished I would be careful not to shock those good Baptists and to say nothing on divorce, but to be "spicy and brilliant on some pleasant topics." Greeley once offered me the columns of the *Tribune* in the same way. I am very busy reading, and writing my speeches, and I have no time to prepare articles nor any desire to submit my ideas to the pruning knife of youngsters. Now do for my sake let them manage matters in their own way, and remember that you did not sell my pen in your transfer of the *Revolution*. I am not to be bought to write at anybody's dictation. You know when I drop any-

---

[1] On May 22, 1870, the ownership of the *Revolution* was transferred to Laura Curtis Bullard, the New York writer, who was aided in the editorship by Theodore Tilton, then editor of the *Independent.*

thing, I drop it absolutely. You cannot imagine what a deep gulf lies between me and the past.

To Susan B. Anthony.

NEW YORK, *June 27, 1870.*

DEAREST SUSAN,—Do not feel depressed, my dear friend. What is good in us is immortal, and if the sore trials we have endured for three years are sifting out pride and selfishness, we shall not have suffered in vain. How I long to see my blessed Susan! Not only have I finished my lecture on marriage and divorce, but I have delivered it. When I spoke in Brooklyn on this subject, I had a splendid audience, and since the Apollo Hall meeting[1] I have received letters innumerable. Women respond to this divorce speech as they never did to suffrage. In a word, I have had grand meetings. Oh, how the women flock to me with their sorrows. Such experiences as I listen to, plantation never equaled. Speaking of divorce, the New York *Sun* has an article about you and me "having dissolved partnership." Have you been getting a divorce out in Chicago without notifying me? I should like to know my present status. I shall not allow any such proceedings. I consider that our relations are to last for life; so make the best of it.

---

[1] Held at New York, May 16, 1870, to express indignation on the verdict in the McFarland-Richardson case. Mrs. Stanton's was the chief address, which was in favor of divorce. Daniel McFarland was a man of dissolute habits, and his wife, Abby Sage, actress, reader, and author, secured a divorce from him and married Albert Deane Richardson, an able New York journalist. Thereupon, McFarland shot and killed Richardson. The verdict was that the former was insane, and so not responsible for the act, and yet he was given the custody of his twelve-year-old son.

As to the newspapers—our critics have overdone their work in the *Tribune*, and the *Sun* has come out with a reply to one of the *Tribune's* attacks on me. With love and faith that all is for the best.

To Elizabeth Smith Miller.

Tenafly, *August 10, 1870.*

Dear Liz,—I have just read your letter. I do not think it too sharp. A friend of mine, a professor and a wise man, says our movement will never come to anything until the women are mad enough to swear. I felt so as I read your letter. There is another thing which almost makes me swear. I am disgusted with the whole system of education, and I am pondering the same problem as yourself concerning the mental development of our girls. But there is one point, Julius, in which I think you are wrong, and that is your complete aversion to schools. It seems to me children need companionship, numbers and variety—children of their own age. I have always felt that it is a great mistake to keep them at home alone. I have looked all around, and the best schools I know for girls are Vassar College and Swarthmore. Suppose we send our daughters to the latter? It is a quiet Quaker institution, in a healthy, warm situation, thorough in its teachings, where boys also go. You know I am a firm believer in the benefits of coeducation of the sexes, which is peculiar to our country, and which we should never abandon. And there is still another thing which makes me swear. I am utterly disgusted with that letter in the *Woman's Journal* on George Sand by Mrs. Stowe. I agree with Beecher, who said to me the other day, speaking of his sister's lucubration: "It is dull and decent."

To Sarah Pugh.

TENAFLY, *August 25, 1870.*

DEAR SARAH,—As Paulina Davis has taken the decade meeting in hand, I hope you will lend her all the aid you possibly can in making it a success. I do wish this approaching coming together might be the means of our reunion. The present divisions in the woman suffrage ranks are frivolous and unworthy of us, while it seems to me most humiliating that both of our associations have men as presidents.[1] There was some excuse for this in 1848, when women were just starting public work. But to-day!

To Susan B. Anthony.

TENAFLY, *February 6, 1871.*

DEAR SUSAN,—I do think the crowning insult to us from the Republican party is Bingham's majority report.[2] He declares we are not citizens, but only "members of the state." Well, you remember in

---

[1] At the anniversary of the National Woman Suffrage Association, held in New York in May, 1870, it was suggested that, as the American Woman Suffrage Association had Mr. Beecher for president, Mrs. Stanton retire, at least for a time, and some popular man be put at the head of the organization. She readily assented, and Theodore Tilton was elected president. He held the office until January, 1871.

[2] John A. Bingham, chairman of the House Judiciary Committee, which made a report unfavorable to woman suffrage.

my 15th amendment speech[1] I said that in the establishment of an aristocracy of sex on this continent, woman would know deeper depths of degradation under this government than she has ever known before. That night in Washington when you said you had never before seen me so on the rampage, I had a vivid intuition of the dark clouds hanging over us; and now they are breaking. In fact, simultaneously with the 15th amendment comes a generally insulting tone in the press, propositions in several state legislatures to license prostitution, and now an open declaration by the most liberal one of the parties that we are "not citizens." Of course, I may add in passing, Mary A. Livermore and those of her kidney can "wait patiently for the suffrage," as she never cared two pins about the right—in fact, laughed at the idea four years ago. But we cannot afford to wait, nor can the nation afford to have us wait. So go ahead and "deal damnation round the land with a high hand," as the *Tribune* says you do; only don't run in debt in order to do it! We will win this battle yet, Susan! With love unchanged, undimmed by time and friction.

To Martha C. Wright.

TENAFLY, *March 21, 1871.*

DEAR MARTHA,—I am so glad that we are to meet again under Lucretia's roof to discuss the affairs of

---

[1] Mrs. Stanton before the Senate Committee on the District of Columbia, at a hearing in January, 1870, on the question of extension of suffrage in the District and in Territories: "By the XV Amendment you have established an aristocracy of sex, sanctioning the unjust legislation of the several states, which make all men nobles, all women serfs. Justice and equity can be attained only by having the same laws for men and women."

state. Now that E. M. D.'s[1] African friends are all in the political kingdom, I suppose he will treat us unhappy women with more patience and tenderness than he did when we last met. To have him pounce on one like a shark with sarcasm and ridicule, all mixed together and simmered down to gall and bitterness; to have Wendell Phillips withdraw his velvet paw as if you were unworthy to touch the hem of his garment—this is enough to rouse one's blood to the white heat of rebellion against every "white male" on the continent. When I think of all the wrongs that have been heaped upon womankind, I am ashamed that I am not forever in a condition of chronic wrath, stark mad, skin and bone, my eyes a fountain of tears, my lips overflowing with curses, and my hand against every man and brother! Ah, how I do repent me of the male faces I have washed, the mittens I have knit, the trousers mended, the cut fingers and broken toes I have bound up! Do you see what Gladstone says? "If women vote, they will hold office, be members of Parliament—and what next? We cannot debate with them in private; how can we in public? The men will be obliged to retire and resign the government to women." I warrant Mrs. Gladstone has driven him to the wall a thousand times. It is too much for   Yours,   E. C. S.

To Isabella Beecher Hooker.

TENAFLY, *April 12, 1871.*

DEAR MRS. HOOKER,—We should change our tactics and belabor these time-serving politicians, as

---

[1] Edward M. Davis, son-in-law of Lucretia Mott.

Garrison and Phillips did in the good old days. A very pretty game of fox and geese they play with us from year to year. They keep the ballot boxes just before our noses, but a little too far off for us to reach, and fools that we are we keep thanking and praising them therefor. In a word, they play with us sweet little kittens, dangling before us feathers and strings, and when tired of us, gently, quite gently, pitch us outside, by the back door, without regard to wind or weather. I enclose a list of the standing committees of our legislature, found in all the leading papers at the time of their appointment. But there is none on woman suffrage. Read the list, and you will find there, well provided for, everything under the sun— fire, water, jails, morgues, canals, etc., etc.—but nothing for the most sacred interests of one-half the citizens of this state. And then some men are astonished, or at least pretend to be, that there is a "shrieking sisterhood." We should do more than shriek; we would be perfectly justified if we were to strike too.

To Elizabeth Smith Miller.

DES MOINES, IOWA, *June 12, 1871.*

DEAR JULIUS,—You see Susan and I are slowly journeying westward.[1] Since I left you, I have filled twenty engagements, speaking twice in nearly every place, once on suffrage and once to women alone. This idea of mine of addressing women by themselves

---

[1] A journey to the coast was planned early in the year. In a letter to Miss Anthony dated February 6th, Mrs. Stanton agrees: "Yes, I will go to California this summer with you. You might make arrangements for me to deliver my lecture to women alone on the way back."

should produce a rich fruitage in the future. What radical thoughts I then and there put into their heads, and as they feel untrammeled, these thoughts are permanently lodged there! That is all I ask. And what a magnificent chance on these lines is in store for us. We have just received letters from Salt Lake City saying that Brigham consents to let "Miss Susan and Mrs. Elizabeth" speak in the Tabernacle. P. S. Later. This letter got into the pocket of my valise rather than in the mail bag. Since it was written we have been at the Utah capital. There were to have been two sessions of our meeting with the Mormon women; but as Susan and I felt they would never be allowed back again, we decided to say all we had to say at the first session. This meeting began at two P. M., and did not end until seven P. M. Every aspect of the institution of marriage was discussed; then the doors of the Tabernacle were closed to our ministrations.

To Elizabeth Smith Miller.

DENVER, *June 25, 1871.*

DEAR JULIUS,—I sit at the foot of the Rocky Mountains, those grand old giants that have stood in the solitudes frowning here for ages. What must they think now to see the valleys at their feet all alive with busy miners, and these fleet iron horses, with long tails, dashing in all directions over the plains and plunging ever and anon into their very vitals? How sad and lonely they must have been before the Adams and Eves came with their fair Cains and Abels.

The inhabitants in this region depend wholly on irrigation, which, Meeker[1] says, "is better than fooling round and waiting, watching and praying for rain." I am going with him to-day to Greeley Colony. Susan went to Laramie yesterday. You see we divide our forces now and then in order to spread our teaching. But for the past few days we have been making our joint headquarters here with Governor McCook, who has a beautiful house and a beautiful wife. I should have put the wife first! I found a letter here from a man who asked me what seemed to me the most impressive example of heroism in history or in my own experience. I told him that, to my mind, the greatest heroes are the satellites of the dinner pot and the cradle —they who toil without reward, who are sacrificed in

---

[1] Nathan Cook Meeker, one of the editors of the New York *Tribune*. In 1869 he founded the Colorado colony, and as president of the organization, named it after Mr. Greeley, who consented to act as treasurer of the enterprise, which was purely co-operative and proved a great success. To-day, Greeley is the largest town in northern Colorado. Ralph Meeker, the son of the founder of Greeley, wrote to the editors: "Mrs. Stanton and Miss Anthony were the guests of my father and mother here in our rough adobé house. They melted into the family life like sunshine, and soon seemed like friends who had lived here for years. We have had gifted visitors at different times, but perhaps we have appreciated most the great catholic soul of Mrs. Stanton, who was long years ahead of her time and yet in the everyday hearts of all whom she met here. She seemed to live in several centuries at once. You know I helped my father in running the Greeley Colony. Most of the members of the colony were old-time readers of the New York *Tribune* and ardent followers of Mr. Greeley and his teachings. But they were radical *Tribune* readers, and gave Mrs. Stanton and Miss Anthony good audiences. As I was a young disciple of their faith, it was a pleasure to me to manage their lectures and help entertain them. In driving over the Plains we had the most charming experiences. In full view of Long's Peak and the Snowy Range, we rode many days. The scene changed every moment. It made Mrs. Stanton more than eloquent. Her conversation, recalling scenes and events in other lands and in her own early life, was poetry; and I fancy few persons could have matched the beauty and inspiring fervor of her noble language."

every household, who suffer that men may shine; heroes whom none envy, to whom none build monuments, whose names even are often not inscribed on the stones which mark their last resting place. But I must end this letter in a less solemn mood. So I put it in this ridiculous envelope.[1] But do not think I am growing sentimental. Just before I left Tenafly, I one day sent my "Son of Erin" down to the village to buy me a little much-needed stationery, and he brought back three packages of these, which he handed to me smiling as if he expected me to be pleasantly surprised. I laughed, of course, took them and have sent them flying in all directions except Boston. What would Higginson[2] say if I sent him a staid letter in such an envelope? This certainly smacks of "free love"!

To Mrs. I. W. England.

February 22, 1872.

DEAR MRS. ENGLAND,—Well, this is the birthday of the Father of his Country. I can just see, 140 years ago, Mrs. Washington, in ruffled cap and embroidered nightdress, sipping panada in a darkened room, while the nurse manipulates little George through a prolonged bath and toilet. How little that ignorant African guessed that she was familiarly flopping about on her capacious lap, puffing every crack and corner, the future first President of these United States, whose continued wailing was then wringing the heart and ears of the feverish mother.

---

[1] Little birds were seen billing and cooing on the flap.
[2] Thomas Wentworth Higginson.

This train of thought was suggested by a call which I have just had from a prominent local orator who is to respond this evening at a public dinner to the toast of "Washington and the Day We Celebrate." But I am sure he will not make the slightest reference to this first scene in the drama of this famous life. And this brings me to the question of the naming of children. In this I have begun a vigorous crusade in behalf of humanity, euphony, and musical harmony. Why in naming a new generation should we mouse round like medical students in cemeteries for old ancestral prænomens, doleful enough for tombstones, but not in keeping with the pretty boys and girls of the nineteenth century? A like objection can often be made to many of our cognomens. When such abominations as Bull, Hogg, Cruckshanks, *et al.*, are fastened upon succeeding generations, is it not wisdom to carefully consider this matter? Think, for example, of a butler shouting out at a reception, "Mr. and Mrs. Hogg," or announcing two lovely girls, in white muslin and blue satin sashes, as "the Misses Cruckshanks"! Let us copy our parents' virtues, but bury their harsh vulgar names with them. In this respect, I may add, "the great Virginian" got off fairly well. Yours for the right—kind of naming.

To Lucretia Mott.

NEW CASTLE, DELAWARE, *April 1, 1872.*

DEAR LUCRETIA,—Since leaving you, I have thought much of Mrs. Woodhull[1] and of all the gossip about

---

[1] Victoria Woodhull presented a memorial to the Congress claiming the right of suffrage under the XIV and XV Amendments, and asking for the

her past, and have come to the conclusion that it is great impertinence in any of us to pry into her private affairs. To me there is a sacredness in individual experience which it seems like profanation to search into or expose. This woman stands before us to-day as an able speaker and writer. Her face, manners, and conversation all indicate the triumph of the moral, intellectual, and spiritual. The processes and localities of her education are little to us, but the result should be everything. Most women, who, like some tender flower, perish in the first rude blast, think there must be some subtle poison in the hardy plant which grows stronger and more beautiful in poor earth and rough exposure, where they would fall faded, withered, and bleeding to the ground. We have already women enough sacrificed to this sentimental, hypocritical prating about purity, without going out of our way to increase the number. Women have crucified the Mary Wollstonecrafts, the Fanny Wrights and the George Sands of all ages. Men mock us with the fact and say we are ever cruel to each other. Let us end this ignoble record and henceforth stand by womanhood. If this present woman must be crucified, let men drive the spikes.

---

legislation necessary to guarantee the rights of women. The Judiciary Committee of the House gave a hearing on her petition January 11, 1871. This called out the famous minority report by Benjamin F. Butler. There was much criticism when Mrs. Woodhull was invited to repeat her Judiciary Committee speech at the Woman's Suffrage Convention then being held in Washington.

To Tryphena Bayard, Harriet Eaton, and
Catherine Wilkeson.

FREMONT, NEBRASKA, *April 21, 1872.*

DEAR SISTERS, 1, 2, 3,—I have had a fearfully hard
week and am glad that this is the Lord's day and
belongs to no Lyceum Bureau. Monday I rode in
an open wagon thirty miles across the prairies, spoke
that evening and the next morning, and in the afternoon rode the same distance back again. Then I
took the cars to Hastings, where I arrived at eleven
P.M., and as there was an exciting murder trial on, I
could not get a place to sleep. So, with my clothes
all on, I lay on a broken-down old lounge, sleeping
on the points of some springs and bumps until one
side of my body was partially paralyzed, and then
getting up and walking for a while before trying the
other side. I thought the night would never end.
The next morning, after a meager breakfast, I was
packed into a long omnibus filled with men, women,
children, babies, bags, and bundles, with a conceited
boy of sixteen in charge of the precious cargo, who
went round the corners as if the devil was after him.
I expected every moment that we would be upset,
and my expectations were realized. Dashing up to
the depot and wishing to show off before a crowd of
men and boys, all in town to attend the trial, we were
overturned, on my side, the blow coming full force
on the back of my head. Several of the passengers
were badly hurt and all emerged from the wreck
with torn garments and disheveled locks. But strange
to say, I came out of the mess without a scratch or

bruise that I can see, though my head and back have ached constantly. Since then I have spoken every night, traveling in the cars during the day. Everybody regards me with wonder for my endurance and cheerfulness, and I must say that, comparing myself with most women, I have come to the conclusion that I was well born, and that my parents put me together with unusual wisdom and discretion; for all of which I am devoutly thankful. I enjoy life under the most adverse circumstances, and am in no particular hurry to be translated.

To Lucretia Mott.

Tenafly, *July 16, 1872.*

Dear Friend,—I try to feel that the Philadelphia splinter—it cannot be dignified with the name of plank—is something.[1] But sometimes it makes me intensely bitter to have my rights discussed by popinjays, priests, and politicians; to have woman's work in the church and state decided by striplings of twenty-one; and to have the press of the country on the broad grin because forsooth some American matrons chose to attend a national convention. Now I know

---

[1] The National Woman Suffrage Association, at its May meeting, appointed a delegation to attend the approaching presidential conventions in order to secure a woman suffrage plank in the platforms. The Liberal Republicans at Cincinnati and the Democrats at Baltimore listened respectfully to the pleas of the women, but did nothing. From the Republicans at Philadelphia this "splinter," as Mrs. Stanton called it, was obtained: "The Republican party is mindful of its obligations to the loyal women of America for their noble devotion to the cause of freedom; their admission to wider fields of usefulness is received with satisfaction, and the honest demands of any class of citizens for equal rights should be treated with respectful consideration."

well how Robert Purvis[1] feels when the "white males" turn round their long left ears at him.   There is one consolation, however, we are in fact the peers of the best of them.

To Susan B. Anthony.

NEW YORK, ELECTION DAY,
Tuesday, November 5, 1872.

DEAR SUSAN,—Well, poor Mrs. Greeley is gone, and I suppose the American people are to-day preparing a death knell[2] for poor old Horace. I had rather see Beelzebub President than Greeley. You say you are tired being the clown of our conventions. I have never considered that you were filling that part. I have always urged you to prepare a set speech for these occasions, though in such a conflict as ours, "thinking on one's feet" is as important as thinking at all. Have you read the *Independent?* Only think of the leading editorial being on our question. Though you and I catch it on all sides, I never cared so little. *E pur si muove!* With love as ever and ever till death do us part.

To Susan B. Anthony.

CHICAGO, *November 30, 1872.*

DEAR SUSAN,—After closing up a speech last evening in which I had been as usual rather severe on

[1] A successful colored merchant residing at Philadelphia who at this period sided with Mrs. Stanton in demanding equal rights for women as well as the negro.

[2] In the presidential campaign of 1872 Greeley carried no Northern state and only six Southern states. General Grant carried thirty-one states. Greeley received forty-seven votes in the electoral college, and Grant two hundred and eighty-six.

Horace Greeley, I was dreadfully shocked to hear that he was dead! Poor man, the disappointment of his defeat was too much for him; he was wholly unprepared for such a fiasco. Well, I think he had done his work, and with his departure one of woman's worst enemies has gone from this sphere, leaving our path to enfranchisement the smoother. But I cannot help thinking of his earlier and better days, when he took a broader outlook, when he and I were on the friendliest of terms, and when he and his journal aided us materially. Here, as in many other cases, you and I have made enemies of old friends because we stood up first and always for woman's cause and would not agree to have it take second place. Expediency does not belong to our vocabulary.

To Sara Jane Lippincott.

TENAFLY, *May 30, 1873.*

DEAR GRACE GREENWOOD,—Yes, I play chess. When I was last in Peterboro, they formed a chess club there. I polished myself up and became the best of any woman member and the equal of any of the men except two. In my younger days, chess was thought to be a necessary accomplishment. But now you seldom meet a woman who knows the game. They all say it is too hard work, as if thinking were not one of the pleasures of life. The picture I referred to is Meissonier's "The Chess Players," which I once saw somewhere either in the original or in a copy, I cannot remember which. But I do remember what a deep impression it made on me. That quotation was from Goldsmith's translation of Vida's poem, "The Game of Chess." It would indeed make a good motto for a chess periodical. Prof. Willard Fiske, whom I once met at Cornell University, could probably give you the original Latin of the quotation. He is a good chess authority, and very probably has the book in his own library. Yours, as ever, especially in chess matters.

To Antoinette Brown Blackwell.

TENAFLY, *June 10, 1873.*

MY DEAR ANTOINETTE,—I am sorry I have disappointed Isabella Beecher Hooker by not devoting more time and thought to the next life. But the fact is I have always been so busy with mundane affairs that I have not had a moment to commune with the angels. If you have any heavenly experiences, do communicate them to I. B. H. and make your letter compensate in a measure for my indifference. To suppose this short life to be all of this world's experiences never did seem wholly satisfactory, but at the same time I see no proof of all these vague ideas floating in Mrs. Hooker's head.

To Matilda Joslyn Gage.

TENAFLY, *June 25, 1873.*

DEAR MATILDA,—As to the verdict in Susan's case, it is not an unusual thing when a case rests on principles of law rather than facts for a judge to do just what Hunt did.[1] Tom, Dick, and Harry can decide questions of fact, but they are not expected to have opinions on constitutional law, nor to bring in verdicts from the realm of abstract principles, without judicial guidance. In this case the facts were all admitted. Susan is a woman, she voted, she would do it again. The judge thought Susan's action in defiance of law, but considering her and her compeers harmless criminals, a fine was the sugar plum to destroy the bitterness of the prosecution. Perhaps I do not comprehend your point of indignation. It is difficult, anyway, to be indignant with the thermometer at 90! And the insult of being tried by men—judges, jurors, lawyers, all men—for violating the laws and constitutions of men, made for the subjugation of my sex; to be forever publicly impaled by party, press, and pulpit, so far transcends a petty verdict of butchers, cab-drivers, and plough-boys, in a given case, that my continuous wrath against the whole dynasty of tyrants has not left one stagnant drop of blood in my veins to rouse for any single act of insult.

To Susan B. Anthony.

TENAFLY, *June 30, 1873.*

DEAR SUSAN,—I have an article in to-day's New York *Times* on your case. I hope it will suit you.

---

[1] At the presidential election in November, 1872, Miss Anthony and fourteen other women voted in Rochester, New York. On June 17 and 18, 1873, Miss Anthony was tried for this offense. Her counsel, Henry R. Selden, made a masterly argument in favor of woman's constitutional right to vote. Judge Ward Hunt, Associate Justice of the United States Supreme Court, who presided, refused to submit the case to the jury, and sentenced Miss Anthony to pay a fine of $100 and the costs of the prosecution.

Unless the Republicans do something for us this
coming winter, our "splinter" will verily dwindle to
a toothpick.[1] I see our very "proper" friend primly
turns up the whites of her eyes in the last *Woman's
Journal*, and says she is so sorry to find women "so
belligerent." I wish they were all roused to the
whitest heat, and then our days of slavery would not
be long.   Your rebellious friend.

To Anna E. Dickinson.

TENAFLY, *August 20, 1873.*

MY DEAR ANNA,—Aristotle could not conceive of
any form of government without slavery.   Modern
writers on social science cannot imagine any kind of

---

[1] This anticipation was fulfilled.   The Congressional session, 1873–74,
brought nothing larger than the discussion of the bill to establish the Territory of Pembina.   This proposed legislation called out from Senator
Aaron A. Sargent the following letter of May 20, 1874, to Mrs. Stanton:
"Thank you for the compliments on my being 'ever on the watch tower.'
I have passed them on to Ellen, for she is the watchman.   I will follow
your suggestions and move when the bill comes up, which will be in a day
or two, to substitute 'every inhabitant of the United States' for 'male.'
The clause protecting the right of suffrage reads just like the XV Amendment
—'on account of race, color, or previous condition of servitude.'   I will
move to amend by putting 'sex' before 'race.'   As ever at your service."
The bill came up in the United States Senate May 28, 1874.   Senator Sargent's amendments caused a long discussion.   They were defeated, as was
the bill itself.   This matter is interesting as giving a glance "behind the
scenes."   When the Woman's Party on in the nineteen hundreds began
to claim for Miss Anthony that she initiated the move for a suffrage amendment to the United States Constitution in 1878, it was pointed out that
she was not in Washington at the time, and that others carried through
the work of that year.   Then a shift of date was made to 1874.   That
was an equally bad pitch, for no suggestion of a national amendment was
made at the suffrage convention in January, and even the Pembina "toothpick" was not whittled out by Senator Sargent and Mrs. Stanton until
four months later.

civil or domestic government without the subjection of woman. So it is our special work to show these blessed sons of Adam that when woman comes to be an equal factor in civilization, the solar system will still move round obedient to law, and that man will still have a place on this planet and enjoy the right of self-government. We will not dominate everything, including him, though many say we dominate him already. By the way, remind me next time we meet to tell you of my experience of how men come in play in terrible emergencies. Once I had one with me at a public entertainment in a burning hall, and he went down two flights of stairs in a twinkling—I suppose to get the fire engine to save me!

To Susan B. Anthony.

TENAFLY, *July 30, 1874.*

OFFENDED SUSAN,—Come right down and pull my ears. I shall not attempt a defense. Of course I admit that I have made an awful blunder in not keeping silent so far as you were concerned on this terrible Beecher-Tilton scandal.[1] The whole odium of this *scandalum magnatum* has, in some quarters, been rolled on our suffrage movement, as unjustly as cunningly; hence I feel obliged just now to make extra efforts to keep our ship off the rocks. There was never anything so base and cowardly as that state-

[1] Miss Anthony happened to be visiting the Tiltons in Brooklyn the very day Mr. Tilton learned of the relations of his wife to Mr. Beecher. She had told Mrs. Stanton, and Mrs. Stanton committed the unpardonable indiscretion of repeating the confidence, that she stood in front of Mrs. Tilton's door for hours assuring the enraged husband that "he could only enter that room over her [Miss Anthony's] dead body."

ment of some of Beecher's supporters, building a footstool for him to stand upon out of the life, character, aspirations, and ambition of a large circle of reputable women. This terrible onslaught on the suffrage movement has made me feel like writing for every paper daily. From the silence on all sides, I saw it was for me to fight alone. I have in fact written several articles, *incog.*, in the *Graphic*. But I am too silent when I know I should be thundering against this wholesale slaughter of womanhood. When Beecher falls, as he must, he will pull all he can down with him. But we must not let the cause of woman go down in the smash. It is innocent.

To Elizabeth Smith Miller.

TENAFLY, *December 16, 1874.*

DEAR JULIUS,—Hearing that you are still agonizing over a name for your book, let me suggest these titles: "What Shall We Eat?", "Artists in the Kitchen," "Our Daily Bread," "In the Kitchen." [1] I like the first. I like, too, "Crown the Cook." It is a charming alliteration and suggests the queenly nature of a cook's work. The frontispiece could be *cordon bleu* being decorated by Brillat-Savarin. Your suggestive

JOHNSON.

To Susan B. Anthony.

CHICAGO, *February 16, 1875.*

DEAR SUSAN,—I have been in Chicago for some three days, and such a rush of people you never saw.

---

[1] The title finally adopted for Mrs. Miller's very successful cook-book.

I had a magnificent audience at the Grand Opera House, with people on the stairs, sidewalks, and even out into the street, who could not get into the building. I was in the depths all night and the day before lest the speech should not be up to the occasion. But when I was fairly launched, and every eye on me, I could feel the pluck slowly rising, and I went through the ordeal with credit to myself and to you; for I believe you are always quite as anxious about me as I am myself. Bradlaugh,[1] who sat on the platform, pronounced "Our Boys" worth giving. I was a week speaking in Iowa. When I arrived in Alden, managers came at once from two adjoining towns and invited me to lecture on Sunday. So at one o'clock that afternoon I went six miles off and spoke at three o'clock, and in the evening I held forth in the other town. I had a hard time with snow blockades, but missed only two appointments. When the day was before me, I took a sleigh, and went twenty miles on one occasion and thirty-eight on another, and successfully filled the engagements. At this last place the audience despaired of me, though I telegraphed I was on the way in a cutter. They did not believe it was possible for me to get through. However, when I stepped on the platform in traveling dress, but supperless, the audience, from miles around, was on the spot and ready to listen. These splendid people are hungry, hungry. Oh, for more power to give out the truth!

[1] Charles Bradlaugh, whom Mrs. Stanton also met several times later, was the leader of the Free Thought movement in England. When he died he was an influential member of the House of Commons.

To Robert Livingston Stanton.

CINCINNATI, *February 3, 1876.*

DEAR BOB,—I have had a delightful call from Doctor and Mrs. Reid from the Seminary at Steubenville. They had a visit recently from Mr. Emerson, and were charmed with his sweetness, charity, and simplicity, notwithstanding they are rigid Episcopalians. Doctor Reid says that after listening to Emerson talk a long while, it seemed to him that the latter had no religious belief; so he asked him squarely: "Mr. Emerson, do you believe in God?" "Really," he replied, "it is beyond my comprehension." When they sat down to dinner, Doctor Reid requested him to ask a blessing; thereupon Emerson closed his eyes and with great tenderness in his voice, said: "Father of all good, make us thankful." At Steubenville my trunk failed me, and I had to borrow Mrs. Reid's black velvet gown to appear in on the stage. After the lecture she told me that it rather alarmed her to hear such advanced sentiments coming out of a gown of hers. By the way, it is very foolish of you to be quite so pronounced about the Bible before you read it. Moreover, it cannot be spoken of as a whole. There are many glorious truths in it. Surely, the maxim, "Do unto others as you would that others should do unto you" is not a "swindle." My soul is to-night so full of love and tenderness for my precious flock that it would be easy for me to die if thereby I could make you all good and happy. Good night.

To Harriot Eaton Stanton.

TENAFLY, *November 8, 1876.*

DEAR HATTIE,—The election is so close that we shall not know certainly about it for several days to come; but we think Tilden will get it. He should succeed whether he does or not. I have not breathed freely in two weeks, I have been so afraid that the corrupt Republican party would triumph again. Just before election day we had a great Republican gathering one evening in Johnson's carpenter shop. Tenafly was out in force. Guns were fired and bands played. The milkman inopportunely drove into town, and his horse, unaccustomed to such hilarity among these Dutch farmers, ran away, breaking the cart and harness into more pieces than the Republican party in this vicinity can boast members. I have just finished reading *Robinson Crusoe's Money*, and am a little shaken in my greenback faith. I am glad you are reading Nordhoff's *Politics for Young Americans*, so that you and I can continue our political discussions next summer as we drive over the blue hills of Jersey.

To Elizabeth Smith Miller.

TENAFLY, *January 23, 1877.*

BELOVED JULIUS,—Susan and I returned from Washington Sunday morning. We had a two days' convention,[1] with crowded houses every session. The

---

[1] This annual convention of the National Woman Suffrage Association, held January 16th and 17th, was regarded as opening a new era in the movement. As the efforts to alter the XIV and XV Amendments, during their passage, in the interest of women had failed, and as the final opinion

day after the convention, we had a reception from
ten to two in the large parlors at Willard's Hotel,
where troops of people called on us—senators, congressmen, judges, lawyers' wives and daughters, and
some girls from the Departments. It was four when
I left the parlor, after having talked six hours without
ceasing, standing most of the time; and then, I was
on the cars all night. Susan is completely used up,
not having my genius for sleep as opportunity offers.

To Harriot Eaton Stanton.

NORTH AMHERST, OHIO,
March 11, 1877.

DEAR HATTIE,—I sit to-day in a forlorn old hotel,
poor bed and worse fare, and yet I am comfortable,
for I have spent the day outside of my surroundings.
These trips have taught me one thing in regard to
myself, and that is that I can be happy under most
conditions. I see so many people fretting and dis-
contented under the most promising circumstances

---

rendered March 29, 1875, by the United States Supreme Court in the
Minor-Happersett case was adverse to the contention that the Constitution as it stood forbade the states to deny or abridge the right of a citizen
to vote on account of sex, the conclusion was reached to bend every effort
to add an amendment to the Constitution definitely prohibiting the several
states from disfranchising United States citizens on account of sex. This
course had been urged by Mrs. Stanton at the convention held in January,
1869, and was for a time pursued, but fell into abeyance during the period
1872–75, when the question as to the political status of women was being
tried out in the courts. During this convention of 1877 thousands of
petitions were presented to the Congress asking for a XVI Amendment,
and both the Senate and the House of Representatives by unanimous
consent assigned time when members presented these petitions from their
constituents and made arguments in favor of woman suffrage. But no
resolution to submit a XVI Amendment to the states was introduced.

that I have come to the conclusion that heaven and hell depend more on our organization than on our environment. I am sorry to hear of the religious excitement at Vassar. I trust you will not attend any of those meetings. I prefer to have you walk in the open air, sleep, or read Plato to listening to the prayers of sentimental girls and to the recounting of their morbid experiences. Our friends are insisting that M. shall not visit C., "under the circumstances." But I think it would be a great shame now that the poor little thing is in trouble to desert her. If C. is the chief of sinners, it does not follow that she should be shunned by all the saints. They might rather constitute themselves a board of missions to carry to her the gospel of purity, chastity, and honor. We take infinite pains to send the glad tidings to the heathen in the remotest corners of the earth, but shun the heathen at our own doors. With kisses many and long for my precious one. Good night.

To Margaret Livingston Stanton.

STARLIGHT PLANTATION, IOWA,
May 16, 1877.

DEAR MAGGIE,—I reached here yesterday. I wish you could have seen Gat and me coming over the prairies. Imagine a lumber wagon laden with a chest of drawers, a spring bed, a box of groceries, a package of meat, two bags of flour, a bag of sundries, a box of freight, my trunk and hand bag, bundles for a half dozen neighbors, a hundred trees from the nursery and a lot of small fruits—all this looming up behind us. We moved along as if in a funeral procession, for the load was heavy, the roads bad and head winds blowing a hurricane. My hair and veil stood out to the four points of the compass. Everybody is in bed now, though it is only eight P.M. But they will be up at four to-morrow morning and breakfast at five. Of course I shall not join this matutinal feast, but will appear on the scene much later, as I did this morning, when I had for my meal a broiled chicken, some flour "gems" as light as a feather, stewed peaches, excellent coffee, cream as yellow as gold and butter as sweet as clover. I hope you[1] will take the head of the house and learn all you can about cooking. Devote the month of May to reading the cook-book and getting all the practical knowledge of the kitchen that you can. It will be a pleasant change from books. Learn a few simple things, such as how to make bread, tea, coffee, cake, and how to cook vegetables. See how washing, starching, ironing and everything of that kind is done. Master the sewing-machine. Then you will know how to direct every sort of household work. Every man and woman should have these acquirements. At West Salem I had three whole days free and I boned down to expanding and improving my lecture on "Our Boys." I wrote two hundred pages and made the whole much better. I begin to think that in time I shall succeed in throwing as bright a halo round "Our Boys" as is the case already with "Our Girls." As recreation I read Mark Twain. His books are more potent than sermons in teaching human duty, and they do

---

[1] Margaret had graduated from Vassar the previous year.

it with a laugh in which we must join in spite of ourselves.

To Susan B. Anthony.

TENAFLY, January 14, 1878.

DEAR SUSAN,—I suppose you are waiting to hear
about the convention.[1] It went off well; there were
crowded houses as usual and $200 in the treasury
after all the bills were paid. I prepared the resolutions[2] a week before and had them in print, so that
there was no worry at the last moment over them. I
devoted my whole vacation to the speech to be made
before the committee.[3] All said, "Very good." The
day before, Senator Sargent had presented in the
Senate a resolution proposing the following amendment: "Article 16, sec. 1. The right of citizens of
the United States to vote shall not be denied or abridged
by the United States or by any State on account of
sex."[4] The day after the close of the convention,
Isabella Beecher Hooker held a regular Moody and
Sankey prayer meeting in the ladies' reception room
right next to the Senate Chamber. Those present
prayed, sang "Hold the Fort," "Guide Us, Oh, Thou

[1] The tenth annual Woman Suffrage Convention was held in Washington on January 8th and 9th. It was one of the very few gatherings of
this kind that Miss Anthony did not attend.

[2] The first resolution called for a XVI Amendment (<i>History of Woman
Suffrage</i>, vol. iii, p. 61).

[3] On January 11th, Mrs. Stanton spoke before the Senate Committee on
Privileges and Elections on "National Protection for National Citizens."
(Given in full in <i>History of Woman Suffrage</i>, vol. iii, p. 80.) The opening
words in her masterly argument against State Rights and in favor of national
protection of the right of suffrage were, "In appearing before you to ask
for a <i>XVI Amendment.</i>"

[4] This is also the form in which the amendment was introduced year
after year and in which it finally passed Congress in 1919.

Great Jehovah" and "The Battle Hymn of the Republic," and made speeches from the tops of tables. In the meantime the Senators were assembling and the corridors were crowded. Senator Sargent told us it was a regular mob. Mrs. Sargent and I did not attend the prayer meeting, for, as Jehovah has never taken a very active part in the suffrage movement, I thought I would stay at home and get ready to implore the committee, having more faith in their power to render us the desired aid. At this same time a debate was precipitated in the Senate, and when a fellow member rallied Senator Sargent on the mob character of his constituency, he cleverly replied: "This is nothing to what you will see at this Capitol if these women's petitions are not heard." Altogether it was a week of constant agitation and I think the result—prayer meeting, mob and all—is good. I reached home Saturday night and found a telegram asking for my speech as the committee intends to print it. So I sat up last night until four o'clock in order to copy it and I sent off this morning 150 pages of manuscript. I was so interested in "National Protection for National Citizens," that the night slipped away and I felt neither tired nor sleepy, though to-day I am like a squeezed sponge and have done nothing. With love, good night.

To Susan B. Anthony.

BATAVIA, NEW YORK,
December 18, 1878.

DEAR SUSAN,—I had a magnificent audience at Ulrichsville, where I so vexed the Presbyterian minister by telling what the General Assemblies and Synods of that church had done against women that he vowed he would get up a protest. But the people were delighted with what I said, and after I finished, flocked up to tell me so. Nor is it only our lectures which sow good seed. Coming from Cleveland the other day, I met Mrs. W. and her daughter, who said she would not have our visits at her house blotted out of her life for any consideration; and I know that hundreds of women feel the same. Perhaps the world is better that we have lived, and so we will not mind the hotels and early hours. But I must get up at six to go to Frankfort. Oh!

To Lillie Devereau Blake.

WASHINGTON, *January 6, 1879.*

DEAR MRS. BLAKE,—My philosophy of life, love, and marriage is quite different from that of many people. I regard them all with reference to individual development. You say you are called upon by a mother to advise her about the proposed marriage of her daughter—my first thought would be concerning the character of this young man; whether he has led a pure life, whether he is honorable in his dealings with his fellows, whether he is high-minded in his ambitions. My next thought would be as to whether his ancestors were strong and vigorous in mind and body. Society has not established the same code of morals for men and women, but nature's laws are equal, and there is no escape for either sex from the penalty of every transgression. If I were a mother about to marry a daughter, the distinction of good, honest, healthy blood is the nobility I would most prize in my future son-in-law. It seems to me that your friend should hail an all-absorbing love on the part of her daughter for her future husband as a most important step in this daughter's development, and no narrow or selfish consideration on the mother's part should mar the child's happiness. Her love for her husband can in no way conflict with her love for her mother. A man's love brings into a woman's existence an inspiration, a completeness, a satisfaction, that a mother's cannot. A true conjugal union is the highest kind of human love,—divine, creative in the realm of thought as well as in the material world. I have great faith in nature's promptings and the sincere love of young men and women for each other.

To Harriot Eaton Stanton.

IN THE WEST, *January 8, 1879.*

MY PRECIOUS LITTLE GIRL BABY,—I am so glad that you have seen and heard Emerson. I have always regretted that I have not seen more of him. But the rare glimpses I have had of him, commencing in the early forties when we lived near Boston, and my occasional conversations with him scattered through the past years, are always bright spots in my memory. I have always liked him ever since he once told me that he wrote in his *Journal*[1] the day of the famous

---

[1] "October 14, 1851. To-day is holden at Worcester the 'Woman's Convention.' I think that as long as they have not equal rights of property and right of voting they are not on the right footing."—*Journal,* vol. viii, p. 258.

Worcester meeting that he was in favor of woman suffrage. I have had rather a hard trip through Missouri; night travel all the time. At one point I took the cars at twelve. There was no sleeping coach, so I had to sit upright all night with another person in the seat, in a car crowded with immigrants to Kansas. It is said that the emigration West was never so great, and judging from what I saw in this train, it must be so. There were babies enough to populate Jupiter and his four moons. I was particularly interested in them, thinking how they some day were to become active American citizens with no memory of the distant lands from which they come. It really made my heart sad to read the criticisms of Anna Dickinson which you sent. Like the student in Longfellow's poem, she forgot her high calling and thought only of making money, thus she lost her power and inspiration. Gold is good in its place, but when it becomes the primal consideration, it turns the heart to stone. Good night.

To Theodore Stanton.

TENAFLY, *January 11, 1879.*

DEAR THEODORE,—Last week in Washington I sat up two nights until three o'clock in the morning to write a speech and the resolutions for the convention which occurred on the 8th and the 9th. I presided at all the sessions during two days. The Washington papers were very complimentary to me as a presiding officer, and Susan says I never did so well. I came home by the night train and now have until

Monday—this is Saturday—in which to get ready for a five months' trip in the West. Some of my resolutions seemed to hit the nail on the head; especially these, which caused considerable amusement in all circles: Resolved, That we cannot have honest money until we have honest men. Whereas, a Sixteenth Constitutional Amendment for Woman Suffrage is now pending on a tie vote in the House Judiciary Committee—Yeas, Lapham, N. Y.; Lynde, Wis.; Frye, Me.; Butler, Mass.; Conger, Mich.—Nays, Knott, Ky.; Hartridge, Ga.; Stenger, Penn.; McMahon, O.; Culberson, Texas;—Absent, Harris of Va., who declares he has never investigated the subject: Therefore Resolved, That it is the duty of Harris of Va. to remain absent when a vote on this question is taken, unless he has given it as much consideration, as if the rights of all men were therein involved. Whereas, In President Hayes' last message, he makes a truly paternal review of the interests of this Republic, both great and small, from the Army, the Navy and our foreign relations, to the ten little Indians in Hampton, Va., our timber on the western mountains, and the switches of the Washington railroad; from the Paris Exposition, the postal service and the abundant harvests, to the possible bulldozing of some colored men in various southern districts, cruelty to live animals, and the crowded condition of the mummies, dead ducks and fishes in the Smithsonian Institution, yet forgets to mention twenty million women citizens robbed of their social, civil and political rights; Therefore, Resolved, That a committee of three be appointed from this Conven-

tion to wait upon the President and remind him of
the existence of one-half of the American people whom
he has accidentally overlooked, and of whom it would
be wise for him to make some mention in his future
messages.   With best love,

MOTHER.

To Elizabeth Smith Miller.

JOPLIN, *March 26, 1879.*

DEAR JULIUS,—Here is Johnson down in a little
mining town in southern Missouri. I have been
wandering, wandering, ever since we parted; up
early and late; sleepy and disgusted with my profession, as there is no rest from the time the season
begins until it ends. Two months more, containing
sixty-one days, still stretch their long length before
me. I must pack and unpack my trunk sixty-one
times; pull out the black silk trail and don it; puff
my hair and pin on the illusion ruffling round my
spacious throat, sixty-one more times; rehearse "Our
Boys," "Our Girls," or "Home Life," sixty-one times;
eat 183 more miserable meals; sleep between cotton
sheets under these detestable things called "com-
forters"—tormentors would be a more fitting name
—sixty-one more nights; shake hands with sixty-one
more committees, smile, try to look intelligent and
interested in everyone who approaches me, while I
feel like a squeezed sponge; and endeavor to affect a
little spring and briskness in my gait on landing in
each town in order to avoid giving an impression that
I am seventy, when in reality I feel more like crawling

than walking.   But, with her best foot forward, I am always,   Your own   JOHNSON.

To Susan B. Anthony.

OMAHA, *April 5, 1879.*

DEAR SUSAN,—The *Woman's Journal* has, I see, some strictures on us for allowing those Mormon women on our platform.[1]   But I think if the Congress of the United States can allow George Q. Cannon to sit for Utah in that body without it being supposed to endorse polygamy, we could permit Mormon women the same privilege in our association without our being accused of embracing their principles.   If Congress can stand Cannon with four wives, we might stand the women with only the fourth part of a husband! And, furthermore, when Congress proposes to disfranchise the women of a Territory, where should they go to plead their case[2] but to the National Woman Suffrage Association?   You ask whether the lady you mention will have the strength to go through one of our campaigns.   I doubt it.   Such pine knots as you and I are no standard for judging ordinary women.

To Gerrit Smith Stanton.

ST. LOUIS, *May 12, 1879.*

DEAR GAT,—Though I reached the convention at the last hour, all the St. Louis papers have given more space to me than to all the others put together, which

---

[1] At the January Washington Convention.

[2] In 1870 the Legislature of the Territory enfranchised its women.   In 1887 Congress withdrew from the women of Utah the right to vote.   When, however, Utah became in 1896 a state in the Union, the Constitution re-established woman suffrage.

rather conceited remark is for your eye alone. And I may add that what they say has been very complimentary, which is perhaps the reason why I am conceited. We were publicly received—the first time in the case of women—in the Merchants' Exchange, an immense building. I had the president's arm, walked the whole length of the great hall, mounted the platform and was given an armchair, whereupon all the ladies present made five minutes' speeches to over a thousand men—the leading business lights of the city—standing with bared heads. We were then escorted to our carriages—seven in number—and driven out to the fair grounds, where a collation had been prepared and where we had toasts, speeches and merriment. I returned half dead, one of the penalties of greatness. Sunday night, that is last night, I spoke in the largest Methodist church in the city to over a thousand people. The edifice was packed when I arrived with the officiating clergyman. As we walked slowly up the center aisle, I heard those in the pews whisper, "There she is," "There she is," which made me put as much life into my steps as possible, though on such occasions I begin to feel that age is upon me. I sat in the pulpit facing the immense throng during the prayer and singing, and had time to get rested and collect my thoughts before giving my "sermon." It was my "simultaneous creation" discourse (Genesis 1:27 and 28), and was published in full in the *Globe*. Though an extra edition was struck off not a copy was to be had by ten o'clock. Ex-Governor Stanard sent copies broadcast over the state. With love and kisses, MOTHER.

To Moncure D. Conway.

NEW YORK, *October 27, 1879.*

DEAR MR. CONWAY,—I find that by mistake I recently destroyed the letter I had from Calvin Fairbank,[1] probably the last he ever wrote. The letter breathed a childlike faith in the final triumph of the cause for which he had so deeply suffered and like the prophets of old he foretold what has since come true. After declaring he would never bow to the slave-holding oligarchy, he puts these lines between quotation marks: "I will neither yield to the song of the siren nor the voice of the hyena, the tears of the crocodile nor the howling of the wolf."[2] I was so struck by these words that I fortunately copied them, and it was later that I tore up the letter. Do you chance to know who said or wrote them? In fact to get an answer to this question is the main purpose of this letter I am writing to you. I may use the quotation in a speech. But before doing so, I would like to know whom I am quoting. What a hard time poor Fairbank had in life. In prison fifteen years!! How did he live through all he suffered? Such self-denial and devotion to principle should make us other reformers quite ashamed of our easy existence. I have such a horror of cells and rats, I fear I would forswear my dearest convictions if I were threatened with incarceration!

---

[1] Twice imprisoned at hard labor in Kentucky for having assisted in the escape of slaves.

[2] "Eastward Ho," act v, scene i, by George Chapman.

To Rosamond Dale Owen.

TENAFLY, *January 2, 1880.*

DEAR MISS OWEN,—Many thanks for your beautiful contribution about Indiana for our *History*. What you tell us about your dear father's work in improving the laws of that state, about his marriage and his home life, so noble and worthy of imitation, brings him back to me vividly. I can scarcely believe that he has passed away. He was often at my house in New York and I have always regarded him as one of the noblest of men.

To Susan B. Anthony.

TENAFLY, *January 10, 1880.*

DEAR SUSAN,—You have not made me take your position. I repudiate it from the bottom of my soul.[1] It is conservative, autocratic, to the last degree. I

[1] The Preface to vol. iii of the *History of Woman Suffrage* contains this paragraph from the pen of Mrs. Stanton: "We are now pressing on the legislature of New York State the consideration that it has the same power to extend the right of suffrage to women that it has so often exercised in enfranchising different classes of men. Eminent publicists have long conceded this power to state legislatures as well as to Congress, declaring that women as citizens of the United States have the right to vote, and that a simple enabling act is all that is needed. The constitutionality of such an act was never questioned until the legislative power was invoked for the enfranchisement of woman. We who have studied our republican institutions and understand the limits of the executive, judicial, and legislative branches of the government, are aware that the legislature, directly representing the people, is the primary source of power, above all courts and constitutions." Miss Anthony took issue with Mrs. Stanton on the correctness of this statement and even consulted lawyers on the subject with a view to modifying this paragraph or wholly suppressing it in the Preface. This called forth a long correspondence between the joint authors of the *History*, which is well resumed in this letter.

accept no authority of either bibles or constitutions which tolerate the slavery of women. My rights were born with me and are the same over the whole globe. I may be denied their exercise in the mines of Siberia, in the empire of China and in the State of New York, through force, fraud, and sophistry; but they remain the same everywhere. Does my watch cease to be mine because some thief has taken forcible possession thereof? Of the three branches of government, the legislative, representing the people, is the primal source of power. I perceive that one of the lawyers you have consulted admits one of my points —that the legislature is above the courts; and yet the courts can declare null and void the acts of the legislature. But if the legislature can be above the courts and yet at times be in conflict with them, why on the same principle can it not be above the Constitution and yet in conflict with it? How do you amend the Constitution? The legislature, directly representing the people, decides that the Constitution needs amending, frames the amendment and submits it to the people, the majority saying yea or nay. Now where is the primary source of power? In the majority of the people. All this seems so plain to me that I wonder you halt so long over it. Think of you accepting the man-made constitution, the man-interpretation thereof, the man-amendment submitted by a convention of aristocrats, and the old secession reverence for a constitution. Why Garrison, who kicked and cuffed the old document for forty years, would turn in his grave to see printed in our *History of Woman Suffrage* your present ideas as to the authority and majesty of any of those constitutions, state or national. Ah, beware, Susan, lest as you become "respectable," you become conservative. One-half of the people have had no voice in the setting up of this constitution of New York, and I, for one, would not let a member of the legislature skulk behind the constitution so as to hold me at bay for years until that document were amended. On the contrary, I would say to him: "You represent me and it is your duty to see that justice is done. Set aside technicalities and accepted interpretations of special acts, and on broad principles recognize my citizenship." The legal rule of interpretation is in the spirit of the document. The legislature has the right to enfranchise the women of New York. Susan, you must rise to the dignity of Lord Mansfield who, when law, popular sentiment, religion, custom, everything and everybody, believed in slavery, declared that no slave could breathe on English soil. You may, if you choose, write ten thousand footnotes giving in your adhesion to these man-made constitutions and appending your own name thereto, but wherever in your last revision of the proofs you have made me responsible for such todyism, I shall always bow my head with shame and sorrow.

To Robert G. Ingersoll.

New York, *February 10, 1880.*

Dear Mr. Ingersoll,—The passage from Charles Kingsley you refer to runs as follows: "I have arrived at conclusions which I keep to myself as yet, and only utter as Greek, φωνάεντα συνετοΐδιν, the principle of which is, that there will never be a good world for woman till the last monk, and therewith the last remnant of the monastic idea of, and legislation for, woman, *i.e.*, the canon law, is civilized off the earth." This has long been a hobby of mine, this condemnation, in the interests of my sex, of the canon law, and I cannot tell you how delighted I was to find such a distinguished and able supporter of my contention in Canon—but I do wish he had not accepted the Chester title!—Kingsley. I may add that the foregoing passage is from a very long letter addressed by him in 1870 to John Stuart Mill, wherein various aspects of the Woman Question are treated, but not always in a way that I so thoroughly approve as I do this bold thrust at the monks and their fabrications. In a letter written in the previous year and also to Mr. Mill, he touches on this same subject when he refers to himself "as completely emancipated from those prejudices which have been engrained into the public mind by the traditions of the monastic or canon law about woman." As regards the exact meaning of the two Greek words which Kingsley quotes above, since my own knowledge of the Hellenic tongue has grown rusty, and you confess that yours was never very bright, I have turned for light to Professor Sterrett, of Amherst College, and he tells me that these words are found in the second Olympian Ode of Pindar, line 93. They mean, according to Professor Sterrett: "Things that have a voice for the wise," and the whole sentence runs: "Many swift arrows have I beneath my bended arm within

my quiver, arrows that have a voice for the wise,"
and then it continues: "but for the multitude they
need interpreters." It seems to me that the whole
passage, especially the last phrase, renders Kingsley's
reference still more pointed. So here you have this
light of the Church of England coming to our support,
himself falling back on Pindar, a rank heathen, while
that arch-rationalist, John Stuart Mill, is his con-
fidant in the matter. Your follower in the faith.

To the Rev. Robert Collyer.

TENAFLY, *February 22, 1880.*

DEAR MR. COLLYER,—I have your communication
about "literary righteousness," criticizing me for
using one of your anecdotes without giving you credit.
But you forget that you belong to a class—white male
citizens—who have robbed me of all my civil and
political rights; so I feel that it ill becomes you to
call me to account for using one of your little anecdotes. I consider you and your sex fair game for
literary pilfering. Moreover, it is man's department
in life to dig and delve for jewels, actual and ideal,
and to lay them at woman's feet for her to use as
she may see fit; and, finally, you should rejoice that
you have ever said anything that is worth quoting!
Sincerely, your guiltless purloiner.[1]

---

[1] Mrs. Stanton's Diary, in referring to this incident, contains this: "Doctor Collyer wrote in reply that he had not one more word to say in the way of accusation, but lay prostrate in sackcloth and ashes, and wondered that he had not taken my view of the case at the start."

To Cadet Whittaker.[1]

TENAFLY, *April 20, 1880.*

DEAR SIR,—Reading from day to day of the insults
to which you have been subjected in the Military
Academy of the United States, while I have blushed
for my country, I have had a feeling of pride in the
young cadet who has maintained, under very trying
circumstances, such self-control and dignity. What
a splendid record for the page of history some brave
young cadet of the white race might have made for
himself, if, in defending you against the contemptible
persecutions and brutal outrages of his fellows, he
had fought and conquered that hateful spirit of caste,
so degrading to every human soul that entertains it.
It would have been a more gallant four years' fight
for some Northern boy to have made at West Point,
than to have been the leader of all the victories from
Fort Donelson to the fall of Richmond. But not
one soldier was there. With all the memories of the
late war, the proclamation of emancipation, the acts
of enfranchisement, the constitutional amendments,
and civil rights bill—not one soldier brave enough
to stand for justice, liberty, and equal rights to all!
In the contemplation of such unworthy sons, such
moral cowards, I do not feel we have any reason to
be proud of our color. Accept my best regards and
sincere sympathy for you in the present trials. Yours
respectfully.

---

[1] Johnson Chestnut Whittaker, the colored cadet from South Carolina,
entered West Point in 1876 and left in 1882 without graduation.

To Isabella Beecher Hooker.

TENAFLY, *May 10, 1880.*

DEAR ISABELLA,—I feel with you that, in spite of all minor drawbacks, the union of the suffrage forces would be a move in the right direction. But our cause is too great to be permanently hurt by what any one individual or group of individuals may do. For over thirty years some people have said from time to time that I have injured the suffrage movement beyond redemption; but it still lives. Train killed it, Victoria Woodhull killed it, the *Revolution* killed it. But with each death, it put on new life. Boston thought that Paulina Davis impaired our best interests; that you did the same; that Susan dealt us a death blow at various times. But every time it is stricken to earth, it comes up again with fresh power. I enclose a letter from Helen Gardener, who, you will see, is distressed about Prohibition and Miss Willard; neither of which harms us a particle. Reforms are not made of blown glass to be broken to pieces with the first adverse wind.

To Mary Clemmer Ames.

TENAFLY, *June 20, 1880.*

DEAR MARY CLEMMER AMES,—The Hebrews in their synagogues say in every service: "We thank thee, oh Lord, that we were not born women, but made in thy image," while the women say: "We thank thee, oh Lord, that we are made according to

thy will." [1]   But from this don't conclude that I am a
Jew-hater; on the contrary, some of my dearest friends
are Hebrews.   But this synagogue service is a disgrace
to them and to the century.

Anne Lynch Botta.

TENAFLY, July 20, 1880.

DEAR MRS. BOTTA,—I am sorry to hear that our
friend is still on the ailing list.   We must take her in
hand and teach her that thoughts are things.   "As
he thinketh in his heart, so is he."   It is not our surroundings but the spirit within us that makes our life
glorious or insignificant.   I refer to the principles as

---

[1] From Felix Adler to the editors, May 11, 1914: "The statement made
in your mother's letter is correct.   But perhaps the following explanation
will not be superfluous.   Nothing perhaps is more characteristic of the
religion of Israel than its benedictions.   Some hundred of them are spoken
day by day—life was embroidered with blessings.   There are in particular
three classes.   One class relates to every kind of enjoyment.   There are
blessings to be spoken in smelling sweet fragrances, when tasting wine,
when seeing the flowers first bloom in spring, when catching sight of mountains or the great sea, when seeing beautiful persons; but also, and this is
characteristic, when seeing those who are afflicted with loathsome disease
—the blessing in this case being a humble acceptance of the divine decree.
The second class of benedictions are pronounced in connection with the
performance of religious duties.   It was esteemed a high privilege to perform religious duties of any kind—a mark of the chosen people; and because
women were exempt from many onerous religious duties and in general
were not required to be students of the Law in the same sense that men
were, the benediction was spoken, 'Blessed art Thou who has not made me
a woman.'   It is in line with the other benediction, 'Blessed art Thou who
has not made me a pagan.'   The phrase sounds so harsh and is capable
of such sweeping misinterpretation, that the above remarks may possibly
be useful to you.   The third class of benedictions are liturgical.   Of course
we must remember that among the Hebrews, despite these discriminations,
the mother and wife was always regarded with tender reverence.   Among
the people who in their sacred books possess the last chapter of Proverbs,
it could hardly have been otherwise."

you find them in Emerson of the power of mind over outward conditions.

To Henry Stanton.

TENAFLY, *August 2, 1880.*

DEAR KIT,—I am now reading Lecky's *History of Rationalism in Europe.* The chapter on Witchcraft is heartrending. How anyone, in view of the protracted sufferings of the race, can invest the laws of the universe with a tender loving fatherly intelligence, watching, guiding and protecting humanity, is to me amazing. I see nothing but immutable, inexorable law, grinding the ignorant to powder. History shows us that by bitter experience man has learned the laws of the universe and their relation to his own organization. With the advent of the Christian religion, came more terrible tortures and persecutions than ever before. And woman has all along been the great sufferer. I note that a large majority of those who were tortured for sorcery were women. And those who will not accept the popular superstitions *to-day* suffer bitter persecutions, more and more refined, of course, as civilization advances. Instead of the tortures of the Inquisition, they endure ostracism. When shall we learn the lesson of individual freedom?

To Theodore Stanton and Harriot Stanton.[1]

TENAFLY, *November 12, 1880.*

DEAR CHILDREN,—This is my birthday. I am sixty-five years old, nearing the seventies. Looking

---

[1] Who were together in Europe.

back through life, I feel that our troubles are fully
compensated by our joys. I have had an existence
of hard work, but I think it has been a success. I
began a Diary to-day, which I shall hope to keep up
with more or less regularity—I fear the latter!—so
that, when I have passed away, you children will have
a better knowledge of some of the things I have thought
and done during the final years of my life. On the 2nd
inst.—election day—I went down to the polling booth,
offered my ballot and argued the case with the inspectors.[1] The Republican wagon and horses, all decked
with flags and evergreens, came for the male part of
the household. I told the driver that my legal representatives were all absent, but that I would go down
and vote. "You flabbergast me," he answered.
But as I am now in the midst of writing the chron-
icles of the woman suffrage movement, it seemed
quite in line with the work to give a practical demonstration of the faith which is in me, so, notwithstanding
the flabbergasted condition of the driver I thought I
would take the risk and go down to the polls with
him. Once there, I had great fun frightening and
muddling these old Dutch inspectors. The whole
town is agape with my act. A friend says he
never saw Tenafly in such excitement. The men

---

[1] After the passage of the XIV and XV Amendments fully a hundred and
fifty women in different parts of the country either tried to vote or succeeded in doing so. Court proceedings were involved in most instances, the
government bringing suit against the officials receiving the vote of a woman
and against the woman voting as in the case United States of America *vs.*
Susan B. Anthony, or the women proceeding against the election officers
for refusing to receive their ballots, as in the Minor *vs.* Happersett case.
The first woman to offer her vote was Marilla M. Ricker of New Hampshire.
This was in 1870. The last was Elizabeth Cady Stanton.

have taken sides about equally. This is a good example of what I have often said of late that acts, not words are what is needed to push this woman suffrage question to the fore. The next evening when I went down for the mail, the postmaster said he would give five dollars for the ticket I proffered. "I would have it framed and hung up in my house," he added. I should add that I really felt quite tired holding that ballot so long and arguing with the judges of election. Good night.

1880

MY DIARY

Grow old along with me,
The best is yet to be.

TENAFLY, *November 12.*

To-day I am sixty-five years old, am perfectly well, am a moderate eater, sleep well and am generally happy. My philosophy is to live one day at a time; neither to waste my forces in apprehension of evils to come, nor regrets for the blunders of the past. Once in a while, in thinking of what I might have done for my children, I feel suddenly depressed. But as I did not see, when I myself was young, all that I now see with age and experience, I dismiss the thoughts from my mind with the reflection that I then knew no better than to have seven children in quick succession. I have no sympathy with the old idea that children owe such immense gratitude to their parents that they can never fulfill their obligations to them. I think the obligation is all on the other side. Parents can never do too much for their children to repay them for the injustice of having brought them into the world, unless they have insured them high moral and intellectual gifts, fine physical health, and enough money and education to render life something more than one ceaseless struggle for necessaries.

TENAFLY, *November 13.*

I find in the New York *Tribune* a notice of the death of my much loved friend Lucretia Mott—eighty-eight years old. Having known her well in the flush of life when all her functions were at their zenith, and in the repose of age when her powers had begun to wane, her withdrawal from our midst seems to me as beautiful and natural as the changing foliage from springtime to autumn of some grand oak tree I have long cherished and watched. Where do we go? On what glories do our eyes reopen? These are the unanswered questions. We can speculate, we can hope, but who can know? A few days before she died Lucretia sent this sentiment with her autograph to Clara Spence:[1] "In the true marriage relation, the independence of the husband and wife is equal, their dependence mutual and their obligations reciprocal." Surely this is a good definition of marriage.

TENAFLY, *November 14.*

Though I could not be at Lucretia Mott's funeral to-day to say my word, yet I have thought of her, read about her, and written of her all alone here by myself.[2] This Sunday was with me a sacred memorial day to her, and as I consider her repose, self-control, and beautiful spirit, and recall how through all our conventions and discussions not one word to sting or exasperate anyone ever passed her lips, I have vowed again, as I have so many times, that I shall in the future try to imitate her noble example. If I go

---

[1] Founder and director of the Spence School in New York City.

[2] Under date of Washington, January 20, 1880, occurs in the Diary this entry: "The opening session of the woman suffrage convention was a memorial meeting for Lucretia Mott. Lincoln Hall was handsomely decorated with flags and flowers. The colored choir sang sweetly and I gave the oration. (See *History of Woman Suffrage*, vol. i, p. 407.) The hall was packed and Mrs. Hayes, wife of the President, was in the audience."

through the coming six months with this *History* [1]
work with equanimity, I shall have hopes of myself!

TENAFLY, *November 15.*

I have fully made up my mind not to budge this
autumn one inch outside my premises.[2] I am so
happy at the thought of staying at home that nothing
that could offer would be so charming as to cause me
to change my mind. I do not believe there ever was
a woman who esteemed it such a privilege to stay at
home. It is often said that if women are given a taste
of public life, they will never be satisfied with home.
But I think experience shows that all men and women
who have been much in the outside world are only too
glad to retire.

TENAFLY, *November 18.*

Lillie Devereau Blake writes urging more aggressiveness on our part. I approve and answer that I
think indeed that we have sat quite long enough on
a limb of the Republican tree singing "suffrage, if
you please," like so many insignificant humming
birds, and that I am ready for any change of method
that will undermine a solid male dynasty.

TENAFLY, *November 22.*

My distinguished good friend C. has been visiting
me but he has not succeeded in stating a definite idea.

---

[1] *History of Woman Suffrage*, edited by Elizabeth Cady Stanton, Susan
B. Anthony, Matilda Joslyn Gage. Volume I was published early in 1881,
Volume II in 1882, Volume III in 1886.

[2] With the season 1879–1880 Mrs. Stanton ended her exacting Lyceum
lecture tours, but for thirteen more years continued as president of the
National Woman Suffrage Association and attended the conventions or
sent addresses or letters.

I never saw so intelligent a man have so much trouble in getting out a connected sentence. Ever since I have known him, he has desired to have a long talk with me, but he never gets started; and yet each time he meets me with renewed zest for the outpouring. It is like getting congealed liquid from a demijohn; you know the jug is large and full, but getting the contents out is the problem.

TENAFLY, *November 25.*

I have just been reading Adler's sermons. He says so well what I have long thought and believed—*viz.,* that religion is life. How much happier life would be, if we made more of man and this world and thought less of future states of which we know nothing.

TENAFLY, *December 1.*

My brother-in-law, Sam Wilkeson, has begun a suit against Henry Ward Beecher for ten thousand dollars, the sum he advanced out of his own pocket towards the publication of *The Life of Christ.* It is expected that this action will have the effect of spurring Beecher on to complete this work, which has been hanging fire.[1] Like many writers of a sanguine temperament, Beecher started in with enthusiasm but grew tired before it was finished. He felt the same way over his first and only novel, *Norwood.* He once told me, speaking of that story, that he didn't know

---

[1] In a later entry Mrs. Stanton says the plaintiff was "nonsuited, but Sam declares it was worth $10,000 to see the expression on the faces of judge and jury when he was on the witness stand and said 'the Beecher-Tilton trial knocked the *Life of Christ* higher than a kite.'"

how to get all his actors off the stage and thought seriously of introducing a railway accident in order to accomplish this result!

TENAFLY, *December 25.*

I have been reading of George Eliot's death. The editorial in the *Sun* is just, appreciative, written on a high plane. How flippant and egotistic Kate Field's article is in contrast, with her two flings at George Eliot's life in warning off others. Why do most women think that they exalt their own virtue if they howl at the flaws in other women? They see but one virtue, while there are many, and they quite forget that "the greatest of these is charity."

TENAFLY, *December 27.*

We are getting on finely with our *History.* We are trying to collect everything that pertains to our cause, to exhume what women have done and to rescue all the facts from being forgotten. Mrs. Gage has been here for a month and we have all been busy. She has gone home for the holidays and Susan and I are tugging on alone. We are scratching from morning till night. We sit in the library surrounded with papers, our writing desk loaded down with encyclopædias, dictionaries, etc. I am so glad that I am not wandering on those Western prairies. Heavens! It makes me shudder to think of my weary lecture tours from Maine to Texas during the last twelve years.

1881

WASHINGTON, *January 25.*

We called on Mrs. Hayes, and spent an hour at the White House. I have heard here but one opinion in regard to her, *viz.*, that she is an intelligent, common-sense woman. I myself noticed that she is good looking, frank and genial in her manners, with no airs or affected graces, no French dancing-master attitudinizing and gesticulations. She has kept the White House morally clean—no whisky and scandals there.

TENAFLY, *February 1.*

On my way back from the Washington Convention I stopped in Delaware, and had a hearing, one evening, before the legislature, the governor, chief justice, and the members of the bar, and another evening addressed the public. Tom Bayard was just elected senator for another six years. We met in the streets of Wilmington by chance, and I congratulated him. He is always a little embarrassed when we meet, and this embarrassment was not lessened on this occasion by one of the local papers asking what our relationship was and another paper replying, "Well, they have the same uncle, anyway," which was incorrect however.[1] But among the newspaper squibs called forth by the stop-over at Wilmington, this from the Philadelphia *Press* is perhaps the best: "Mrs. Elizabeth Cady

[1] He was the nephew of Edward Bayard, Mrs. Stanton's brother-in-law.

Stanton has made an attack on little Delaware. In justice, she should take a state of her size."

TENAFLY, *February 22.*

William F. Channing has made us a short visit, which I have enjoyed very much. We sat in the parlor and talked hour after hour on the dual humanity; of what men and women are to each other and what we can, would, and should give to each other. Susan attacked Mr. Channing the next morning in her blunt way, calling a spade a spade, permitting no mysticism, pinning him down most mercilessly with some plain questions. I went to his relief and silenced Susan's guns. Doctor Channing brought me a little poem on motherhood, which, however, I do not like as it expresses the old idea of maternity being a curse. I have come to the conclusion that the first great work to be accomplished for woman is to revolutionize the dogma that sex is a crime, marriage a defilement and maternity a bane.

TENAFLY, *April 4.*

I have just read aloud to Miss Anthony, Mrs. Crawford's [1] letter on Russian affairs, *à propos* of the assassination of the Czar by the Nihilists, on March 13th. I am sending word to her that we both approve of the broad view she takes of the event. I think there is a general feeling of satisfaction here, as well as in Paris, that Russian despotism has thus received a telling blow. I cannot help expressing the hope that the son too will soon repose in Abraham's bosom.

[1] Emily Crawford, journalist, then Paris correspondent of the New York *Tribune.*

Not all the royal blood of Europe could atone for
what humanity has suffered in one hour in sustaining
these thrones.   The time is close at hand when all
governments must be, as Abraham Lincoln said, "of
the people, by the people, for the people."   "The
holiday of miserable men is sadder than the burial
day of kings."

BOSTON, *May 29.*

I have been having a grand time here, where I
came to attend the annual meeting of the National
Woman Suffrage Association.   The Governor[1] received
us at the State House and he came out squarely for
woman suffrage.   I congratulated him on his neat
little speech and also on his recent translation of
Vergil's *Æneid,* and as is always the case with authors,
he was evidently more pleased with the second than
the first congratulation.   "On my way from New
York to Boston the other day," I said to him, "I
bought and read your volume and never did time
pass more quickly"; which was quite true, for when
I get absorbed in a book I am oblivious to everything
else.   I have also spoken before the Free Religious
Association, following Adler, whom I heard and whom
I enjoyed exceedingly, his views are always so large
and noble.

TENAFLY, *June 1.*

I began to-day the second volume of the *History.*[2]
In reading up on woman's work in the Civil War, I

[1] John Davis Long.

[2] On July 3, 1881, Mrs. Stanton makes this entry in the Diary: "To-day both the *Tribune* and the *Sun* have splendid notices nearly two columns in length of the first volume of our *History.* We could ask for nothing

could but feel how little her labors are appreciated and remembered. Who can state all the ills the women of a nation suffer from wars? They bear the misery and enjoy none of the glory. What rewards have our women of the last war received for all their labor in the Sanitary Commission, in the military hospitals and on the battlefields, alone with death and darkness; for the terrible hours of solitude in their home waiting and watching for those who will never return, and in many cases weighed down in helpless poverty, struggling even for bread? No monuments are erected to their memory, no wreaths of immortelles mark their last resting place.

TENAFLY, *July 2.*

What startling news we have to-day! Our good President shot; perhaps dead by this time. Such tragedies do not speak well for a republic. I am sorry to give despots the satisfaction of thinking "the people" are as restless in liberty as in slavery; for the former will no doubt blame the people for the folly of this crazy loon. This barbarous act teaches at least one lesson, and that is the danger of berating political opponents as some of our papers have been doing. In this case, as I have often said of the outrages on women, I blame the men in high places for the overt acts of the lower masses. If Guiteau had read the *Sun* since the inauguration of James A. Garfield, he could have but felt that he did God's service in shooting the President.

---

better. Both compliment the Introduction, the former giving from it several entire paragraphs." The Introduction was from Mrs. Stanton's pen.

TENAFLY, *August 6.*
To a young man, about to wed, I have just written:

In marrying, there is everything in starting right. Be scrupulously refined and delicate. Always be reverent and worshipful towards your wife. Never ridicule her, nor joke or use badinage with her. Never argue nor dispute with her, for nothing so soon rusts the marriage link as contention. Never join in that common course of sneering and berating "the sex." Weak and frivolous women have been made so by false education, customs and conventionalities. Do not feel that your courtship ends with the wedding breakfast. Do not be self-willed about trifles. Leave your wife free to go ahead and do as she pleases in ten thousand little things. By constantly interfering, saying, Go here, Go there; Say this, Say that; Think thus, Think so—men drill all spontaneity out of women until the mass of them look and act as if they were not certain of anything.

TENAFLY, *October 7.*
To a young wife who expects soon to be a mother, I have written to-day as follows:

You must keep yourself on a high plane, and mould this new life the very best you can. His character and destiny, which you hold in your hands, are infinitely more important than his clothes, which, however, I deem very important too. Ah! it is a sublime mission to be a true mother. Live in the open air as much as possible, in admiration of the glorious scenery about you, and keep yourself in a peaceful frame of mind. Never be laughed out of sleeping. All who live to a good old age have a genius for sleep. Cultivate it. If you don't want that future boy crowing and laughing and pulling your hair at five o'clock in the morning, stay in bed and sleep yourself until a Christian hour. These early risers are always uncomfortable people, keeping everybody on the rack. We who believe in sleep must assert ourselves, and defend our superiority. They always act as if they considered that they hold the vantage ground because they *cannot* sleep, whereas we who can sleep when we choose, under all circumstances, and awake when we *must*, certainly occupy the better position. When I was in Paris, a relative of Thiers told me that the famous statesman often took five short naps during the day; that in a drawing-room he could disappear behind the curtains and sleep for ten minutes and come forth as fresh as a rose. This is very common among great men who use their brains. Let us exalt the goddess of Sleep, and with the immortal Sancho Panza chant the sentiment, Blessed is the *woman* who invented sleep.

TENAFLY, *October 28.*

I am in the toils of another thousand-paged volume— the second of our *History*. My large room with a bay-window is the literary workshop. In the middle is a big library table, and there Susan and I sit *vis-à-vis*, laughing, talking, squabbling, day in and day out, buried in illegible manuscripts, old newspapers and reams of yellow sheets. We have the sun pouring in on us on all sides, and a bright wood fire in the grate, while a beautiful bouquet of nasturtiums of every color stands on the table with a dish of grapes and pears. These last came from Julius. Susan has taken charge of them. She has put them in a dark closet, examines them every day and selects those for our dish which have reached the right stage of ripeness. At noon, we take a walk in the sun, then I have a nap, and we dine at two. My only regret is that we have not more experience in book-making. But this labor will at least produce what the French call a collection of documents *pour servir.*

II.—13

1882

WASHINGTON, *January 22.*

We tried an experiment at our annual three days' Convention by sending to the hearing before the Senate Special Committee on Woman Suffrage the new and young blood of the suffrage host. Miss Anthony had heard in England of the advantage of putting forward the "young and attractive," and she decided to keep out of sight the "same old set." The amusement was great when at the close of the hearing, the Committee expressed a wish to hear the old war horses, and appointed Jan. 21st at ten o'clock for our appearance. When introduced by the Chairman, I said, "When the news of the appointment of this committee[1] was flashed over the wires, you cannot imagine the satisfaction that thrilled the hearts of your countrywomen. After fourteen years of constant petitioning, we are grateful for even this slight recognition. I never before felt such an interest in any congressional committee, and I have no doubt that all who are interested in this reform share in my feelings. Fortunately your names make a couplet in rhyme—

Lapham, Anthony and Blair,
Jackson, George, Ferry and Fair

[1] A resolution was introduced in the Senate December 13, 1881, calling for the appointment of a select committee of seven Senators to whom should be referred all petitions, bills, and resolves for the extension of suffrage to women. It was carried in January, 1882.

—which will enable us to remember them always. This I discovered in writing your names in this volume, which allow me to present to you." Each one of the Committee rose in turn and I presented him with a copy of the first volume of the *History*. George of Mississippi asked why no Southern women appeared to urge their right to vote. I told him to turn the pages of our *History* and there he would find that many from the South, such as the Grimké sisters of the early days, were among our most powerful advocates.

S.S. *Château-Leoville*,

At Sea, *June 6.*

Hattie and I sailed for the south of France May 27. Our stewardess is a beautiful French girl whom I love to look at. She wears a ring. I asked her if she were married, and she replied sadly, looking as lovely and as pensive as a Madonna, "No; I was engaged, but the young man died." I think my friends on land would have laughed heartily if they could have seen me the first night out. The sofa was so narrow that I could not stir. I might as well have been in my coffin. At last, in desperation, I took up my bedding and went into the ladies' salon and lay down there, where I should have done very well had not two cats waltzed round all night. The next day my sofa was widened a foot and the felines shut up, so that my sleeping hours were less burdensome. But we sit up late reading and writing, and so make the nights, the most disagreeable part of a voyage, much shorter. It is a shame to shut the eyes on the ocean, which in its grandeur compensates for all discomforts. The majestic waves, glorious moonlight nights, the sunsets so rich and varied— all these are a continuous pleasure.

TOULOUSE, *June 15.*

This is an old university town and has quite a literary circle. Hattie will study here until October. These queer old places and superstitious people are an endless source of amusement to me. You seem to see decline and death stamped on everything, though I know that the fact is that a rising up from decline and death is now going on under the enlightened influence of a liberal republic.[1] I have been into many of the ancient cathedrals—grand, wonderful, mysterious. But I always leave them with a feeling of indignation because of the generations of human beings who have struggled in poverty to build these altars to the unknown god. In a chapel of one of these churches, before the altar to one of the saints, lies a large open book in which you are invited to write your name, pay a franc and then make a wish, which you are assured will be granted. I put down my name and the coin, and then asked that American

---

[1] An entry a month later reads: "The antiquity of these queer old towns does much to make them appear to be the center of a dead civilization, which, however, is not so dead as it seems, as I have already found out. At first blush you would say that these southern Frenchmen are a hundred years behind us, and perhaps this is so in some things. The collars of the horses, for instance, are enough to make an American groan. Three great prongs half a yard long shoot up from them, and the whole thing is so heavy that it is a load in itself. Again, I saw women to-day working beside men paving the street at half the wages given to these men. I do pity the horses, the donkeys and the women,"

women be enfranchised. Of course this is to come
to pass in the near future, and then the pious Romanists
could say that it was due to the intercession of this
saint. But I would not object to this way of getting
the ballot. In fact, it would be much easier than
the more mundane methods to which we are forced
to have recourse.

TOULOUSE, *June 22.*

I have asked Mrs. Spofford [1] to be the interpreter
of my thanks to the Association for the complimentary
resolutions forwarded to me on May 24th, and which
I have just read with sincere pleasure. The sight
of all those familiar names signed thereto brought
tears to my eyes and almost made me ashamed for
having dropped out even for one year from the ranks
of such a noble band fighting so hard and protracted
a battle. Such words from women like these pay
one richly for years of weary struggle. I tell them I
shall not be idle here.

TOULOUSE, *July 20.*

Quite a number of "lady boarders" are received at
this Convent de la Sagesse—what a happy name!—
in order to help pay the cost of the education of the
children who are taught here. Several large buildings
enclose a spacious garden filled with trees, shrubs,
fruits, and flowers. The large beds of Easter lilies
look just as the sisters do in their white caps and
aprons when they sit round in a circle, some two or
three dozen of them together, at the twilight hour to

---

[1] Jane S. Spofford, treasurer of the Suffrage Association.

perform some homely household task. A few evenings since, while sauntering in the grounds, I stopped and told them what they looked like from my window, which seemed to amuse them immensely. We have large pleasant rooms in the second story of the main building of the convent, with two spacious French windows in each. We could not be more delightfully situated. At eight o'clock every morning a little *bonne* with an immaculately white cap brings me a cup of coffee, a piece of bread and some hot milk—no butter or cream—which I sip and eat sitting up in a small high-curtained French bed. I then read a bit, write a postal or two, bathe, dress, and take a walk in the garden. Returned to my room, I read, write, and at half past eleven our mignon *bonne* again appears and spreads a small round table where is served a soup, some mysterious dish of meat, a vegetable, bread, fruit, and wine. I never know what I am eating, as the little dishes are new to me. I only know that I would give five francs for a good meal of Amelia's cooking. I bemoan the absence of butter, which seems to be an unknown quantity in this part of France, and I long for muffins, and oatmeal, and cream. We eat our strawberries with a fork. There is no powdered sugar—I called it *sucre poudre* the other day, much to the amusement of the *bonne*—though by rubbing two lumps together I get a poor substitute for it. In the afternoon we go on some exploring expedition, visit some savant or remain in the convent to receive some interesting caller. Dinner is at six and consists also of soup—soup is

the dish in France—meat, vegetable, bread—another
staple—fruit, and wine, which I care little for, though
it is very pure in this region, one of the vineyards of
France. If I grow thin on this diet, I shall feel fully
compensated for my many culinary deprivations.
After dinner, we walk in the garden, where the birds
sing and the fountains play, or we sit in our room, I
mending stockings while Hattie reads Emerson aloud.

TOULOUSE, *August 13.*

There is much to enjoy about this convent life—
it is so tranquil. Though there is a school of fifty
children in an adjoining building, and all the servants
are still young, having come up from this school,
everything goes on like clockwork. You never hear
any quarreling or complaining. Everybody seems
happy and contented. Many of the sisters are very
pretty, and some of them have been making considerable effort to convert us. We have had to look
through innumerable books about the church and its
ceremonies and beliefs. As an antidote, Professor
Joly,[1] a delightfully companionable savant, lends us
Voltaire's volumes, of which he has a fine old edition
printed during the author's lifetime. We have now
under way a volume containing this arch-skeptic's
views of the Holy Bible—the verses of the scriptures
being at the head of the page and the philosopher's
notes and comments underneath. They are amusing,
to say the least. The interview between Mother
Eve and the wily old serpent, who is standing upright

---

[1] Nicholas Joly, French zoölogist, professor at the Toulouse University.

and skipping round on the point of his tail, is surpassingly comical.

> He it was, whose guile,
> Stirred up with envy and revenge, deceiv'd
> The mother of mankind.

TOULOUSE, *August 20.*

Professor Joly has written a most glowing review of our *History of Woman Suffrage,* and published it in three numbers of the liberal newspaper of this city. He really shows great enthusiasm for our movement and for me as one of its representatives. When I bade him good-by the other day in the presence of the children, he asked if he might kiss me, which is quite French. Here even men embrace one another, especially in this demonstrative Midi. And so he kissed me! Apropos thereof, I have written to Susan: "Pray do not let this fact reach the ears of Boston, for I suppose even an old man of seventy and a woman of sixty-seven should not look at each other with feelings of regard. Let this indiscretion be known to you alone!" I have to-day finished my letter [1] to the Convention, and have sent off an article [2] to the *North American Review.*

TOULOUSE, *September 25.*

We took a delightful drive this evening round the suburbs of the town and along the banks of the Garonne. I left the young people on the top of a high hill to see

---

[1] See *History of Woman Suffrage,* vol. iii, p. 244.
[2] "The Health of American Women," *North American Review,* December, 1882.

the sunset and returned alone, thinking of the many centuries that had rolled by since these old convents and cathedrals were built. What a wonderful organization the Catholic Church is! In these convents and sisterhoods, it realizes in a measure the principle of co-operation. My dream of the future is co-operation. But is there any other foundation outside of religion on which it can be based? Can a belief grounded on science, common sense, and love of humanity sway the human soul as fears of the torments of hell and promises of the joys of heaven have done?

Toulouse, *October 1.*

I have just given a farewell dinner at the Hôtel Tivollier to some of my pleasant French friends here, the principal guest being Doctor Joly, who at dessert proposed, in French, this toast:

To the worthy, amiable and valiant defender of the rights of women in America. May her example find numberless imitators in France. May French women soon resolutely enter on the liberal and really republican path which their sisters of the new world have opened to them, for upon this the future of our Republic depends. I drink to the health of Mrs. Elizabeth Cady Stanton, to the fruitful union of the two worlds,[1] and to Science and Liberty.

I had been informed in the afternoon that I was to be toasted, and so I prepared a rhymed response, the closing stanza of which ran as follows:

> Now fill to full your flowing glasses,
> Ye old and young, ye lads and lasses,
> And, though we may indulge in folly,
> Let's try to-night to be all Jolly!

---

[1] A reference to Elizabeth Cady Stanton, Jr., the infant daughter of Marguerite Berry and Theodore Stanton.

The dear old professor has a good reading knowledge
of English, but is weak on doggerel, I fear. So I
don't suppose he saw my pun, which, however, is not
very deep. But we all had a good time, however
poor my verses may have been.

BASINGSTOKE, ENGLAND, *October 20.*

While out taking a drive to-day in the neighborhood
of this Hampshire town, I noticed a little wayside inn
called "The Four Alls," a most significant sign, which,
whether painted by a wag or a philosopher, gives the
working classes the key to their hopeless slavery.
In the center of the sign was the word "All." On
one side stood a soldier in military dress, who, pointing
to the word, says, "I fight for." On the other side
was a bishop in his sacred vestments, who, with the
index turned towards the same word, exclaims, "I
pray for." Above, sat the King, who, pointing down,
declares, "I rule for." Underneath, you see a laborer
in ragged garments, hollow-eyed, bent, and bony, and
he says, "I pay for." No comments are necessary.

LONDON, *November 13.*

Hatty's marriage [1] occurred to-day at Portland
Street Chapel, William Henry Channing officiating.
I wanted to have Mr. Conway associated with the
ceremony, but this seemed impossible. When I
approached the latter on the subject, he said:

I hardly know what to reply. Channing has such dread of my
opinions that I fear his dislike extends to myself personally. I

---

[1] To William H. Blatch of Basingstoke, Hampshire, England.

have only the kindest feelings towards Channing, and have just been writing in my book on Emerson how Emerson loved him and thought him the only minister pure enough to christen the Emerson children.

LONDON, *November 20.*

I have been pleasantly occupied the last few days. I spent an agreeable half hour with John Bright in his modest flat overlooking Hyde Park. He spoke with warmth of America, but said he was too old now to accept the pressing invitations to visit us. "The threatened attentions would kill me." The interview was arranged by his niece, Mrs. Thomasson. In her note fixing the hour, she said: "Be very cautious in alluding to the suffrage question. Who knows but that with caution you might assist him to see more clearly in the matter?" But as the topic did not come up naturally, I thought it best not to speak of it, especially as I fear I could do nothing with a man who, after hearing Mill's able presentation of the subject, and after having at first voted with him, finally changed his mind. Late one afternoon, I went to the House of Commons and heard Gladstone, Fawcett, Parnell, and Sir Charles Dilke. They all equaled what I expected, which is not generally the case. Gladstone looks thin and care-worn. It is evident that his responsibilities press heavily upon him. Seeing Bradlaugh seated outside the charmed circle, I sent him my card and he joined me and we had a little chat. I asked him if he expected eventually to get his seat, and he replied promptly and earnestly: "Most assuredly I do; I shall at the opening of the next session make such a row as Parliament has rarely seen." [1]

LONDON, *November 25.*

I have dipped into Darwin's *Descent of Man* and Spencer's *First Principles,* which have cleared up many of my ideas on theology and left me more than ever reconciled to rest with many debatable ideas relegated to the unknown. Bradlaugh and Annie Besant called on me this afternoon, and we had some interesting talk. They seem to complement each other very well. He is rather cold and slow of speech, she more sympathetic and voluble. It is rather a pity they have not been man and wife, as this would probably have been one of those rare instances of a really happy union. And yet perhaps it is better that they have worked together independently.

LONDON, *November 26.*

Spent the afternoon with some Positivists whom I was invited to meet at Mrs. William Hertz's.[2] Though clear on religious questions, I found many of them narrow in their ideas as to the sphere of woman. The difference of sex, which is the very reason why men and women should be associated in every circle of activity, these Positivists make the strongest argument for the separation of the two sexes.

---

[1] Repeatedly refused admission to the House of Commons because he would not take the required oath, he was finally admitted in 1886.

[2] Fanny Hertz and her husband, William D. Hertz, made their London home a social rallying point for intellectuals at this time.

Lunched with Mrs. Lucas and went with her to a great meeting of the Salvation Army in Exeter Hall. In England just now this is quite a remarkable movement, which its leaders propose to carry round the world. The heads of it seem to be a Mr. and Mrs. Booth, who, with their followers, not only hold public meetings, but march through the streets singing and playing on instruments. Women as well as men join in the parade, and perform on tambourines. To-day the exercises consisted of prayers, hymns, and exhortations by Mr. and Mrs. Booth. The immense hall was packed, the audience numbering full four thousand. The hymns were emotional, the large crowd joining in the chorus with great effect. It all reminded me of one of our old-fashioned Methodist revival meetings, especially when the proceedings were enlivened by shouts of "Glory halleluiah!" "Amen! amen!" "Hear the Lord!" I purchased a copy of their organ, *The War Cry*, which is full of the most extravagant sentiments. In spite of the ridicule attached to it, this movement is nevertheless an aspiration. The first thing the converts are urged to do is to give up drink and all their old affiliations. If some other movement could only take them at this point and supplement their emotions with ideas of reason and common sense bearing on the practical duties of every-day life—then much good might result from this initiative step.

LONDON, *December 11.*

For the last three days London has been visited by
one of the blackest and most dense fogs ever known.
It was as dark as night. The gas was lighted in all
the houses and streets, carriage lamps were burning,
and other conveyances had flaming flambeaux. It
was considered dangerous to go out. I was surprised
by the call of a heavily-veiled lady, who, when I
entered the drawing-room, threw off her concealment,
and there stood Victoria Woodhull. She insisted on
my going with her in her carriage to a beautiful home,
where she lives, the legal wife of an Englishman of
wealth and position. She has passed through great
suffering. May the good angels watch and guard her.
I will not condemn.

LONDON, *December 13.*

I met James Russell Lowell and wife and George
W. Smalley and wife. All four, especially the men,
impressed me as snobbish. But I suppose that they
are afraid, particularly the Lowells, that all Americans whom they meet over here are in pursuit of
some favor or service, and so by immense mock dignity and reserve ward off all friendly approaches.
There is no better evidence of true greatness and
nobility than to be kind and gracious when suddenly
raised to positions of honor and power. The marked
courtesy with which John Bright received me was in
strong contrast with that of my own countrymen.
Perhaps, too, they were a little frightened at my
"isms." But as both of these men have gone through
the antislavery struggle, they ought to know that it

is highly probable that when the rhymes of the one and the newspaper letters of the other are quite forgotten, some of the reforms which I have mothered will still be full of life. I could not help recalling the days when the now lofty *Tribune* correspondent was sub-editor of his father-in-law's *Antislavery Standard*, in the shabby office in Beekman Street, and the rather exclusive Minister was teaching Harvard Freshmen.

LONDON, *December 15.*

Spent most of the day in a hansom driving about making calls. In the morning I saw Jeanne Deroine Desroches,[1] whose letter from the Paris prison of St.-Lazare to the Worcester Woman's Rights Convention is in the Massachusetts chapter of the *History of Woman Suffrage.* She is a little, dried-up woman, though her face still beams with intelligence. She is living in great poverty and obscurity at Shepherd's Bush. In the afternoon I called on Ernestine L. Rose, and found her very feeble. I sat with her for an hour talking over the past. She was as bright, witty, and sarcastic as ever. It is sad to be as alone in the world as she is, with not one soul with a drop of her blood in their veins living, not one life-long friend at hand on whom she can call. I urged her to return to America. She said she would like to do so, but feared she had not strength enough for the voyage.

---

[1] One of the enthusiasts and martyrs of the French Revolution of 1848.

LONDON, *December 18.*

Lunched with Mr. and Mrs. Hertz. Later, we attended Mrs. Orr's[1] reception, where I met Browning. He is a fine-looking man of about seventy, with gray hair, mustache, and goatee—little if anything of the conventional poet about him. He was frank, easy and playful, and a good talker. I was a bit embarrassed and surprised when at one of my sallies he gave me a little flick on the shoulder with the big handkerchief he held in his hand and said, "No, no, Mrs. Stanton, you do not mean that." We discussed the merits of Henry James' *Life of Hawthorne*, and on the whole he was complimentary thereto. He then asked me if I had known Hawthorne, and when I replied that I had caught glimpses of him once or twice at Brook Farm, he put many questions to me about Hawthorne's personal appearance. On my side, I was about to ask his opinion of Hawthorne's writings, when he was switched off by our hostess to be introduced, or perhaps re-introduced, to Lowell, who had just come in. As I saw them in rapt conversation, I recalled a fine critical article by Lowell on Browning, which appeared many years ago in the *North American Review*, and which was one of my earliest, if not my earliest, introductions to the genius of Browning.

---

[1] Alexandra Sutherland Orr, author of *Life and Letters of Robert Browning* (1891).

1883

BASINGSTOKE, *January 4.*[1]

With Gambetta's death, Prince Kropotkin's trial
and the manifesto of Prince Napoleon, French affairs
occupy much space in our journals just now. I do
hope there may be enough wisdom in the French
nation to maintain the Republic. Vacillating as the
French people have been in the past, it is no small
achievement to have brought even to a partial success,
midst the plottings of kings and popes, the idea of
self-government. Well, well, we hear of rebellion
and revolution on all sides, and I suppose we shall
have a general unrest among all the nations until the
principle of equality is vindicated everywhere in
government.

LONDON, *February 6.*

Took tea with Lady Harberton[2] yesterday, and
met there Miss Cobbe *and her dog.* Fortunately
they arrived late, for Miss Cobbe, like many a mother
of a spoiled child, let her little pet take the center of
the stage. The dog was put through all his tricks,
and each time his skill was repaid by one of the thin

---

[1] This entry also carries the item, "Mailed my letter to Washington," to
the 15th Annual Convention of the National Woman Suffrage Association.
(*History of Woman Suffrage,* vol. iii, p. 260.)

[2] Viscountess Harberton was also a strong advocate of woman suffrage.
Her "rational dress movement" came to nothing, as Mrs. Stanton feared
would be the case.

slices of bread and butter from the tea table. The delicate viands disappeared like snow before a hot sun. Our hostess, who is a charming woman, is very much interested in dress reform. To-day, she and other ladies spoke at a public meeting in favor of the innovation. They all wore the bifurcated skirt, which was so skillfully arranged that no one would have noticed the fact. I thought of my bloomer days, and I ask myself if this, like that effort to improve our cramping gown, is doomed to failure. I fear so.

LONDON, *February 11.*

I went this Sunday morning to hear the Rev. Stopford Brooke preach. But we reached the hall an hour too early and found the doors closed. Instead of returning home, however, I slipped into a neighboring church, ensconced myself comfortably in a back pew and went to sleep until my escort called me in season to go back to listen to a very good discourse from Mr. Brooke, which I enjoyed all the more after my refreshing nap. After having been the Court Preacher, he seceded from the Church of England three years ago. I had a brief conversation with him after the service. "My reason for the step I took was that I had ceased to believe in miracles. But as the Established Church founds its whole scheme of doctrine on the miracle of the Incarnation, disbelief in that miracle put me outside of the doctrines of the Anglican sect." Judged by to-day's sermon, Mr. Brooke is a sort of philosophical Unitarian, much like our O. B. Frothingham.

LONDON, *March 7.*

I attended to-day Fanny Hertz's reception. On taking leave of her I thanked her for having "contributed so largely to the pleasantness of my English experiences." Thereupon she said: "The thanks are all on my side, for to have made the acquaintance of a woman who represents American womanhood with so much dignity and charm as you do has been a true pleasure to me." I admit this compliment pleased me, especially as it was said with genuine feeling, as I could plainly see.

BASINGSTOKE, *April 30.*

We took a delightful drive this afternoon through Strathfieldsaye, the estate of the Duke of Wellington. This magnificent property was given by the English Government to the hero of Waterloo. Our guests, Mrs. Mellen[1] and her two daughters, were with us. A drive of a few miles further brought us to Eversley, where Canon Kingsley lived and preached for many years, and where his ashes now lie buried. We wandered through the cemetery, among the moss-covered tombstones, visited the church and went into the house where he spent the last years of his life, and which is now empty and desolate. Silence reigns, the family scattered in different quarters of the globe! We returned home laden with flowers, moss, and ivy

---

[1] Mrs. William Proctor Mellen, whose husband was associated with Gen. William J. Palmer in the development of Colorado Springs. Canon Kingsley was a guest of the Mellens at Glen Eyrie, Colorado Springs, when he visited America. His son was tutor to the Mellen children,

from the spot sacred to the memory of this noble, broad-minded preacher.

BRISTOL, *May 21.*

I have been here since the 16th, and am leaving this afternoon for London. I am stopping with sisters-in-law[1] of John Bright. When my husband and I were here in England in 1840, we spent several days with their parents. They have told me just how I looked when a bride, what I wore, and the amusing things I said and did. We were the first Americans they had ever seen; hence made a deep impression on them, which half a century has not effaced. On the evening of the 17th, I spoke before the Liberal Club on the various questions before Parliament, and the next day I gave in a church an address to women alone. Saturday evening, the 19th, Helen Clark, John Bright's daughter, invited a large number of her friends to meet me. The parlor was crowded. I was asked to give them some account of the state of affairs in America and to explain the woman suffrage situation. Thereupon, some clergymen who were present made the mistake of asking me if the Bible was not opposed to woman suffrage, when I seized the fine occasion thus offered to give them "a piece of my mind." I gave quite a Bible exposition and wound up by stating the limits—I noticed that my clerical friends squirmed a bit at this word "limit" —of its authority. Mrs. Clark was considerably

---

[1] Mrs. Tanner and Anna and Mary Priestman, active in the suffrage and other reform movements.

stirred up, fearing that I had shocked the saints and the clergy. The result showed the wisdom of my having spoken out, for the next morning the Primitive Methodist minister, who had been present the night before, called to invite me to occupy that evening his pulpit and repeat exactly what I had said Saturday. I accepted. Accordingly, I went to the modest church. The minister led the services and I preached the sermon, taking as my text, Genesis i, 27 and 28. It was plain that the congregation was pleased, especially the women, who were evidently glad to learn that man and woman were a simultaneous creation, that Eve was not an unfortunate afterthought, and that the curse was not a direct fiat from heaven, but the result of violated law, to be got rid of by observing the rules of life.

LONDON, *May 25.*

Went with Louise Chandler Moulton to dine with a friend, where we met the blind poet, Philip Marston. There was one topic on which we both agreed. Like me, Mr. Marston is an ardent eulogist of Sleep, and has devoted several sonnets thereto. Two or three of these, which he said had not yet appeared in print, he recited to us. One of them, "In Praise of Sleep," especially pleased me. I asked him to dictate for me the final lines, which he did, signing them:

> I am in love alone with tender Sleep—
>   Dew on my sad, unfruitful flower of life
> Of which no man the memory may keep.
>   O most divine forgetfulness of strife,
> My sky is not too dark, my path too steep,
>   While Thou art mine, for Friend, for Love, for Wife!

BASINGSTOKE, *June 1.*

For the last three days I have been working with might and main on a sketch of Susan B. Anthony for Worthington, the Hartford, Connecticut, publisher, for his book, *Our Famous Women.*[1]

LONDON, *June 25.*

Susan[2] and I were invited to speak on the suffrage movement in America at Princess Hall. We had a fine audience. Jacob Bright presided, and made a very good opening speech. Our friends said we spoke well; but we were not at all satisfied with ourselves. Lady Wilde[3] introduced herself to me and congratulated me on my speech. She made a pleasant impression on me. Moncure D. Conway also complimented me, and invited me to fill his pulpit. "You are a born preacher," he said.

BASINGSTOKE, *July 8.*

I have written a letter to Mrs. M'Laren and Mrs. Lucas, which I ask them to read to the Brights and Thomassons, on the wisdom of broadening their platform.[4] I impress on them the fact that to get the suffrage for spinsters is all very well, but their work is also to elevate the position of women at all points, and that in calling attention to every form of injustice and laying bare every inequality, they take

---

[1] Published in 1884. The sketch in the same book of Mrs. Stanton, perhaps the best of its kind, was written by Laura Curtis Bullard.

[2] Miss Anthony had come to Europe in February.

[3] Jane Francisca Elges, Lady Wilde, author, and mother of Oscar Wilde.

[4] Mrs. Jacob Bright did later launch a broader association. Among the young women who were on the executive board of this Equal Franchise Society were Emmeline Pankhurst and Harriot Stanton Blatch.

the shortest way to educate women into rebellion and self-assertion, and men into consideration of women's rights and wrongs. That the married women in this movement in England consent to the assumption that they are, through marriage, practically represented and protected, supported and sheltered from all the adverse winds of life, is the strongest evidence of their own need of emancipation. Any other course is as illusory as was working for the black man's emancipation and enfranchisement at the close of our Civil War.

LONDON, *July 21.*

I retired last night feeling very nervous over my sermon to-day in Mr. Conway's radical South Place Chapel, and this sensation of lack of confidence steadily increased until I reached the platform, when I again felt cool and happy, and never more enjoyed giving a speech than this one. My subject was: "Has the Christian Religion done aught to Elevate Woman?" This idea has long been revolving in my mind. I had to give an answer in the negative, although I know there is much special pleading on the other side. My friends were all pleased with my discourse, and I had many warm compliments. Mrs. Conway said: "I think it the finest thing I ever heard a woman do."

LONDON, *July 22.*

I am staying with Mrs. Conway. Mary Clemmer Ames dined with us this evening along with her new husband.[1] He says that when he escorted his wife

---

[1] Edmund Hudson, American journalist.

to her seat in the ladies' gallery behind the grill in the House of Commons, she wept because of what she felt was an indignity to her sex. That was just like the Mary Clemmer of yore, weeping instead of speaking out her deep feeling over the disgraceful way womanhood is treated at Westminster!

LONDON, *July 23.*

Here is what one leader says on the present state of the woman suffrage cause in England:

> It is not Moses who is wanted—it is Joshua. We are not so "utterly demoralized" as you think. Our trouble is a surface trouble, and if Joshua would wake up and shake up the lazy ones, we should hear no more of it.

But to me the woman suffrage situation in England at present does not appear so rosy. Neither a Moses nor a Joshua would be the man for the hour; it is rather a fighter like David that is needed.

BASINGSTOKE, *September 6.*

We were six ladies at dinner this evening. No men. We had a free and cheery time. Now and then it is a great relief for either sex to have a little occasion to themselves. I have been reading *Leaves of Grass.* Walt Whitman seems to understand everything in nature but woman. In "There is a Woman Waiting for Me," he speaks as if the female must be forced to the creative act, apparently ignorant of the great natural fact that a healthy woman has as much passion as a man, that she needs nothing stronger than the law of attraction to draw her to the male.

BASINGSTOKE, *September 18.*

To-day we gave a party to the wives of the old cottagers to try and interest them in a co-operative laundry Hattie wanted to give them. I talked to them on health, air, diet, and babies. I found, as usual, none of them gave their little ones water. They said they never knew that nurslings needed it. I also spoke to them of over-population. I think I made them clearly understand that so long as they filled their homes with infants their own conditions grew worse and worse with every generation. We offered them a nice supper, Hattie presented her plan, and Alice Blatch[1] played some fine classical music, and then, as the twilight deepened, they returned to their isolated cottage homes. When one reflects on what might be accomplished by co-operation, it is pitiful to observe all our unnecessary miseries arising from competition, in the midst of which the finest and most spiritual natures are totally wrecked. ·

BASINGSTOKE, *October 7.*

Nora was a week old yesterday. As I sit beside Hattie with the baby in my arms, and realize that three generations of us are together, I appreciate more than ever what each generation can do for the next one, by making the most of itself and thus slowly building the Jacob's ladder by which the race shall at last reach the divine heights of perfection.

[1] The sister of Mr. Blatch was a type of the public-spirited English woman, a member of the Basingstoke School Board, and later in London was elected again and again to the Board of Guardians in the largest Metropolitan district. She married George Edwards, the secretary of Scotland Yard.

LONDON, *November 4.*

I am the guest of Henrietta Müller,[1] 58 Cadogan Place, whose house has a charming outlook over the park. We went this evening to hear Helen Taylor. It was an able address in favor of the soil being as free to all as the air. It was a speech full of startling facts, logical and eloquent. She spoke without notes an hour and a quarter. She showed that no other country in the world but England had such vast possessions held by single proprietors; reviewed the history of England from William the Conqueror down, pointing out how, by confiscation and grabbing, the public lands that belonged to the people had been filched from them; and concluded that as by acts of parliament the land had been legislated into the hands of the few, so it might be legislated by acts of parliament into the hands of the many. During the lecture I often thought of the high compliment paid her by her distinguished stepfather[2] in his famous *Autobiography.*

ALDERLEY EDGE,

CHESHIRE, *November 15.*

November 12th was my birthday and my last day at Basingstoke. The next day I started for this spot, where I am the guest of Mr. and Mrs. Jacob Bright. When Hattie and I parted, we stood mute, without a tear, hand in hand, gazing into each other's eyes. My legs trembled so that I could scarcely walk to

---

[1] Was a member of the London School Board, and active in various branches of the English Woman Movement.

[2] John Stuart Mill.

the carriage. The blessed baby was sleeping, one little arm over her head.

ON BOARD THE *Servia,*

AT SEA, *November 22.*

The sail from Liverpool to Queenstown was smooth and pleasant. We tarried there several hours. The harbor is beautiful. Crowds of gulls hovered over us. After taking on the U. S. mails, and many passengers, we sailed out for the broad ocean and then our sorrows began. Some blunder must have been made in the arrangement of the ballast, for the ship rolled beyond all endurance. Most of the passengers were sick. I was not; but as it was impossible to walk on deck, I was compelled to remain seated in the dining saloon. My reading during the voyage has been confined to Howells's works, a complete set of which was given to me by my children just as I left Basingstoke. It seems to me there is a lamentable want of common sense in all his women. They may be true to nature, but as it is nature under false conditions, I should rather have some pen portray the ideal woman, and paint a type worthy of our imitation.

NEW YORK, *November 27.*

The sail up the harbor this morning was most delightful. The sun rose in all its splendor, and the air was cold and bracing. Coming from England with its leaden sky and heavy, damp atmosphere, the change to our clear, bright heavens was striking. I was unspeakably happy to set foot on my native shores once more. Driving up Fifth Avenue I felt quite proud of the beauty of our metropolis.

NEW YORK, *December 3.*

I am glad to see that at the New York State election last month, Attorney-General Russell, who was up for re-election, was defeated. He openly opposed us at the Constitutional Convention in 1867, and last year, when called upon by the Assembly for advice concerning the constitutionality of a proposed bill enfranchising us, he drew up a formal opinion against us. But what particularly pleases me is the fact that his defeat is attributed largely to the way the women worked against him at the polls. It is in fact a repetition of what happened in 1879, when women were potential in the prevention of the re-election of Governor Lucius Robinson, who had vetoed our school suffrage bill. This aggressiveness on the part of New York women will cause the politicians to think twice before they oppose our demands.

1884

JOHNSTOWN,[1] NEW YORK, *March 1*.

How frequently we hear those in all ranks of life deplore rather than rejoice in existence. To me, as far as my own individual happiness is concerned, life has been a boon. I find compensation in what I have been able to do in rousing women to new thought and in securing for them higher privileges. I have finished my appeal to the Committee. "Self-Government the Best Means of Self-Development," is my theme.[2]

NEW YORK, *April 30*.

My speech ready, I came down here on the 28th and spoke last night before the Nineteenth Century Club in the large parlors of its president, Courtlandt Palmer, in Gramercy Park. I had a fine audience, but my opponents came without preparation, and nothing worthy the name of a debate was had. Nobody controverted one of my statements, but each one at random set up his or her own man of straw and then knocked it down.

NEW YORK, *May 1*.

To-day I lunched with the Bigelows. Mr. Bigelow showed me the *Autobiography of Benjamin Franklin* in the original manuscript, yellow with time. It was

---

[1] Mr. and Mrs. Stanton had rented their Tenafly home, and had opened the Cady residence at Johnstown.

[2] See *History of Woman Suffrage*, vol. iv, p. 40.

very interesting to look through the old family letters and read the quaint sayings in Franklin's own hand.

JOHNSTOWN, *May 14.*

This evening I gave in the Presbyterian church my lecture on "Our Boys." The pastor of the congregation introduced me, and I had a fine audience. The young ladies presented me with a beautiful bouquet and complimented me on my speech.

JOHNSTOWN, *May 19.*

Old Oxford has at last opened her doors to women! This is a great event. Would that Harvard, Yale and Princeton would do the same. The journals report every day some advance step in woman's cause. All will come in time. Patience, my soul. We have been busy all the week housecleaning. Would that women had the control of the streets and premises around public buildings; then order and cleanliness might reign. For the past six weeks I have been writing articles in the *Democrat*—the town paper—on the untidiness of our Johnstown streets, urging the passage of a municipal ordinance prohibiting the throwing of papers on the pavements. As a nation we need an immense amount of education on this question. Our public squares and conveyances are a disgrace to the decency of the 19th century.

JOHNSTOWN, *May 27.*

Early in the month Susan B. Anthony arrived with a number of appalling boxes of papers in which we are to be buried for the coming six months preparing the rest of *The History of Woman Suffrage*.[1] At this labor we work all day. In the evening, we take a walk, then chat for a while, look over the daily papers, drink a glass of lemonade or eat an orange, and then we part for the night. Susan retires early, but I spend an hour or two before going to bed reading and thinking about the great world. I go to church every Sunday evening to enjoy the music. There is always something in the deep-toned organ that inspires me with new hope for progress.

JOHNSTOWN, *June 28.*

I have been devoting my energies this week to writing for the *North American Review* an article on divorce[2] in answer to Judge Noah Davis, who proposes an amendment to the national Constitution which would make the laws on divorce homogeneous from Maine to Texas. My reply is that there should be no further legislation on the subject until woman has a word to say in the law-making; that when there are uniform laws from the Atlantic to the Pacific on woman suf-

---

[1] The third volume, not completed until 1886. Similar "appalling boxes" had been attacked in the preparation of volumes I and II. They were appalling in more than size, containing as they did masses of unassorted Congressional and suffrage reports, and wholly unsystematized newspaper clippings. It was like putting a race horse at the plow to put Mrs. Stanton at the work of reading and co-ordinating this material. But she bore her share of that burden, and carried the full weight of the literary work. The manuscripts received from co-workers from the different states are often referred to "as illegible, a sore trial to old eyes." The three volumes, of a thousand pages each, were compiled without the services of a stenographer for a single day.

[2] "The Need of Liberal Divorce Laws," *North American Review,* September, 1884.

frage, then women will be in a position to help adjust the marriage relation.

JOHNSTOWN, *July 13.*

A day or two ago the ratification of the nomination of the Democratic presidential candidate, Grover Cleveland, was celebrated here by a torchlight procession, a band of music, bonfires, and cannon firing. I hope when women take part in these observances, we shall have something more rational.

JOHNSTOWN, *July 16.*

Found time to sit under the trees and read Blaine's letter of acceptance. It is a well-digested, able paper. The Republicans had a ratification last evening. Susan and I perambulated about the streets to hear the music and see the crowd, but mainly for exercise. As we are not electors, we felt that we should keep thus in the background, though of course we know more about the issue than one in a hundred of these blatant males.[1]

---

[1] Mrs. Stanton took a lively interest in this campaign, though no part, as later entries show: "On Oct. 16 Ben Butler spoke in the Court House yard to an immense gathering. He was our guest while in town. I rode with him to the meeting and sat in the carriage while he spoke, where I heard him very well. On the 23d Cassius M. Clay was our guest, and spoke in the rink to a large audience. Henry presided and introduced him. We found him a very gentle personality. Henry made a set speech later in the Court House. He retains much of his old fire and oratorical power. A large number of ladies were present, and many of them felicitated me after the meeting." "The night of November 4th—election day—we were up until one in the morning waiting for a telegram from the *Sun* office giving us election results. It read: 'Pivotal states doubtful. I suppose Cleveland has them. Dana.' All day during the 5th and the 6th we were kept in suspense, the election is so close. A young neighbor actually wept when she heard that Cleveland was chosen. And yet they

JOHNSTOWN, *August 28.*

On the 8th we held a woman's convention in the old Court House, where in the past my father argued more than one case. Several times during the sittings I wondered if his spirit was present. I presided, and Lillie Devereux Blake, Susan, and I did the speaking. Of course such a gathering is but a drop in the great bucket of the United States. But it has always been my rule "to keep the pot aboiling." We formed a Fulton County Association, of which I was made president! The chief matter of discussion was school suffrage. Besides writing on the *History* every day, Miss Anthony and I did missionary work in stirring the women up to vote at the school election, which came off two days ago. We held several preliminary meetings to see how many we could get to vote and if any could be persuaded to stand for trustees. When the day came, the large upper room in the old academy was filled with ladies and gentlemen. The chairman opened the proceedings, welcoming the ladies to their new duties. One of them was appointed teller, and she performed her part creditably. We had one woman candidate and she was elected by seven majority. The announcement called forth loud and hearty cheers with which were mingled a few hisses from the Democrats. Miss Anthony and I enjoyed in silence this little revolution, and thought of what a great step in advance all this meant, happening in

---

say women care nothing for politics! I am not so disconsolate as our young friend, as I can see many advantages in the disintegration of the Republican party. It has been in power too long, and has grown very corrupt. Some far better party may spring from its ashes."

our sleepy old Johnstown, where my father once refused to have me visit him because of my radicalism. Tears came to my eyes as I thought of that dead past and this dawning future. Yesterday I drove out to Gloversville to see what had been accomplished there, and learned that two of the leading ladies of the town had been elected unanimously, the men in both cases behaving like angels, not offering the slightest opposition. We are winning over to our side the American man, who is at bottom peculiarly under the influence of the American woman. But we must elevate our women still higher and make them more worthy of this confidence, for it is this silent sway of the American woman over the American man that is one of the greatest assets in this struggle for our complete emancipation. I have never been a man-hater. In our long and often discouraging combat I have sometimes been blamed by co-workers for my easy-going way with the other sex. But my response to this criticism has always been: *Suaviter in modo, fortiter in re.*

JOHNSTOWN, *October 30.*

In the way of writing, I have been preparing an article for the Boston *Index*, and I have been busy for the past two or three weeks reading Lecky, Maine's *Ancient Law*, and Newman Lord, and preparing an article for the *North American Review.*[1] It is to form part of a Symposium.

---

[1] "Has Christianity Benefited Woman?" *North American Review,* May, 1885. An entry in the same month says: "Dr. Shaw of the Auburn Theological Seminary has been paying his respects to me *à propos* of my recent article. But I have no fault to find with Jesus or his teachings. My

JOHNSTOWN, *December 15.*

I have received from England the text of the suffrage bill. It is absurd. But all legislation is piecemeal. One paragraph says: "Women shall have the same rights as men," and the next practically says they shall not, as marriage is made a disability for women and not for men. We are descendants of animals. Here, in this instance, comes out the little fox. The friends of the bill cunningly say, "We will make single women the entering wedge, who will render the gap by degrees wide enough for all to rush in." When the English women first explained their position to me, their eyes twinkled as if they had a nice little game all concealed from the sight of their legislators. But the debates in Parliament clearly showed that the members took in the situation. To my daughter in England, who is depressed over all this, I am writing as follows: "Nothing runs smoothly. Even Dame Nature has her hurricanes and earthquakes, her fogs and extremes of heat and cold. If your cook is perfection, take courage and enjoy your food. If your baby is well and her nurse reliable, rejoice again. If the friction outside your home is more than you can stand, shut your door and rejoice that you have one to shut. Smile with Emerson, growl with Carlyle, satirize with Thackeray, caricature with Hogarth, but do not waste one effort in trying to

---

complaint is of the co-called Christian *Church*, the *canon law* and the action and *discipline* of all the sects. In my article I do not leave the careful reader in the slightest doubt as to what I mean. The sectarian press and the pulpit dishonestly evade what I do say, and reply to what I do not say."

make people consistent. We are none of us that. We are all built in water-tight compartments."

JOHNSTOWN, *December 30.*

Our old cook has left me to go home to rest for the winter, and the new one makes housekeeping rather onerous. But the necessary exercise is just what I need. Susan was here at the beginning of the month. We passed the time writing resolutions for the Washington, and a letter for the Providence, Conventions. I have written a speech on "The Disabilities and the Limitations of Sex." [1]

---

[1] Delivered at the National Convention held at Washington on January 20, 1885. (See *History of Woman Suffrage,* vol. iv, p. 57.)

1885

RIGGS HOUSE,

WASHINGTON, *January 22.*

Our woman suffrage convention, which went off successfully, closed its three days' session this evening. To my mind, the main feature in the meeting was the attempt to pass the following resolution:

> Whereas the dogmas incorporated in religious creeds derived from Judaism, teaching that woman was an afterthought in creation, her sex a misfortune, marriage a condition of subordination, and maternity a curse, are contrary to the law of God as revealed in nature and the precepts of Christ; therefore, Resolved, That we call upon the Christian ministry, as leaders of thought, to teach and enforce the fundamental idea of creation, that man was made in the image of God, male and female, and given equal dominion over the earth.

I was made chairman of the committee of resolutions, and at first wrote a short one.[1] The committee thought mine rather too pronounced, and favored the wording just given, which places all the blame on Judaism. This form raised a row among some Jews in the convention, and precipitated a discussion on the whole question. Finally the resolution was withdrawn; but it was published in the newspapers, widely discussed, and called out several sermons in different parts of the country.

---

[1] Mrs. Stanton's spirited defense of her resolution may be found, in part, in *History of Woman Suffrage*, vol. iv, p. 60.

WASHINGTON, SUNDAY, *January 25.*

This morning the Rev. Doctor Patton, President of Howard University, preached a sermon on "Woman and Scepticism," in which he took the ground that freedom for women led to incredulity and immorality. Susan and I occupied front seats, and at the close went forward, and shook hands with the preacher, when Susan remarked earnestly: "Doctor, your mother, if you have one, should lay you across her knee and give you a good spanking for that sermon."

NEW YORK, *January 29.*

I had hoped to get ahead of Susan's "spankade," so as to present it to my friends in its best light. But alas! on my way from Washington, I saw every paper I took up announced it under various imposing headlines. Some presented the incident as if Susan had interrupted the services with a loud and vehement harrangue. But the *Graphic* sustains us in an editorial. I have just written to Susan as follows: "The more I think of your Patton volley, the better I like it, for it was the most contemptuous thing that could have been said. It was an attack, a defiance and an argument all in one. Like that shot at Lexington, it ought to go round the world. It is done. Don't regret it. By the way, did you see that the 'funny man' of one of the papers said we were 'a spanking team'? That's not bad."

TROY, *February 10.*

I have been spending ten days here with friends. On the evening of the 5th, I spoke in the Senate Chamber at Albany, before a large audience, in favor of women's rights, and on Sunday, the 8th, I preached in the Unitarian church in this town.

NEW YORK, *February 17.*

On the 11th, I came down here. On the 12th and 13th were meetings at Steinway Hall, I speaking both days. One afternoon recently I went all over the new building of the Union League Club and saw what a nice time men have when released from all the carking cares of wife and children.

DELEVAN HOUSE,

ALBANY, *February 19.*

To-day we had a splendid hearing in the Assembly Chamber before the Committee on Grievances, most of whose members are favorable to our pending suffrage bill. After the general hearing, I talked with the committee alone for an hour.

JOHNSTOWN, *February 20.*

Returned home to-day quite satisfied with myself bodily and mentally, having been on "the go" for over a month.

TENAFLY, *July 15.*

The last three months have been busy ones for me both as regards hands and brain. Moving from Johnstown here and repairing my home, rented during the past three years, occupied April and May. It seems very pleasant, after wandering for so long in the Old World and the New, to be once more in my home, where everything is so lovely and quiet.

TENAFLY, *July 20.*

I have just finished reading George Eliot's biography. If all her headaches, low spirits, etc., etc., were left out, the whole would make one readable volume. We have here the history of the struggles and triumphs of a great soul, faithful, conscientious. What avail the aspersions of bigots and worldlings? Their poisoned arrows cannot touch so high a mark. The list of the books she read is enough to make the head of an ordinary mortal swim. Here we have another noble life to prove the dignity and grandeur of human nature in its best estate.

TENAFLY, *September 30.*

The days pass along pleasantly with driving, reading, writing, and conversation. At the end of July Susan returned, and we went to work with a vim on Volume III of the *History.* When it is completed, I shall feel as happy as when delivered of a male child. Oh, what dreadful manuscripts some women do send us! It is enough to destroy our old eyes. It is astonishing also what dry bones we receive from most of our collaborators. Susan and I take moonlight walks now and then. When weary, we sit on the benches which I have had scattered along the hillside road, and we gaze at the moon, which I enjoy more than walking. We sometimes drive out. We have my very easy phaeton, but we sold dear old Jule[1] some time ago; so they send us up from the livery the most stolid beast in the stable. Susan plies the whip, while I jerk the reins and "get up" continually. Verily we "work our way." If we drop into a conversation and forget the animal for a moment, he soon comes to a dead standstill.

TENAFLY, *October 24.*

Henry drove over to Ridgewood the other evening to fetch me back from the Englands, and we had a lovely return in the twilight. How I do rejoice in the lights and shadows of the sunset hour, the rich autumnal colors, the moon, the eternal stars, and the rustling leaves, the gentle breezes whispering to them as they fall: "Grieve not, for you shall live again in some other form," interpreting in imagination the voices of nature. The whole drive was a pleasant dream to me, and before the end, came the moon and the stars. Nature is full of mysteries.

TENAFLY, *November 15.*

Three days ago my seventieth birthday was celebrated. Elizabeth Boynton Harbert devoted the November number of her monthly, the *New Era*, to me. It was quite a flattering issue. The suffrage associations all over the country held meetings and I was invited to speak on "The Pleasures of Old Age" at the New York City reunion held in the hospitable

---

[1] Named for the Hon. George W. Julian, who introduced the resolution in Congress calling for a XVI Amendment in 1869.

home of Dr. Clemence Lozier. It took me a week to think up all of the pleasures of old age, and Longfellow's *Morituri Salutamus* helped me considerably. Following my essay, were short speeches by old friends, by Jennie June and recent converts to our suffrage ideas. On the morning of the 12th, telegrams, letters, and express packages began to arrive. Every Northern and Western state was represented, the message in some instances being in the form of books, pictures, silverware, bronzes and mosaics. From California came Indian blankets, fruits, and flowers. I received cablegrams from England, France, and Germany. A delightful letter came from Grace Greenwood,[1] who is now in Milan.

TENAFLY, *November 30.*

I have written and thanked Robert Collyer for his neat little letter about me sent to the editor of the *New Era*. I was especially pleased with these words: "I was proud when we were all younger to welcome her to my pulpit"—that is, when he preached in Chicago. I fully appreciated that privilege then, and I re-thank him now for the aid he thus gave the ideas which I advocated and which were not then—

---

[1] She wrote: "I am too late! I have always been too late except in the untoward event of my birth. Then I was at least half a century too early. I cannot, *cannot* believe that you have passed your seventieth birthday! Your dear, beaming face has always seemed to me to shine with the light of the rising, rather than the glow of the setting sun. I do not congratulate you on having seventy years on your brave shoulders, but I do congratulate your friends and country on the fact that you are able to bear them so lightly, that they were as yet no impediment in your noble work. May God bless you and spare and strengthen you for that work many years."

this was in the 'sixties and 'seventies—quite so accept-
able as they are becoming to-day. In the same issue
Mrs. Harbert has another letter which touched me—
that of Frederick Douglass; especially this passage:

Five and forty years ago in Boston, before the snows of time
had fallen upon the locks of either of us, and long before the cause
of woman had taken its high place among the great reforms of
the nineteenth century, Mrs. Elizabeth Cady Stanton, then just
returned from her wedding tour in Europe, did me the honor to
sit by my side and by that logic of which she is master, successfully endeavored to convince me of the wisdom and truth of the
then new gospel of woman's rights.

I have just written Mr. Douglass: "I had quite forgotten that incident. I have, I know, made many
converts to woman suffrage, but I was not aware
that I had been so instrumental in adding a black
diamond to our suffrage diadem!"

December 31.

We have been moving on from day to day much
the same save that we pass, in our *History* work,
from one chapter to another—reading, writing, cor-
recting proof. In fact, we have finally penned the
last page of this work, and thus brought to an end a
labor begun ten years ago. The general interest
which I feel sure the women of the present and the
future will take in reading these records, which would
otherwise have been lost, will richly repay us for our
arduous toil. There has been but little variation in
our days; no time or eyesight to read more than the
imperative documents for this *History*. How often
have I wearied of these endless and oft-repeated dry
facts! I am now actually hungering and thirsting

for some other mental pabulum. Success in our
demands begins to seem so hopeless that at times
courage fails me.   But lifting woman into her proper
place in the scale of being is the mightiest revolution
the world has yet known, and it may be that more
than half a century is needed to accomplish this.
The weather still continues warm and delightful,
and these moonlight nights are bewitching.   It is a
glorious evening as I write.   I have just been promenading on the piazza and looking at the stars.   Orion
lies stretched out like a great lion.

1886

NEW YORK, *January 13.*

To-day I went in to the city to lunch at Laura Curtis Bullard's to meet Madame Durand - Gréville, the French novelist, who has come over to lecture in this country. I was not particularly impressed with her. Her manners are not polished, and she seemed a politic rather than an earnest woman of high principle. I fear also that she is too weak in body to stand the severe strain of a lyceum tour in America.

NEW YORK, *January 20.*

Miss Anthony writes me to invite Mme. Gréville to take part in our next convention. But I answer that I feel sure she would not like to stand on our platform. I have seen much of her since she landed, and I was not long in discovering that she has not the spirit of the reformer.[1] Her wish is to make money by being as popular as she can. In her lecture on Russia, she narrates merely the pleasant things she saw there. She makes no reference to the horrible crimes of that civilization. She is doing what a certain countess advised us to do—cultivate

---

[1] Mrs. Stanton had very definite ideas on the feasibility of reform by indirectness. In the Diary she says of a co-worker: "She impresses me as a person of policy rather than principle, who evidently thinks she can carry the world by claptrap and sweep the people into reforms without their knowing whither they are going. But she is mistaken. I am an old hand at this business, and I know that is not the path which leads to victory."

the artistic and æsthetic. But try and imagine an æsthetic view of injustice. I have written Miss Anthony: "Suppose at our next convention we all dress in æsthetic green, deck our platform with sunflowers and lilies, subdue the gaslight with pink shades, put our speeches in verse and chant them to guitar accompaniment!" How to reform the world æsthetically is the puzzle. Oh, that the good countess had told me how to do it!

TENAFLY, *February 28.*

I see in the Congressional debates that it is proposed to make an appropriation to erect in Washington a monument to General Grant. I am weary seeing our laboring classes so wretchedly housed, fed, and clothed, while thousands of dollars are wasted every year over unsightly statues. If these great men must have outdoor memorials let them be in the form of handsome blocks of buildings for the poor, such as George Peabody built in London, a grander reminder of him among the living than would be the purest Parian shaft rising among the sepulchers of the departed. *Monumentum ære perennius.* The strikes, mobs, and discontent of the people warn us that, though we neglect and forget the interests of the people, we do it at our peril.

TENAFLY, *April 27.*

I am very happy just now in the consciousness of a good thing that has happened through my influence. Mr. Henry Phipps has given $25,000 for the erection of plant houses in the Allegheny Park in Pittsburgh, on *condition* that they shall be kept *open on Sunday.* He states that he decided to attach this condition to his gift after reading my article in the *Forum* on "Our Boys on Sunday." [1] The clergymen and deacons are making a great row over this, and are urging the city to refuse the offer.

TENAFLY, *August 31.*

Frances Lord, of London, reached us on the 4th instant. I laid before her my idea of preparing a "Woman's Bible"; and as she entered into my enthusiasm on the subject, we immediately began the work and invited others to join us.

AT SEA, *October 31.*

As we sailed out of the harbor Tuesday morning, we had a fine view of Bartholdi's Liberty. It seems to me that the very early sun brings it out better than the light later in the day. I never saw it looking so bold and sturdy. The voyage has been delightful, and with whist and letter writing the days have passed pleasantly and quickly.

BASINGSTOKE, ENGLAND, *November 30.*

We have been reading Doctor Holmes' *Elsie Venner,* which is full of admirable philosophy and keen touches of human nature. I was much amused with a quaint description of a young lady's efforts to show off her neck and shoulders to two old gentlemen, and the deliberate survey one of them took, spectacles on nose.

---

[1] April, 1886.

BASINGSTOKE, *December 29.*

Dowden's *Life of Shelley* I find amusing and pathetic. Here we see a refined, sensitive nature, full of noble purposes, thrown out when too young to meet all life's responsibilities, with no wise, loving Mentor at hand to point out youth's blunders and help him to retrieve the consequences. Had Shelley been surrounded with a few true friends of broad ideas whom he could have trusted, who would have admired what was great in him and would have pitied what was weak, his existence would have been entirely different. His father was hard, exacting, unreasonable, and hence had no influence over him. His mother had neither the wisdom to help him nor the courage to stand by him. But, poor woman, herself in thraldom to conventionalities, how could she understand a boy who set at defiance all these conventionalities? It must be said, however, that in spite of all his shortcomings, poor Shelley tried to lead a worthy, noble life; though, while very sympathetic and generous, he did not possess a clear sense of justice.

1887

BASINGSTOKE, *January 12.*

I have been busy getting off my promised letter
to our next National Convention.[1] I am devoting a paragraph to the question of "the ballot and
the bullet." There is more than one way of fighting,
and I am sure that woman's ingenuity will find means
of rendering herself useful in case of a conflict. The
recent evictions of Irish tenants on the immense
estate of Lord Clanricarde, is an illustration in point.
It appears that the women rendered active service
in holding the enemy at bay by pouring scalding hot
lime water on the heads of their assailants. If all
the heroic deeds of women recorded in history and
our daily journals have not yet convinced our opponents that women are possessed of superior fighting
qualities, the sex may feel called upon in the near
future—I see many signs of this even here in slow old
England—to give some further examples of their
prowess. Of one thing men may be assured, and
that is, that the next generation will not argue the
question of woman's rights with the infinite patience
we have displayed during half a century.

BASINGSTOKE, *January 12.*

This morning, while I was taking breakfast in my
room, Hattie entered with a cablegram from New York

---

[1] For excerpt see *History of Woman Suffrage*, vol. iv, p. 113.

announcing the death of her father. Death! We all think we are prepared to hear of the passing away of the aged. But when the news comes, the heart and pulses all seem to stand still. We cannot realize that those we have known in life are suddenly withdrawn, to be seen no more on earth. To be with them during their last sickness, to close their eyes, to look upon their lifeless form for the final days, and to go through the sad pageant that follows, helps one, little by little, to realize the change. But when the boundless ocean rolls between you and the lost one, and the startling news comes upon you without preparation, it is a terrible shock to every nerve and feeling, to body and mind alike. Then well up regrets for every unkind, ungracious word spoken, for every act of coldness and neglect. Ah! if we could only remember in life to be gentle and forbearing with each other, and to strive to serve nobly instead of exacting service, our memories of the past would be more pleasant and profitable. I have lived with my husband forty-six years, and now he leads the way to another sphere. What the next life is, whether this one is all, or we pursue an individual existence in a higher form of development, are the questions not yet answered. My daughter and I have sat together and talked all day long of the mysteries of life and death, speculating on what lies beyond.[1]

---

[1] On this page of the Diary was pasted a part of a newspaper wrapper with canceled stamp dated "New York, 1-6, 1887," addressed to Mrs. Stanton. Underneath is this note: "This is probably the last time Henry wrote my name in sending to me the Sunday *Sun*. The writing looks tremulous."

ELIZABETH CADY STANTON, BAS-RELIEF, BY
PAUL W. BARTLETT, 1887

[See p. 146, vol. I

BRONZE TABLET ON WESLEYAN CHAPEL,
SENECA FALLS, N. Y. DEDICATED, 1908

BASINGSTOKE, *March 6.*

I gave up the day to Tolstoy's *Anna Karenina,* which is said to offer a good picture of Russian life. I do not like it very much, as all the women are disappointed and unhappy; and well they may be, as they are made to look to men, and not to themselves, for their chief joy.

BASINGSTOKE, *March 15.*

Here, just now, the main subjects of debate are the Queen's Jubilee and the Irish Question. All over the country, ladies have formed societies to collect funds to build a monument to Prince Albert for the Queen. As Her Majesty is worth, I am told, some 10,000,000 pounds, one would think she might build this monument herself, if she really wants another. Every little village even is divided into districts, and different ladies go the rounds begging pennies of servants and the laboring classes. One of them came here a few days ago and asked of the maid who opened the door to see the servants. So they assembled, and she then solicited a penny from each one of them. Doing justice to her Irish subjects and giving the half of her worldly possessions to the poor and suffering would be a more fitting way to erect a monument to her dead consort. In this world of plenty, every being has a right to food, clothes, a decent shelter, and at least the rudiments of an education. There is something "rotten in Denmark" when one-tenth of the human family, booted and spurred, rides the masses to destruction. I detest the words royalty and nobility and all the ideas and institutions based on them.

BASINGSTOKE, *April 6.*

These April days have come in bright and beautiful. The crocuses, white, yellow, and purple, have pushed up their heads all over the grounds, looking so gay and giving promise of speedy spring. A kindergarten teacher arrived to-day to take charge of Nora. It is indeed a charming system. What a blessing Fröbel has been to the rising generation. What an improvement on the old system of little children of five sitting on a bench learning from books. I feel so happy that Nora is to have this great advantage. But the plan will have to be carried through surrounded by opposition on all sides, as we are living in a circle of old-fashioned conservatives who would be only too content to run in one groove forever.

BASINGSTOKE, *April 12.*

Yesterday a great meeting was held in Hyde Park to protest against the Irish Coercion Bill. It is encouraging to see that there is a democratic as well as an aristocratic England. The papers this morning give very contradictory accounts of the meeting. The Tories say it was a mob, and inconsequential. But reason teaches that you cannot get up a large and enthusiastic out-of-door gathering unless there is something abroad that touches the heart of the people. Those who declare that Ireland has no grievances are ignorant alike of human nature and the facts of history.

PARIS, *August 25.*

I have seen quite a good deal this summer of Doctor Chapman and his wife, the editors of the *Westminster Review.* Doctor Chapman is an excellent conversationalist and has many good anecdotes to tell of English and American literary celebrities whom he knew when he resided in London. At that time he saw a good deal of George Eliot, and at the side of the chimney-piece in his drawing-room is a small crayon portrait of her which he pronounces a remarkably good likeness. It reminded me very much of portraits I have seen of Mrs. Browning. But when you are with Doctor Chapman he is always apt to get off on the ice bag as a preventive of seasickness—one of his hobbies— and then he becomes, as the French say, *insupportable.* He even wants me to try one the next time I cross the ocean. *I.* But I am never seasick. *He.* But this bag will make you doubly sure. *I.* But according to homeopathy, in which I am a firm believer, this bag ought to give me seasickness. *He.* That might be well, as it might cure you of such quackery as homeopathy.

PARIS, *October 14.*

To one of our receptions Bjornstjerne Bjornson brought with him one of his daughters, who told me afterwards in her girlish northern simplicity: "Papa said to me as we approached your door: 'Look well at this woman, for she is one of the most famous of America.'" This is the kind of compliment that touches the heart and makes amends for so many rebuffs.

LONDON, *November 1.*

On October 29th I reached London from Paris, and have been spending three days with Henrietta Müller. The other evening we saw Mary Anderson in "The Winter's Tale." She was very beautiful and graceful, with the true talent of a great actress. She carried her audience with her and she seemed to be treated with special favor—not a very common thing for an American in London. The average Englishman, especially if a Tory, cannot believe that any good thing can come out of Kentucky. But I believe that Mary Anderson's father was an Englishman, which fact may partly account for the friendliness of her British audiences, though her talents alone would seem to suffice.

BASINGSTOKE, *November 6.*

I have been reading John Paul Richter's *Levana.* The closing chapters in the second volume are on woman. He says many good things, wise and true, about the sex, but quite as many ridiculous things, as is the case with all men writing of woman, on the assumption that the sexes have no feelings, sentiments, or opinions in common. He has no more data to go on than if he were writing of the angels in heaven.

BASINGSTOKE, *November 12.*

This is my birthday—seventy-two years of age. I have been reading Ruskin's *Præterita.* All these great men seem to have had such pitiful childhoods.

Too much restraint and directing make very one-sided fragmentary characters. Had Ruskin mingled more freely with children and gone more into general society, he would have been a happier and more harmonious man. In spite of all these pessimists, I think we have a right to happiness. Suffering may serve a purpose, but I feel that we should get our best development in understanding and obeying the laws of our being. Ruskin was very fond of the society of girls, but never knew how to approach them. He says he was always happy in serving them; that he would gladly make a bridge of himself for them to walk over, a beam on which to fasten a swing for them—anything, in a word, but to have to talk to them. Perhaps it was a case of:

> Awkward, embarrassed, stiff, without the skill
> Of moving gracefully, or standing still;
> One leg, as if suspicious of his brother,
> Desirous seems to run away from t'other.

BASINGSTOKE, *November 23.*

We have all been greatly stirred with the scenes in London on the 13th—"Bloody Sunday," as the *Pall Mall Gazette* calls it. The people had announced a meeting to protest against the bad treatment of William O'Brien, the M.P., in an Irish prison, and the government ordered out the military to prevent it. The papers tell us the crowd numbered 100,000, and the police and soldiers 5,000. Many persons were killed, many injured, and many arrested. From what I learn from private and public sources, the political prisoners in the jails of Ireland are subjected to the most abominable outrages.

BASINGSTOKE, *November 27.*

This is the first time in my life that I have had uninterrupted leisure for reading, free from all care of home, servants, and children. Mill, Richter, and Ruskin have been occupying my attention of late. What an impeachment of English wisdom and honesty the works of the last named!

ROYAL HOTEL,

WINCHESTER, *December 15.*

We are down here to hear John Dillon, the Irish M.P., speak on Home Rule. Speaking in public on a platform is not like speaking in an easy-chair in a drawing-room. If one is an easy-chair speaker, one should not speak except in an easy-chair. What would one think of a woman who is a good home-cook trying to take charge of the kitchen of a big hotel? That post is for a *chef.* Mr. Dillon thoroughly understands Home Rule, and it may be also home-cooking, but he is not a *chef.*

BASINGSTOKE, *December 16.*

To-day I am reading George Eliot's essays. The one on Heine is admirable. She quotes one of his characteristic sayings about women, which, on account of its wit, should not offend us because it comes from a man who always felt that he had been jilted. Let us thank our stars, also, that Heine, as regards the

treatment of our sex, was not another Schopenhauer.
Here is the quotation:

Oh! the women! We must forgive them much, for they love
much and many. Their hate is properly only love turned inside
out. Sometimes they attribute some delinquency to us because
they think they can in this way gratify another man. When they
write, they have always one eye on the paper and the other on a
man. This is true of all authoresses except the Countess Hahn-
Hahn, who has only one eye!

1888

LONDON, *New Year's Day.*

We dined pleasantly this evening at Mrs. Fannie Hertz's, and went later to Newton Hall to hear Mr. Harrison, president of the English Positivist Committee, give his annual résumé of the steps of progress thus far achieved. The English Positivists, I learned at Mrs. Hertz's table, group themselves mainly around Mr. Harrison, Prof. Edward S. Beesly, editor of the *Positivist Review,* and Dr. John Henry Bridges. They form a sort of triumvirate, being united by a close friendship that dates from their college days, and having alike devoted their best energies to the dissemination of Positivist ideas. It appears that there is another smaller group in Chapel Street, of which Richard Congreve is the center. It is distinguished from the Newton Hall group, says Mrs. Hertz, by its tendency to accentuate the development of a cultus and a ritual. Though woman holds a very subordinate place in the calendar of saints according to the Positive philosophers, still it appears to me that Mrs. Hertz is at least the social center of the English movement. Although she supports strongly the theory of the superiority of man, one of the dogmas of the Positivist philosophy, and which they hold is necessary to social order, still I noticed this evening, as I have noticed before, that in argument Mrs. Hertz is quite able to maintain her opinions with the best of the fraternity. When we arrived at Newton Hall, we found the place tastefully decorated with evergreens, the bust of Auguste Comte occupying the central point in front of the dais, while those of other distinguished Positivists filled prominent spaces about the hall. Sitting on a front seat, I soon lost myself studying the features of the great philosopher so loved and honored by his worshipers. The small head and thread-like facial muscles, indicating the sensitive nervous organization which he possessed, fully account for the extremes of happiness and misery he at times experienced. In thought I contrasted the homage now paid him the world over with the bitter antagonism called out when his principles were first enunciated. My reflections and observations put me in a kindly receptive mood, so that I greatly enjoyed Mr. Harrison's interesting lecture. As I was reading recently Harriet Martineau's admirable translation of Comte's great work, I found myself recalling vividly the trials of his youth, the hardships of his early manhood and the disappointments of his later years. But in spite of poverty and an inharmonious wife on the one hand, and with the ridicule and the violent opposition of philosophers, metaphysicians and theologians on the other, Comte made a noble fight, and though often wounded was never vanquished. His deep attachment for Clotilde de Vaux may have called forth mockery from frivolous contemporaries, but posterity will read in it a serious lesson, and will perceive that this modern Beatrice played a considerable part in the evolution of Positive Philosophy.

LONDON, *January 4.*

Since my day with the Positivists on the first of the month, I have again met Professor Beesly and had an interesting conversation with him. It is odd that this man, who, as Professor Harrison says to me with a politeness characteristic of so many Englishmen, "has been a life-long opponent of that mischievous fad of entrusting political power to women," has accepted the offer of Morley to write the biography of Elizabeth in the *Twelve English Statesmen* series. He is full of his subject, and when I twitted him on his rather inconsistent position—"you are even calling the Queen a statesman"—he replied in the words of Tacitus, "*Sine ira et studio, quorum causas procul habeo.*"

LONDON, *January 30.*

We came up to the city a few days ago to attend a peace meeting held in the studio of Felix Moscheles. Though an artist by profession, Mr. Moscheles is a most ardent friend of international arbitration. Theoretically I am in favor of the peace movement, though I am ready to accept war under certain conditions in the present state of society. International arbitration, though not so easy of realization as some idealists imagine, is more practicable. My old friend Alfred Henry Love—how well named!—the war horse of the peace agitation in America, was always so warm a friend of woman, that I have had to be a peace advocate. Not a very sound reason, but exceedingly human! On Sunday we called on Mr. and Mrs.

Jacob Bright. I had a long talk with the former on Home Rule. Among other things, he said: "It must be granted in the end; but when is this end to come? That is the question." Such was his rather dreary conclusion. The gloom was relieved by this story: Mr. Bright had recently visited Eton, and when watching a cricket match asked a boy standing in front of him the name of the boy at the wicket. The reply was, "Oh, that's Cobden." Mr. Bright inquired with interest, "Is he related to *the* Cobden?" In a withering tone came the reply, "He is *the* Cobden." Very human again. Each one looks at life from his own angle.

BASINGSTOKE, *February 8.*

I have written Miss Anthony that now that the temperance women have made a move in the direction of tests, we should devote a session of our next convention to a discussion of the question. An effort should be made to accomplish three things. 1. To keep the Federal Constitution as it is—the rights of man recognized. 2. To keep our public schools free from all sectarian teachings. 3. To keep the seventh day holy for the happiness and improvement of the masses by opening all libraries, picture galleries and places of amusement on that day. These women do not seem to see that all this special legislation about faith, Sabbaths, drinking, etc., etc., is the entering wedge to general governmental interference which would eventually subject us to an espionage that would soon become tyrannical in the extreme.

BASINGSTOKE, *February 19.*

In the early part of the month Mrs. Ashton Dilke spent a day with us. As she is going to America, she wished to talk over the voyage and the International Convention. I am busy writing my speech for that occasion.[1] Mr. Naylan called this evening and gave me a photograph of John Dillon. I am so interested in the success of Home Rule that I have a special fondness for these leaders. Dillon's father was a "rebel" in 1848, the very year that I, in Seneca Falls, urged the rebellion of American women. Though I was not shot or hung, or imprisoned therefor, I have been insulted, mocked, mobbed, and ostracised. So I always have a fellow feeling for all those who are kicking against the pricks. When last in London, one Sunday afternoon, we went to Harrow to see Prince Kropotkin. We found him upstairs in his study, if so simple a room can be so named. The house was the usual two-story cottage built in dreary rows all over England. The room devoted to his work contained nothing but a kitchen table acting as a writing-desk, and two rush-bottom chairs. To accommodate herself and the visitors Madam Kropotkin brought in extra chairs from another room. As we were ushered upstairs we found Kropotkin seated at the table busy with a manuscript, with his slippered feet wrapped in an old shawl under the table. A tiny fire burned in the grate. The minute

---

[1] In an entry on January 15th, Mrs. Stanton said: "Every day I am receiving letters from the faithful imploring me to come home for the Washington Convention. I dread a winter passage, but for blessed Susan's sake I suppose I must go."

I saw him I felt as if I were in contact with a galvanic battery. When we shook hands my hair seemed to rise and stand out just as his does. I noticed how thin and fine his hair is, and yet how bushy. He is short and very slender and as active as quicksilver, all smiles, all charity and hospitality. He told us about his imprisonment in France, and how his wife lived near by and visited him whenever permitted. They seemed greatly attached, and he spoke with a genuine touch of pathos of how he was brought to see her in his prison and placed behind one iron screen and she behind another. They could not touch each other, but they could talk. He described how a beam of light sifted down from a window high above their heads, and how, if he lifted himself up on the grating, the light fell on his face and his wife could see how he looked. He added with a sweet smile, "She asked me to climb up every time." He spoke without a bit of rancor. A beautiful nature shone out. After we had talked a long time and had tea—very good tea, by the way—he turned to Madam Kropotkin and asked her to bring in their baby girl, a splendid specimen, dark and solid like its mother. He said as he looked proudly at the child, "She's our little anarchist. All children are anarchists—perhaps all women too." We had two hours of interesting talk. He told us of his prison experiences in Russia, so painful and unjust. He said that the series of articles in the *Century* by George Kennan was not too highly colored, that the suffering of men and women in Siberia and the Russian prisons cannot be overdrawn. I came back to London with a heavy heart.

On the 24th Mrs. Gustafson gave us a reception, where I met Rider Haggard, whose books, *She*, *Jess*, and *King Solomon's Mines*, I have recently read and do not like. I do not understand his books. So I asked the author to explain to me the first of these novels, which he did to the best of his ability. But he gave me no new idea concerning it. I am still in the dark concerning the "true inwardness" of Rider Haggard's romance. But his method of taking his afternoon tea was clear and decisive. His hostess, knowing his tastes, had supplied an immense cup, the biggest I have ever seen. He stirred the sugar at the bottom of four or five inches of liquid so vigorously that I was reminded, by the results, of a bird taking its bath, and edged my chair a bit further away.

WASHINGTON, *April 4*.

On Sunday, the 26th ult., the International Council of Women opened and continued for a whole week most successfully, the splendid agitation closing with hearings before the committees of both the House and Senate. There can be no question that Susan and I have been well inspired in always advocating the securing of these hearings, which educate the large public throughout the Union and modify the prejudices of the senators and representatives sitting on these committees, and who there make their first acquaintance with "strong-minded women" and do not find them "such a bad lot, after all," as a certain prominent congressman once remarked to me. I am convinced that these hearings are doing much to leaven the whole lump, so that when the suffrage wave begins to roll East, as it will some day, a careful observer will find in them and the progress of suffrage cause and effect. Then those of us who have kept "pegging away" for these many years, in season and out of season, will come into our just reward, though we will probably be under the sod. I do hope the departed can see what is going on on this earth, for I admit that such tardy recognition will give me pleasure even though I be enjoying the bliss of paradise.

CLEVELAND, *August 20.*

I have been spending ten days here with my old friend Louisa Southworth. I have attended several receptions, at one of which I met for the first time Mr. Rockefeller, the oil king, who reminds me in several ways of my friend Russell Sage. Both men are so quiet and retiring, you would not think it possible that they possess such executive and tireless ability. You imagine such men must be always bustling about, continually giving evidence of activity. But John D. Rockefeller and Russell Sage offer a striking proof of what I have often remarked, that it is the quiet who are the strong. While here, I have been writing an appeal bringing forward the right of women to vote for members of a constitutional convention, Ohio intending to revise its constitution this fall. Mrs. Southworth is to have 50,000 copies of this document printed and distributed at the State exhibition now under way at Columbus. Of course I do not imagine that this paper will get women delegates into the convention, but it will set people thinking on the whole question of woman's political disabilities, and when men and women begin to think on any subject, half the victory is won. If I were to draw up a set of rules for the guidance of reformers, such as Franklin and other celebrities tell us they did for their own use, I should put at the head of the list: "Do all you can, *no matter what,* to get people to think on your reform, and then, if the reform is good, it will come about in due season." If ten righteous men could save Sodom, all the brilliant women I have met here should save Ohio from masculine domination.

1889

In the matter of the union of our two national woman suffrage societies now on the carpet, I am urging simplicity in everything. I especially do not like article 12 in the proposed constitution, which makes possible the election of a man to the presidency of the organization. I would never vote for a man to any office in our societies, not, however, because I am "down on" men *per se.* Think of an association of black men officered by slave-holders! Having men pray or preside for us at our meetings has always seemed to me a tacit admission that we haven't the brains to do these things ourselves. Perhaps "always" is a little too strong in my case, for I must admit that at our first convention, that of Seneca Falls, I insisted on James Mott being in the chair. But I have outgrown that feeling, I am happy to say. So I have written Susan suggesting that this article might be dropped out and nothing said on that head, though if ever an angelic man with wings full-fledged should appear at one of our gatherings, we might take him into consideration either for an invocation or for some office. On the whole, I find the suggested constitution very wordy and obscure. It is a very mannish document. It makes my head whirl to read it. One would think it was written to hedge in a pack of foxes. I ask Susan what is the matter with our little old constitution, which we simple-minded women drew up back I do not know when? I tell her that I get more radical as I grow older, while she seems to get more conservative.

OMAHA, *January 14.*

I like the reincarnation idea. That each soul should in turn pass through every form of human existence, and thus learn the temptations and miseries as well as the privileges and joys of all, seems so just and equal that I am quite willing to run the gantlet, so that the Czar of Russia may trudge in chains in Siberia, toil through long years in the mines and taste the bitterness of his dreary prisons; so that every man with a dozen children may return in woman's form and suffer the pangs of maternity an equal number of times. This would indeed be justice for all.

OMAHA, *January 20.*

The Story of an African Farm I read and sent away, and was sorry afterwards that I did so, for I wanted to read portions of it again, when lo! to-day it came bound in a pretty red cover from Julius. I think parts of this book are exquisite. But I do not understand clearly why Lyndall did not marry that mysterious unknown. I feel so proud that the four novels which have commanded the most attention during the past year have all been written by women.

OMAHA, *January 31.*

I have made many pleasant acquaintances here, and among them the Rev. Mr. Durree. My agreeable relations with this ecclesiastic has set me to thinking that, notwithstanding my very pronounced opinions concerning woman and the church, I must after all appear very gentle to these gentlemen of the cloth, since I have always been on friendly terms with so many of them. Away back in the Seneca Falls days, I was in the good graces of the parsons, the Episcopalian, Mr. Guyon, being a favorite of mine. In fact, we all used to go to his church more or less regularly. Of course Beecher, Frothingham, Bellows, Channing, Conway, Cheever, Collyer, Tyng, Parker, May, Hinckley, Furness, and preachers of that ilk, were congenial to me, and I, probably, to them. I suppose that the cause of much of this good relationship was due to the fact that I often spoke in the churches, when I would sow as much good seed as possible, though I was careful never to try and set out full-grown plants, especially if they were of a prickly nature, which was more often than not the species taken from my nursery. My experience has been that clergymen are much more liberal than their people, particularly if they have to do with liberals, even of my advanced school, who am ready to say, "I am most truly a protestant, for I protest indifferently against all systems and all sects."

OMAHA, *February 12.*

Frances Ellen Burr, of Hartford, sends me this new plan of campaign and asks me what I think of it. Here is her radical and excellent proposal:

Have as many women as we can—a hundred if possible, the more the better—go to the State Capitol after the Legislature has been in session a few weeks, meet in some convenient room there, form in line, and, after having pinned on our yellow suffrage badges, proceed to the doors of the House. Once there, we will send in by messenger for a good friend who is a member and ask him to tell the Speaker that a hundred women are at the doors who wish admission and a hearing of ten minutes. If we are refused, I think we will walk in and demand the right to be heard in the name of the Eternal and thirty millions of women. The reasons are imperative why women should no longer sit down and suck their thumbs, but walk straight up and beard the lion in his den. When we reach the august presence of our women-paid, as well as men-paid, legislators, we will present the Speaker with a bill accurately drawn in every detail, asking for all the suffrage that is in the gift of the Legislature. Then several women could speak a few minutes; for if we once gain entrance and a hearing, I think we will not leave in exactly ten minutes! If the Washington Convention could raise an army of two hundred women to besiege the doors of our nation's Capitol and demand their God-given rights, it would be better than hearings before committees in the old way. If a dozen states with their armies of women would all do this on the same day, it would certainly tell. Let us march on their works—on the enemies' works!

The tone of this document shows that our women are growing impatient, and with just reason. Our men should bear in mind that we earlier advocates of women's rights were bred in the pacific school of the old Abolitionists, dominated by the non-resistance ideas of Garrison, and where the presence of so many Quakers spread about an atmosphere of brotherly love. But we are passing away, and the new American woman is coming to the front. *Cave canis!*

OMAHA, *March 10.*

Julius writes me to know whether she or I first wore the Bloomer costume in public. Here is my reply:

You put on the short dress the fall before I did. But what interests me most now in the history of that episode is to try and determine how we could ever have had the courage to make that experiment. Do you recall how horror-stricken our friends were when we came down on them in the metropolis? And viewing the situation from to-day, I can't blame them. Sister Tryphena actually wept. My father said no woman of good sense and delicacy would make such a guy of herself, and he expressed the hope that we would not come to Johnstown. But we did! We honored our whole circle of friends and mortified them at the same time. But then the cause was a good one, for can there be anything worse than our dress of to-day? There was much truth in your father's assertion that woman could never take her right position in the world so long as she is hampered by her petticoats. But what can we do? Nothing, I fear.

OMAHA, *March 19.*

I have a woman's column in the Omaha *Republican.* Have had several articles in the *Bee,* and have sent the first installment of my autobiography[1] to the *Woman's Tribune.* As usual, I have been utilizing the press. Everybody in America reads the newspapers, bad as many of them are, and the editors

---

[1] Published in book form in 1898 under the title *Eighty Years and More.* Mrs. Stanton's method of literary labor was to have on hand one, and often two, big pieces of work to which she gave some time day by day. Underneath every mention of other efforts, the *Autobiography* and *Woman's Bible* were being carried on. The latter was published in two parts—Part I, The Pentateuch, 1895, and Part II, The New Testament, 1898.

have awakened to the importance of their women
readers. Some say the "Woman's Column" will
become the "Woman's Page." The part my sex is
to play in the United States eventually is only just
beginning. I have felt its coming for many years.
Hence the courage to fight on in spite of the blind
ones of both sexes, "which have eyes, and see not,"
to say nothing of those "which have ears, and hear
not."

HEMPSTEAD, LONG ISLAND, *May 19.*

I am here for the summer with my son Gerrit in
this quiet old spot, whither came the other day a
jeremiade from an over-pious friend, troubled by
religious anxieties. I hadn't much patience with her,
so I simply sent her this rhyme written on the back
of a postal card—(but for the life of me I cannot tell
whether these lines are mine or whether I have picked
them up somewhere in the present or the past; however, the origin of this doggerel does not weaken its
philosophy):

> Take example of the roses
>   That live alone on sun and dew.
> They never trouble about Moses,
>   And why in heaven's name should you?

I know. Oh, Hafiz forgive me!

HEMPSTEAD, *May 30.*

I am trying to recall on the piano some of my old
airs. My voice too has suddenly cleared up so that
I can sing again. They say that the nightingale

sings his sweetest songs when about to die; so it may be I am nearing the end. At all events, I intend to revive my music.

HEMPSTEAD, *July 20.*

Always considering it my mission to "stir up," the other day I went with some friends over to Coney Island and spoke before some two hundred women in one of the summer hotels. I said a good many radical things, but being well sugar-coated their deglutition was easy. I was the guest of the Seidl Club, named after the excellent orchestra leader, who is giving concerts this summer at Coney Island. I had been invited to speak after the lunch. But I did not go to the table until the feast ended, as I never like to eat or talk before speaking. Accordingly when the time arrived, the committee came to escort me to the table. As I entered, the whole body of banqueters arose and welcomed me with generous hand-clapping. I stood an hour and seven minutes, and what I said was much to the edification of my audience, as I was assured when I closed. Later we went to the concert hall, Mme. Seidl and I arm and arm leading the club down the main aisle to the reserved seats. And such music! I was in the seventh heaven. During my stay I attended three of Seidl's concerts. Altogether it was a charming trip—a perfect day, cool and bright, ending with a glorious moonlight night. I sat on the piazza until midnight watching the silver light on the moving waters, and listening to that plaintive monotone of the ocean which is so ravishing to the senses.

1890

I am busy preparing speeches, resolutions, etc., for Washington, where, next month, we are to celebrate Susan's seventieth birthday, hold an important convention and address both committees of Congress. As I have decided to revisit England, I am tempted to escape from all this excitement at the capital. But Susan commands me to come, and so I have finally written her: "You will have me under your thumb the first of February."

WASHINGTON, *February 8.*

The hearing before the Senate's Select Committee on Woman Suffrage occurred to-day. I was the only one who spoke, and after my address,[1] a rather lively conversation took place.

SENATOR VANCE, chairman: Would women be willing to go to war if they had the ballot?

I: We would decide first whether there should be war. You may be sure, Senator, that the influence of women will be against armed conflicts. Women will do their share of work in the hospitals as elsewhere, and if they were enfranchised, the only difference would be—and it is an important one, Senator—that they would be paid for their services and pensioned at the close of the war.

SENATOR VANCE: Would not women lose their refining influence and moral qualities if they engaged in men's work?

I: But we must first define what is "men's work." I find men in many avocations—washing, cooking, selling needles and tape over a counter—which might be considered the work of women.

---

[1] Given in part in *History of Woman Suffrage,* vol. iv, p. 158.

The consideration of questions of legislation, finance, free trade, etc., certainly would not degrade woman, nor is her refinement so evanescent a virtue that it could be swept away by some work which she might do with her hands. Queen Victoria looked as dignified and refined in opening Parliament as any lady I have ever seen.

SENATOR ALLEN: Your point is well made, Mrs. Stanton. But then you know I am in favor of woman suffrage.

I: But, Senator Vance, may I ask how Mrs. Vance stands on the question?

SENATOR VANCE, laughing: Well, I suppose I must admit that I have got the worst of this discussion.

WASHINGTON, *February 11.*

To-day I repeated my address, this time before the House Judiciary Committee.[1]

NEW YORK, *February 18.*

I made the opening address[2] at the Washington Convention this morning. It was the first meeting of the united woman suffrage associations, of which I had just been elected president. Ida Husted Harper said it was "one of the best speeches of my life." I opened with the remark: "I consider it a greater honor to go to England as the president of this association than would be the case if I were sent as minister plenipotentiary to any court in Europe." When I arose to say farewell the entire audience began waving handkerchiefs and the men cheering. Needless to say that I was deeply touched by this hearty demonstration.

---

[1] Following this address, and for the first time in the history of the agitation before Congress, a majority House report, favoring an amendment to the Constitution granting woman suffrage, was obtained. (See *History of Woman Suffrage*, vol. iv, p. 163.)

[2] See *History of Woman Suffrage*, vol. iv, p. 165.

On Board the *Aller*,

At Sea, *February 25.*

We have had a comparatively pleasant and smooth voyage so far. I have stayed in the ladies' salon night and day. The air in my stateroom was insufferable at night. When will these ship architects learn to properly ventilate their vessels? The delicious sea air is all about, but they haven't enough science to get it inside the steamers. Here is a chance for some intelligent woman graduate of our scientific schools to show up man's incompetency! A sea voyage is a good time to take hold of these sons of Adam and argue with them all the phases of the Woman Question, for then they will listen to you as at no other time. They have nothing else to do. A little touch of seasickness is also often a great help in the argumentation, as it gives a man a feeling of dependence. When the grand central organ of his being is in rebellion, he is less defiant and in a more receptive state. Throughout the voyage we have kept on the rack a retired captain of the German army, examining with him all the rights of women and children, and on the ninth day, he was quite reconciled to heresies that made every nerve in his body quiver on the first.

Basingstoke, *March 17.*

Of late I have seen much of Mrs. Jacob Bright. She unquestionably stands at the helm of the woman suffrage movement on this side of the ocean. She is doing her uttermost to get a bill through Parliament for the enfranchisement of all women with the same qualifications as for men. Those advocating the bill for widows and spinsters have always declared that when they were safely in the political kingdom, they would then labor to get the married women in. But as these same widows and spinsters have had municipal suffrage for twenty years, and are now asking married women to let them have also parliamentary suffrage first, which may mean another twenty years' wait, married women have come to think that they had better look out for number one. So Mrs. Jacob Bright, who is very clear-sighted and has great force and tact, is determined, if possible, to get concessions for married women from the present Parliament. The Married Woman's Property Bill was carried through chiefly by her efforts, and I shall be surprised if she does not accomplish something this session. Her husband, who is an M.P., and one of the noblest and purest public men in England, has always been a champion of the political rights of women, giving freely of his advice, sympathy, and money to aid the movement, and of course, in this instance, he will warmly second his wife's labors.

BASINGSTOKE, *May 28.*

I have received this note from William T. Stead:

I am delighted to learn from Mrs. Jacob Bright that you are in this country again and that there is a prospect of my seeing you. Mrs. Bright warns me that I will find you somewhat uncompromising. I do not suppose you are more uncompromising than *Truth.* I read your article in last month's magazine,[1] and have

---

[1] On Divorce, in the *Arena*, April, 1890.

referred to it in my new number of the *Review of Reviews*,[2] a copy of which I am sending you.

I want to see Stead again, though I must admit that I am always somewhat prejudiced against him.

LONDON, *June 25.*

I spoke to-night on "Over-Government" before the Personal Rights Association at the Westminster Palace Hotel in Victoria Street. The soul of this society seems to be Emilie Venturi, the biographer of Mazzini, who said to me, very truly: "Surely all women ought to value such an association, for they have few enough admitted rights, though they are God's creatures too, and were not created from man nor for man." Amen!

BASINGSTOKE, *August 30.*

Among our recent visitors have been Priscilla B. M'Laren, her sister-in-law, Mrs. Jacob Bright, Annie Besant, Frank Sanborn and his wife, and Moncure D. Conway and his wife. We of course talked on all manner of topics, radical and otherwise. Mrs. Besant was full, too full, of theosophy, to which she says she became converted last year. I liked her better when she was associated with Bradlaugh in the Free Thought and democratic movements. "The Fabian Society can do more for the amelioration of humanity than the Theosophical Society," I ventured to remark. But I saw this pained her, so I let her go on in her enthusiasm for Mme. Blavatsky, "of whom I am a devoted pupil," she said. Mr. Conway was almost

[2] May, 1890.

as tiresome about Thomas Paine, whose life and works he is now busy over, as was Mrs. Besant with her *Isis Unveiled* and its mystic author. We liked him better when he talked of Emerson and the ante-bellum days.

BASINGSTOKE, *September 4.*

Nora is very amusing. We were speaking to-day of a Miss G. who is studying at Girton, and some one said that as her father would not pay a tutor to coach her, she had "slipped up on her tripos." Whereupon Nora asked, "What part of her is that?" The roars of laughter were intensified when the child looked at us all and added reprovingly, "You should not make fun of the poor girl."

BASINGSTOKE, *September 8.*

When I heard last spring that the bill admitting Wyoming as a state had passed the House, I restrained my feelings, waiting for the measure to pass the Senate and be signed by the President. It seemed too good to be true. But in July the complete success of the measure was accomplished and the new state with suffrage for women as well as men was admitted into the Union on the tenth of that month. I cannot express the joy that this victory has brought to my soul. This triumph is enough for one year. The last number of the *Westminster Review*[1] contains an article by me, my formal rejoicing on the subject. This paper has served me in several ways. First as a tract which has been scattered throughout Dakota;

---

[1] September, 1890, "Wyoming Admitted as a State into the Union."

secondly as a speech at two meetings over here; thirdly for this article.

BASINGSTOKE, *October 1.*

We have all had colds. I have doctored myself homeopathically. I tried in succession Bryonia, Sulphur, Arsenicum, China, Phosphorus, Carbo Vegetabilis, and Spongia, and I am well; but which of the seven remedies did the work, I do not know. But Hattie took nothing and got well too! But these colds, and drawing-room and public meetings, at most of which I spoke, and various society distractions during the past summer have not prevented us from reading many volumes of philosophy, history, and romance. There is nothing like having plenty to do to keep well and happy. This remedy is even better than the homeopathic ones!

LONDON, *October 7.*

At a dinner given in my honor the other night by Mrs. Charles McLaren, I met many interesting people. Mr. Rice of the *North American Review,* with his charming wife, was there. I was much amused by Oscar Wilde simulating great irritation with our host after the departure of the Rices, for not having made it known that the editor of an American periodical was one of the guests, "for there might have been opportunity to dispose of some literary wares." Mr. Wilde invariably added to the conversation a touch of wit or humor. To my reference to Tolstoy having said ninety-nine per cent of men were immoral, he protested with grief in his voice, "Oh, no, no, not ninety-nine, not more than—ninety-eight per cent."

Another guest was Henry Lucy, who has made himself famous as "Toby, M. P.," of *Punch*. He is a very interesting man, having traveled much—on the European Continent, in Canada, going around the world, crossing the United States, and visiting Japan, India, etc. He is full of anecdote. He has been connected with many newspapers and seems to have met all the interesting people, especially those of the Liberal party. After he had given us some good stories, Hattie thought it her turn to contribute to the general entertainment, so related one of my psychic experiences, which appeared to particularly interest Mr. Lucy, who put some questions about the rather hair-raising occurrence.[1]

---

[1] In his diary published in the *Cornhill Magazine*, Sir Henry gives this account of Mrs. Stanton's experience: "Some years ago she was at Washington, at a time when Congress was sitting. On applying for a room at a hotel she had been accustomed to frequent, she was told the house was full. After some hesitation the clerk, observing her distress, undertook, if she would wait half an hour, that a room, not the best in the house, but all that was possible, should be got ready for her. It was a small, plainly furnished room on the sixth story. It had to serve, and she was disposed to make the best of it. She went to bed early and slept soundly till she was awakened by the sensation of a hand touching her face, and a voice cried, with piteous accent, 'Oh, Mother! Mother!' She was profoundly startled, but argued with herself that it was only a dream. She determined to go to sleep again, and succeeded. Again she was awakened with the hand nervously stroking her face and the blood-curdling cry, 'Oh, Mother! Mother!' It was no use trying to sleep. She got up, half dressed, lit a candle, got a book, and sat in the armchair till daybreak, nothing further happening. As soon as she heard the servants moving she rang the bell, and the chambermaid came in with startled look. To her the visitor related her experiences. 'Yes, marm,' said the chambermaid, 'I told them they ought not to have put you in the room. He was only carried out an hour before you came.' 'Who was carried out?' said the lady. 'Why, the young man who has been lying here for a fortnight in delirium tremens and died. He was always stretching out his hands, feeling for something, and crying in heartbreaking voice, 'Oh, Mother! Mother!'" [It was I who related the story, much to my mother's dis-

II.—18

BASINGSTOKE, *October 15.*

To a rather timid young woman, I have just written: "If you want to go to the theater, just ask your brother to take you. Make your brothers useful; don't wait for them to anticipate your wants. Men seldom do that in their own family. It is one of the duties of sisters to makes their brothers attentive. Women have to keep alive the flame of family devotion."

It is a bright beautiful day and we have just returned from a drive through Hackwood Park, where we met Kitty[1] and Agnes[1] driving with their nurses and children—four women and six children, all in one carriage! Bless me, how the children do swarm here. All the baby-carriages are made to carry two!

LONDON, *November 4.*

We have been to see Mary Anderson and were charmed. How graceful she is. How I do enjoy going to the theater. But I am probably in my dotage, for I see few people on the shady side of seventy drinking in these worldly joys at the midnight hour, especially in rainy and foggy London. But after you admit that you know nothing of the next stage of existence, and hence cannot decide what preparations to make for the journey, you gradually settle down to enjoy the passing days as well as you may.

---

comfort. She told me afterwards there were "sufficient isms attached to her name without adding spiritism or the like." Mr. Lucy did not connect the story apparently with her, and erred in substituting Washington for Springfield, Illinois, where the occurrence really transpired.—H. S. B.]

[1] Katherine Blatch Stark and Agnes Blatch Conran, sisters of Mr. Blatch, the son-in-law of Mrs. Stanton.

BASINGSTOKE, *November 28*.

A friend of Parnell dined with us to-night. We had a talk over the social earthquake—the O'Shea divorce suit. All England is up in arms to compel Parnell to retire. But I hope he will stick. Strange that the critics should want to relegate him to private life, where they hold he has been a failure, and exclude him from public life, where no one can deny he has been a great success. Human beings lose their logic in their vindictiveness. Mrs. O'Shea is fifty years old, a determined woman who has paid assiduous attentions to Parnell for years. He is a bachelor of forty. I should think she is old enough to take care of herself. The political cauldron is boiling, and no one can predict what the outcome will be.

BASINGSTOKE, *December 21*.

I had a letter yesterday from John Chapman, editor of the *Westminster Review*, concerning my forthcoming article,[1] "Patriotism and Chastity," in that periodical. He said that he and his wife are much pleased with it. Stead and a set of canting saints

---

[1] Of this article, which appeared January, 1891, the Diary reports: "The little set of Social Purity people who are down on my *Westminster* article do not choose to understand it. I simply state facts when I say that men are not educated to consider chastity an imperative virtue for them, and that they are educated to practice patriotism; hence they may fulfill the duties of the one virtue without fulfilling those of the other. There have been statesmen, soldiers, poets, scientists, philosophers, and even clergymen who were not chaste according to the standard of the nineteenth century. I do not apologize for Parnell. I only show how our civil and canon law, Blackstone and the Bible, educate men. The sole remedy for our present chaos is the mental development and the political emancipation of the great factor in social life, namely, woman. The papers that represent me as an apologist for immorality do so willfully; no such conclusion can be fairly drawn from my words."

are the leading hounds on Parnell's track, trying to drive from public life the ablest leader Ireland has ever had. The British public is like the fabled chimera in its many-headed cants and hypocrisies; it is a whole nation hounding one man. As men have not been educated to chastity, why look for it? We might as well require that women, who have never been trained to patriotism, should be public spirited. Let us condemn the system which makes men and women what they are and not crucify the victims of our false standard of morals. The one lesson these social earthquakes teach is to cultivate in woman more self-respect. Instead of hounding men, emancipate women from all forms of bondage. But so long as women are slaves, men will be knaves.

BASINGSTOKE, *December 27.*

To a correspondent I have just written: "You exclaim, 'Why are we born women?' I am sending you by this same post a paper containing an article of mine in which I show the superiority of woman as a factor in civilization. Our trouble is not our womanhood, but the artificial trammels of custom under false conditions. We are, as a sex, infinitely superior to men, and if we were free and developed, healthy in body and mind, as we should be under natural conditions, our motherhood would be our glory. That function gives women such wisdom and power as no male ever can possess. When women can support themselves, have their entry to all the trades and professions, with a house of their own over their heads and a bank account, they will own their bodies and be dictators in the social realm."

1891

BASINGSTOKE, *January 3.*

I have received a letter of twenty-two pages from Susan, which I have duly considered. As to the presidency[1] of our national organization, I have written in reply that I do not want to serve "to keep out any objectionable person" but I will accept what those on the ground think best. I write them that I would prefer to see Susan made president rather than anybody else, and that if I were present I should give my vote for her. I would also be ready to vote for Lucy Stone.

BASINGSTOKE, *January 31.*

After six months' reading about the matriarchate,[2] I am amazed to find how much more we are indebted to woman than to man for not only the intelligence and the morality of the race, but for many of the greatest steps in material progress. Two things are strikingly evident—that woman has not always been the slave of man, nor has she always been his inferior

---

[1] Mrs. Stanton was re-elected. Her long expressed wish to retire could not be granted until it was quite certain Miss Anthony could be elected as president.

[2] The subject of the address written by Mrs. Stanton and which was read by Miss Anthony at the triennial meeting of the Woman's Council held in Washington in February. "The Degradation of Disfranchisement" was the subject of her address for the convention of the National Woman Suffrage Association. (See *History of Woman Suffrage,* vol. iv, p. 176.)

in physical strength. In early savagery he looked out for himself alone, while she looked out for herself and her children. No historian until within thirty years ever noted how long women reigned supreme, and the great physical development and strength they possessed in freedom. Maternity was the source and center of all the first steps in civilization. Because of the variety of things she was forced to do, woman necessarily cultivated many faculties; hence she was better developed physically than the man by her side; and, forced to provide for others, her moral sentiments were roused long before his were.

BASINGSTOKE, *March 2.*

This is Neal's birthday. Had he lived, he would have been forty-nine, nearly half a century. And yet it seems so short a time since he was a baby—my first one—in my arms. I dreamed of him last night. We seemed to be on the piazza at Tenafly, talking to Bob. I said: "Why, Danny, they told me you were dead." "Ah, no," he said with a sweet voice, "not to you, dear mother." I then said to Bob: "Do you see Neal and hear him talk?" "No, I do not," he replied; "Neal is dead." "Why, no, he is not; he sits right here by me talking." It was but a dream, a pleasant one. Well, if he can come to me in dreams with sweet messages of love, I shall sleep with new pleasure.

LONDON, *March 25.*

Hattie was to have spoken last night before the National Liberal Club, and had her speech all ready when, at the very last moment, she was suddenly taken ill. So I went and filled her place. Jacob Bright presided. Quite a debate followed. When such an evening can occur in the greatest of the Liberal clubs, it shows what progress the suffrage cause is making. However, the proverbial obstinacy of the average Englishman is a big obstacle. Can it be got over? Yes, eventually, of course. But when? Will the English women, who are also obstinate, wait indefinitely? I do not think so.

BASINGSTOKE, *March 26.*

I began yesterday Renan's *Life of Christ* and have found it deeply interesting. I have just finished *The Wages of Sin*, by Lucas Malet. It is one of the most powerful novels I have ever read. Because of the author's masculine *nom de plume*, many have supposed the book was written by a man. But to the initiated, it is plain enough that the story comes from a woman's heart and head.

BASINGSTOKE, *May 21.*

I learned on the 11th of the death of my sister,[1] dear, handsome, noble Tryphena. Though her last testament, beautifully written in her own clear hand and fully illustrating her thoughtfulness and generosity, is perfectly plain to the ordinary mind, yet the lawyers have rendered it as intricate as a Chinese puzzle. I do believe that half a dozen commonplace

---

[1] Tryphena Cady Bayard was a woman of striking executive ability. She was throughout her life an active member of the Brick Presbyterian Church, on the board of trustees of the Wilson Ragged School, and from its founding a trustee of the Woman's Homeopathic School and Hospital.

attorneys could so mystify and misconstrue the Ten Commandments, and so confuse Moses' surroundings on Mount Sinai, that the great law-giver, if he returned to this planet, would doubt his own identity, abjure every one of his deliverances, yea, even commend the very sins he so clearly forbade his people.

BASINGSTOKE, *July 12*.

Hattie and Margurite[1] went up to London a few days ago. The children were delighted to have the two mothers go, knowing that I would let them run wild. "Now," said Lizette,[2] "we will have five days of peace; no lessons, no scales, no scolding." "Yes," said Nora, "Queen Mother always says 'yes' to everything." I have been very busy dressing dolls, working, as Lizette said, "like a nigger." Harriot, Lucy, Beatrice, and Alice are now all arrayed. Last evening we took a drive to the park and all the dolls went. I carried Lucy.

BASINGSTOKE, *July 18*.

Mrs. Jacob Bright, Emmeline Pankhurst, and Herbert Burroughs came down for a day this week. I said to Mr. Burroughs that I regretted so much Mrs. Besant's having joined in hounding Parnell. "Please say to her for me that I have just written of her in a letter which is to be published that I consider her the greatest woman in England." He evidently delivered my message, for to-day I received from her a letter written in London yesterday in which she

---

[1] Mrs. Stanton's French daughter-in-law.
[2] Elizabeth Cady Stanton, Jr.

says: "What I objected to so strongly in Mr. Parnell's conduct was that he kept on friendly terms with a man while living with this man's wife. This appears to me to be a mean and dishonorable action; and I said so. None the less, as I have no right to judge other people, I should have done better to remain silent. After the single expression of my view, I kept silence; but I should have done better not to have spoken at all. So I agree in the justice of your criticism." I consider this a very noble letter, which few people would write. So now more than ever I regard Mrs. Besant as one of the greatest women of England.

CASTLE HOWARD, *July 29.*

Hattie and I have been spending a week with Lord and Lady Carlisle.[1] This castle, constructed on an open square, two stories high, is worth seeing on account of its galleries of pictures and statuary and its splendid library. It was designed by Sir John Vanburgh. The reputation of the architect won by this building was so great that he was employed to design Blenheim House for the Duke of Marlborough. On the Castle Howard estate, just as at Blenheim, Vanburgh gave loose rein to his rather affected taste. The park is dotted with triumphal arches, Grecian temples, mausoleums, useless bridges, and memorial columns. In the picture gallery I noticed two beautiful busts

---

[1] The Earl of Carlisle and his eldest son, Lord Morpeth, were Liberal Unionists at the time of Mrs. Stanton's visit and bitterly opposed to Mr. Gladstone. Lady Carlisle, on the other hand, was a stanch supporter of the latter's Home Rule policy, and a leader of the Women's Liberal Federation.

of the Duchess of Sutherland[1] and Lord Morpeth. Lord and Lady Carlisle with their ten children form a notable family group. Lady Carlisle is a large, strong woman with an intense nature and a loud voice. She dominates the household and manages all the business affairs of the estate. She is nobly trying to do her duty to humanity by sharing the good things of life with the poor. A large number of children from the neighboring cities spend in turn several weeks among her cottagers and enjoy picnics in the groves. It is not unusual for her to entertain at lunch all the participants in a cricket match, and during our visit the whole Unitarian congregation from Leeds has been invited to a picnic in the grounds. A constant succession of guests is coming and going.

CASTLE HOWARD, *July 30.*

I think the introduction of American pie would cause a civil war on this estate. Pastry caused two amazing upheavals to-day. Just as Lady Carlisle was about to take a bite of puff paste at luncheon, her daughter, Lady Mary Murray, rose from her place at the big round table with a deprecating cry and dashed to her mother's elbow, seized her hand, saying, "No, no, you must not eat that, the doctor forbids it!" My sisters accuse me of being ruled by my children. I wish they could have witnessed this scene! The second attack on the deadly effects of pastry occurred at tea time out on a lovely lawn under some noble trees. I was seated next Lord Carlisle

---

[1] Whom Mrs. Stanton described in her Reminiscences in 1840. The Lord Morpeth of that time became the seventh Earl of Carlisle.

in the big circle of guests gathered round the tea
table. We were quietly conversing. Suddenly two
of the sons were in a hot fisticuff in our very midst.
I felt as if I were at a prize fight. My knees trembled.
Lord Carlisle rose, stood paralyzed, white as a sheet.
Lady Carlisle dashed at the combatants, crying,
"Stop, stop, don't you see how pale your father looks?"
She separated the boys, and we got the explanation
that one of the two had started to eat a bit of pastry,
an article forbidden in the dietary for the young bloods
of Howard Castle, who were preparing for a rowing
race, and that his brother, the captain of the crew,
made him bite the dust instead of the titbit.

HOWARD CASTLE, *July 31.*

I am amused at the way in which Professor Murray[1]
at dinner each night is singled out for an intended
reprimand. He wants his glass of wine, but the
Carlisle mansion is a strict, temperance household.
Every night regularly when soup is finished, Lady
Carlisle says to the waitress—(there are no men servants here, our hostess having determined when she
first came to the Castle as mistress to manage the
household with women only)—"Place the decanter
and a glass before Professor Murray." Then follows
a remark or two on total abstinence and the meal
proceeds. Last night when Gladstone was under
discussion, Lord Carlisle said, "Mr. Gladstone always
sees principles involved in anything he wishes to do,"
and began to give an illustration. Lady Carlisle

---

[1] Gilbert Murray, the Greek authority, married the eldest daughter of
the Carlisles.

called, "George, you must not tell that." But he told Hattie and me later in a quiet corner of the drawing-room—and here it is: At the time of the Bulgarian atrocities Lord Carlisle was chairman of the Committee organized to rouse England to the horrors of Turkish rule in the Balkans. Gladstone was present at a committee meeting at which it was decided to arrange quietly and carefully for public meetings to be held all over the country on one and the same night. Unanimity, he agreed, would carry to the nation a sense of spontaneity. The meetings came off, the desired effect was achieved. Lord Carlisle as soon as he read the newspaper accounts the next morning started for Gladstone's house to congratulate him on the success of the plan. He saw Gladstone coming down his doorsteps. As he caught sight of Lord Carlisle, he seemed to rush forward to get in the first word, and said very seriously and earnestly, gazing off into space: "Have you seen about the marvelous, spontaneous outburst against the Bulgarian atrocities? Is it not wonderful? The nation has risen of itself and calls us to action." The G. O. M. is a great old fox.

BASINGSTOKE, *August 5.*

At a recent London reception I met a learned Irish-British surgeon and physician, Doctor Wright,[1] who talks intelligently on other subjects than medicine. We got off on woman's rights, when I found him very much opposed to woman suffrage. Some of his scien-

---

[1] Sir Almroth Edward Wright, author of *The Unexpurgated Case Against Woman Suffrage* (1913), "the future book" referred to in the text.

tific objections were plausible, and unquestionably well presented. Of course I did not try to convert him to my views. A reception is not the place for such work; and then, again, I always feel that when superior minds begin to examine our demands seriously, that is a great step in advance and can in the end bring us only good. So I congratulated Doctor Wright on his benighted treatment of our cause, and closed the conversation on my side with these words: "You should put your ideas in print so that they can be studied, examined, and answered." "Perhaps I may do so," he replied. "And if you do so, perhaps I may answer them," I responded, and we parted good friends.

On Board the *Ems*,

At Sea, *August 30.*

As I am crossing alone, I have had a special stewardess all to myself, a healthy, stout German woman about fifty years of age who has proved to be very kind and reliable. This evening we had a farewell entertainment over which I was invited to preside. I introduced the speakers and performers, and I was called upon for a speech at the close. As it is always a man who acts this part at these shipboard festivities, I made a special effort to do my best that the sex might be considered equal to such occasions. There is always curiosity among men and women—especially the latter—as to how a woman will acquit herself in an unusual position, and this acts on me as an excitant.

ROCHESTER, *October 12.*

I have been here with Susan since September 24th. Susan has given a large reception in my honor, which was attended by several professors of the University. One of the questions discussed with them was the propriety of opening this institution to the girls of Rochester. President David Jayne Hill, whose wife has just given him twins of the opposite sexes, remarked wittily that "if the Creator can risk placing male and female in such close relations, I think they might walk on the same campus and pursue the same curriculum together." The reporters and comic papers got hold of the matter, and the whole question was well aired in the public prints, much to the delight of Susan and me.

1892

WASHINGTON, *January 18.*

With others, I appeared this morning before the House Judiciary Committee and gave my address, "The Solitude of Self,"[1] which I repeated at this evening's sitting of our convention. It was well received on both occasions. Yet when I first read my effort to Susan—in fact, she was the first person I read it to—she did not like it—a striking example of how the executive and business side of her remarkable make-up overtops the literary and more intellectual side. She used often to say: "I can do anything but write." Though this self-depreciation is much exaggerated, it is true that she seems to be afraid of a pen as soon as it is required to do other than simple epistolary work.

WASHINGTON, *January 20.*

This morning, before the Senate Committee on Woman Suffrage, I repeated my "Solitude of Self." So this makes three times that I have given this paper in this city. I am very much complimented on its character, and I am much inclined myself to think it is the best thing I have ever written, at least in

---

[1] By general consent this address was the greatest Mrs. Stanton ever wrote. Dr. Anna Howard Shaw once said: "It is one of the finest pieces of literature in our language. It is an English classic." Given in part in *History of Woman Suffrage*, vol. iv, p. 189. It was printed as a tract twice and widely distributed.

my declining years. Senator Vance, one of the members of the committee who is opposed to our measure, said to me as I was leaving the committee room: "Well, Mrs. Stanton, the speeches of you ladies, taken as a whole, surpass any I have ever heard on a single subject, and their logic, if used in support of any other measure, could not fail to carry it." As I shook hands with him and went out into the marble corridor, I gave him this as a parting shot: "Well, Senator, when you make your unfavorable minority report, for I suppose you are going to be guilty of such a political blunder, I mean to get out a special edition of it with a big N. B. at the end, followed with what you have just said." Senator Vance: "But that will kill the report." I: "Better kill the report than let it kill you." Senator Vance: "You ladies wish at least to be charitable to your enemies."

NEW YORK, *February 25.*

When at the Washington Convention last month I declined to be re-elected President[1] of the Woman Suffrage Association, and resolved that I would speak no more. But I soon found that this latter resolve would be impossible, and I have been wheedled into several engagements. A day or two ago, for instance, I spoke before the Brooklyn Woman Suffrage Club. Perhaps it is only right that we veterans should help our successors to get well under way, for they have a big work before them—much bigger, in fact, than they

---

[1] The office of president in the National Suffrage Association was held by Elizabeth Cady Stanton, 1869–92; by Susan B. Anthony,1892–1900; Carrie Chapman Catt, 1900–04; Anna Howard Shaw, 1904–15; Carrie Chapman Catt, 1915–21.

imagine. We are only the stone that started the ripple, but they are the ripple that is spreading and will eventually cover the whole pond.

NEW YORK, *March 22.*

Yesterday I was the principal guest at Sorosis. Mrs. French Sheldon,[1] the woman who has explored Central Africa, was the other guest of the day. After a half hour of digital embracing, the folding-doors were thrown open into a large square ballroom, and to a very inspiring march we walked in two by two, the President of Sorosis, Mrs. Jenny Lozier, and myself at the head. Three long tables were spread for two hundred guests. Ours was elevated above the rest and was beautifully decked with smilax and flowers. Before the speaking began, we enjoyed a most luxurious lunch. The speeches, recitation, songs and music were all fine. Mrs. Lozier presides and speaks very well. I was proud of my country and our women. Probably in no other land could such a gathering as this have occurred.

NEW YORK, *April 3.*

Mrs. Chenoweth[2] called to-day and gave me her experiences with the State Department some years ago. Here is what she said:

When Hamilton Fish, then Secretary of State, complimented me upon my administration of my husband's affairs between the United States Consulate at Canton, China, and the State Depart-

---

[1] American traveler, lecturer, and author, was made in 1892 Fellow of the Royal Geographical Society of Great Britain.

[2] Caroline van Deusen Chenoweth, professor of English literature at Smith College (1883–4), associate editor of the New York *Medico-Legal Journal*, and author.

ment at Washington, our conversation was, almost verbatim, this: Mr. Fish: "It is seldom that the business of a foreign office is turned over in so perfect a condition. You have done splendidly." The Retiring Vice-Consul Chenoweth: "I managed the Consulate, Mr. Fish, during my husband's illness extending through a period of four or five months, and following his death, and all persons concerned seemed satisfied. It is now necessary for me to support myself and my two little boys. Are you willing to return me to that post? My friends earnestly desire that it be done. Senator Hoar endorses me warmly, and President Grant says that he will approve if your consent can be had." Mr. Fish: "No, I cannot give my consent to this innovation; a woman of your ability will have no difficulty in obtaining a position." The Retired Vice-Consul: "I have collected my salary as Acting Vice-Consul at the rate of $4,000 per annum, for work which I am abundantly able to do. But you think that I should take up some new occupation. Can you suggest one?" He had no timely suggestion to make, and we politely parted. And thus ended my career in the United States consular service.

Here is offered a fine example of the necessity for women to have the ballot. The fact that the only voter in her family, her husband, was dead, and that the acting Vice-Consul did not have a vote herself, rendered Mrs. Chenoweth absolutely uninteresting from the politicians' point of view. But if this efficient consular officer had been a real American citizen, she would have gone to the State Department accompanied by her congressman or senator, probably by both, and the conservative, old-fashioned Hamilton Fish would have treated her in a very different fashion.

NEW YORK, *May 6.*

I have been honored by a luncheon given under the auspices of the New York Woman Suffrage League. The feast and the speaking lasted from noon until six o'clock. Lillie Devereux Blake presided with wit and taste. I spoke on "Fifty Years of Progress," a theme rich in material. There were some two hundred guests, many of them being women known for their ability in different spheres of activity. More than once during the afternoon I thought of the Seneca Falls days. Who would have believed then that in less than half a century, I, at that moment the laughing-stock of the press and public that deigned to notice the convention of 1848, would to-day receive such a tribute in the very metropolis itself? The *Herald*, which was then insulting, leads in a worthy report of the festivities. Courage! What will not be the advance in another fifty years?

PETERBORO, *July 1.*

I am spending the hot weeks in the fine old Smith mansion, so full of tender memories. The walls seem to echo still to the deep rich voice of Cousin Gerrit in prayer, and I am ever thinking of the friends and kindred who gathered here year after year, but who are now all gone. A younger generation fills the vacant places, and "I feel like one who treads alone some banquet-hall deserted." Of this new generation, perhaps young Gerrit Miller[1] is the most interesting. Though still a student at Harvard, he shows remarkable aptitude for natural history, devoting himself especially to birds and mice. While conversing with him the other day, he put his hands into his pockets and brought out a dozen of these little rodents, which he handled most dexterously,

---

[1] Gerrit Smith Miller, Jr., Harvard, '94, zoölogist, curator of mammals in the National Museum, Washington, great-grandson of Gerrit Smith.

expatiating on their beauties with as much interest
as a miser would count his gold coins. It appears
that he sets traps for these mice in swampy places,
as these are their favorite spots for congregating. I
may add in defense of my sex that when this gifted
boy showed us these mice all the ladies present
remained quite calm, though I will confess in the
secrecy of this diary that I breathed more freely when
the animals were all safely back in Garry's pockets.
I am very proud of a Holstein cow on this estate which
gives 48 quarts of milk per day. She is milked four
times during the 24 hours, at 4 in the morning, at 10
A.M., at 4 in the afternoon, and for the last time at
8 in the evening. The Misses Thursby are interesting members of our circle. Emma is the well-
known soprano who has sung in all the chief cities
of Europe and America. Her voice is wonderfully
clear and flexible, and she is very generous in singing
for us on all occasions without prolonged coaxing,
which is not generally the case with women who have
gifts. She has with her quite a remarkable bird
from India, named Mynah, which has much interested us. He is devoted to Wyntje,[1] and when out
of his cage, runs after Miss Thursby up stairs and
down and all round the lawn and garden, never show-

---

[1] Daughter of Dr. Gerrit Smith, the composer and organist. She was
then a small child. "My bird was devoted to her," Miss Thursby writes
to us, "as he was in fact to all little children, for whom he had a perfect
passion. There was always some uncertainty as to the origin of this wonderful bird, but after he died, we found under the flap of the letter which
contained directions for his care, the words 'African Mynah.' The day
he died, he said three times, '*Au revoir*,' and the American papers published
columns about him. Dr. Holbrook Curtis, the distinguished New York
laryngologist, has his larynx, which he exhibits during lectures."

ing a desire to fly away. He speaks five different languages, Japanese and Chinese being two of them, and imitates many instruments. He sings Chinese songs. Miss Thursby has always supposed that the bird comes from India, but when asked, he replies, "Aus Africa." He was once stolen, and after his return was kept indoors, when he would go to the window, flap his wings and say: "Mama, I want to go out." This was the first time he ever spoke English, and then he added: "I'll come back."

PETERBORO, *July 28.*

Susan is still on the war-path. All through this hot weather she has been following the political conventions. I wrote the addresses to all, and she read them and signed them as President of the Woman Suffrage Association. By resigning that office, I had hoped to have done with all "State Papers." But I am at it still.

PETERBORO, *August 1.*

I still believe in Congress compelling every state to establish within its borders a true republican form of government. If Congress can forbid polygamy under the national flag, it can forbid disfranchisement.

PETERBORO, *September 8.*

This afternoon I spoke in a neighbor's drawing-room which was full of ladies. My speech lasted two hours. I was not fatigued, and all seemed pleased with what I said. I had learned that the Methodist church in this village has two men and fifty women communicants, and while the latter support the church with fairs, donation parties, and constant begging, the brace of males do all the managing and expending of the funds which the women gather. So, among other things, I talked to these ladies, most of whom were Methodists, of their duty to assert themselves and demand equality in the church.

DOBBS FERRY, *September 30.*

We have been spending two days with the Villards, who have a beautiful home on the hills, with magnificent views of the Hudson. Mr. and Mrs. Villard are charming hosts. Among the other guests are William Lloyd Garrison[1] and his daughter and the Ingersolls and their daughters. This evening we had a long talk on tariff and free trade—Mr. Villard and Mr. Garrison for the latter, and Mr. Ingersoll for the former. Finally, I summed up and told the free traders that they seemed to me to have the best of the argument. But Mr. Ingersoll said my summing up was partial, and that at heart it was evident that I am a free trader, which is quite true.

NEW YORK, *October 15.*

The Columbus celebration has been a great event this week in New York. The city has been crowded. It is estimated that a million strangers were here the

---

[1] American publicist, son of the distinguished abolitionist. Writing to Mrs. Stanton from Boston on July 26, 1899, Mr. Garrison says: "Your letter of the 21st arrived simultaneously with news of Colonel Ingersoll's death, which brought to mind the last time I saw you when we were at Dobb's Ferry, and you egged me into a discussion with him on the protective tariff. It was a memorable evening and I often recall it."

day of the military parade and the unveiling of the monument, which is quite near us. The procession was from ten in the morning until six in the evening passing a given point. In this pageant were soldiers and civilians, governors, senators, and legislators on horseback or in carriages; but not a single woman to represent one-half of the people of the United States was invited to take part. And yet how much Columbus owed to a woman for success in his great enterprise. I thought, as I saw the thousands of men moving in long procession hour after hour, how for every one of them some woman had gone to the gates of death to give them life and immortality; how it was women who had taught the little feet to march to time and tune; how they fed the young soldier long before he could forage for himself; how in sickness and in health, in triumph and in failure, in defeat and in victory, men have ever found one fast friend in a mother; and yet neither in the government nor in the religion of the nation is woman anywhere honored as an equal.

NEW YORK, *November 1.*

I have been busy the past month reading and writing. Reading: Mrs. French Sheldon's *Travels in Africa.* It was a brave thing for a woman to do to go to the heart of that wild country with one hundred native attendants. Prentice Mulford's White Cross series of essays, which I find thoughtful and suggestive. Bulwer's *Rienzi.* It is the third time I have read this book, and I am more than ever impressed with the beauty of the author's style. *David Greive,*

Mrs. Humphry Ward's last. It is very sad and not one satisfactory woman in it; neither was there in *Robert Elsmere*. Writing: Several letters to conventions and an Appeal to the women of this state to arouse themselves and demand their right to be represented in the coming constitutional convention. Louisa Alcott once told me that it distressed her to see her father in his last years display his waning powers in public. I can still do good work with my pen, and it shall be at the service of our reforms so long as its powers last. But I cannot clamber up and down platforms, mount long staircases into halls and hotels, be squeezed in the crush at receptions, and do all the other things public life involves. That day is passed for me.

NEW YORK, *November 10.*

At the elections the Democrats have carried everything, and the Republicans stand staring into the heavens with amazement. To me the most interesting feature of the result is the large vote secured by the People's Party. It is high time that we had a new party with some fresh issues. The old organizations are equally corrupt. But when will this desideratum be attained?

NEW YORK, *December 25.*

A day or two ago we celebrated for the first time "Foremothers' Day." For a long time men have been commemorating, as each December rolled round, "Forefathers' Day." Mrs. Devereux Blake had the happy idea of suggesting that we do the same thing for the Pilgrim Mothers. So we did it, and did it with success. Two hundred ladies, many of whom were descendants of old and distinguished families, sat down at the tables in a large dining hall, which was handsomely decorated with evergreens. The speeches were good, Mrs. Beecher-Hooker and Anna Shaw being particularly pointed and humorous. Mrs. Blake, who presided, did well. I also spoke.[1] It is remarkable that nearly three centuries should have passed before women ever thought of celebrating their own landing on the Rock. Henceforth Foremothers' Day should be the feature of this eventful December season. I tried to scatter through my address humor as well as wisdom. Of the former quality, I gave this: "From the *Mayflower* we hear much of Elder Brewster and his eloquence in exhortation, but nothing of Mrs. Brewster and her twelve children, shut up in a slow sailing vessel, nursing them, no doubt, through chickenpox, whooping cough, and the measles, for the little ones always choose the most inopportune moments to indulge in these popular infantile diseases. It is safe to assume that while Mother Brewster watched night and day over the young fry, the good Elder sat comfortably on deck during the waking hours, enjoying his pipe, while at night he slept midst pleasant dreams in his berth." This sally at the expense of the ruling elder was warmly applauded.

---

[1] Address given in full in *The Woman's Tribune*, Saturday, December 31, 1892.

1893

NEW YORK, *February 11.*

We had a pleasant entertainment at Mrs. Villard's to-day. The African and Indian students from Hampton Institute were there and sung for us. What cause for reflection! Representatives of these two subordinated races standing side by side to amuse the arrogant dominant race. Well, my conscience was clear, for my very first efforts in reform were for the negro.

NEW YORK, *April 26.*

Among recent callers have been Mme. Isabelle Bogelot, the well-known worker among the fallen women of Paris, who has come over for the World's Fair, and Mr. and Mrs. Fisher Unwin, of London. Mr. Unwin is the active English publisher, while his wife—they are on their wedding tour—is my old friend Jane Cobden, daughter of the great free trader. Both are warm woman suffragists and they have given me the latest news in England on that subject. The reform does not seem to be moving there as it should. Those rather obstinate Englishmen need a good stirring up of some kind. I have always said so, and from what the Unwins report, I am still more convinced of the necessity. But how are they to be stirred and who is to do the stirring? This is the problem. I have been busy for a month writing speeches[1] to be read at several of the Exhibition congresses. I do not intend to be present. It is better for me to stay quietly here with my books, my pen, and my piano. I really do get much pleasure out of my piano, recalling all the tunes I used to know, vocal and instrumental, and even learning new ones. I sometimes find myself actually "practicing"! The naval display a day or two ago with the big warships of all nations anchored in the Hudson was a beautiful sight. The little Columbus caravels anchored near shore were particularly interesting. I drove up and down the Riverside Drive several times in order to see it all.

NEW YORK, *May 10.*

There is a conflict on at Chicago about opening the Fair on Sunday. Well, I find comfort in the fact that I have labored faithfully for two years to get public sentiment right on that question. I have had printed and scattered 10,000 leaflets on the subject, published articles in the daily press, in the magazines and in the reviews[2] and spoken on every possible occasion in and out of season. My main point has been that Sunday is the people's day. With all our

---

[1] She wrote for Miss Anthony to read five addresses. This entry on July 1st is in the Diary: "As I had the sewing fever on, I spent a good part of a week mending my son's stockings! All this proves that if you emancipate us we will not quit the needle! But Susan has come to ask me to write another speech for one of the exhibition congresses. Perhaps she got wind of my sewing!" And on July 11th: "Mrs. Sage came over and spent the day with me in order to talk over the Emma Willard reunion to be held in Chicago. She urges me to attend. I have written a speech for the occasion, which Susan is to read, but I cannot take the journey and endure the heat."

[2] "Sunday at the World's Fair," *North American Review*, February, 1892.

boasted love of liberty and equality France can teach us a lesson in respect for the people. I was in Paris once when the 14th of July fell on Sunday. The city was beautifully illuminated to celebrate the downfall of the Bastile, and magnificent fireworks were set off in all the most conspicuous places. In order to get as near as possible and avoid the crowd, we took a carriage and drove about. But all the desirable points were enclosed for the pedestrians with ropes and chains through which horses and carriages were not allowed to pass. How different from the merciless manner in which the crowds are treated by English officials. On gala days in London, I have seen old men, women, and children pushed into the gutters by the batons of the police to make way for the royalty and nobility in carriages.

New York, May 18.

I am much worked up over the infamous Geary bill against the admission of the Chinese into the United States. How my blood boils over these persecutions of the Africans, the Jews, the Indians, and the Chinese. I suppose the Japanese will come next. I wonder if these fanatical Christians think that Christ died for these peoples, or confined his self-sacrifice to Saxons, French, Germans, Italians, etc.?

Glen Cove, July 23.

We were sitting on the piazza the other evening drinking lemonade and beer, when a carriage drove up and in came Charles A. Dana and family. They live about two miles from here on an island near the shore. We returned the call and later dined there. Dana is now seventy-four, but seems hale and hearty, and he is as good a conversationalist as ever. I never see the Dana of to-day that I do not recall him of the Brook Farm community. I lived near Boston then and used to go out to West Roxbury. Speaking of those old times with our host the other evening, this dialogue occurred: I: If I am not mistaken, the last time we dined together was at Brook Farm, in 1843, just fifty years ago! Dana: Yes; but did we really dine *together* on that occasion? Didn't I dine after you? I: Yes, that may be, for I remember that you waited on the table that evening. Dana: I passed around the beans. Beans were our most successful vegetable, and it was my duty to serve them. I remember this perfectly well.

LAWRENCE, *August 10.*

Theodore and I have been spending a few days with Mr. and Mrs. Russell Sage. During a drive with Mrs. Sage this morning we spoke about Cornell matters. I urged Mrs. Sage to see that if her husband did anything for Ithaca that it be the strengthening of the girls' side of the University.[1]

---

[1] This was the first step towards interesting the Russell Sages in Cornell, and the effort eventuated nearly twenty years later in the gift to the university of the fine women's dormitory, Risley Hall. An entry in the Diary, February 9, 1895, reads: "Mrs. Russell Sage called this afternoon. She tells me that President Schurman is trying to get her husband to endow a civil engineering chair at Cornell. I told her, as he stands with us, he should help the girls and not the boys. The latter are always well provided for. She said she would convey my message to him, and that she quite agreed with my view."

GLEN COVE, *August 18*.

Frances MacDaniel, sister of Mrs. Dana, spent the day with me. I am engaged in writing a paper for the religious congress at the Exhibition. I read her some of my notes for this paper. She liked this:

The usual masculine grace has long been a thorn in my flesh. It is enough to make all the feminine angels weep to see a bumptious man, with a good appetite, spread his hands out over a nicely roasted turkey which his little wife has basted and turned for two hours in a hot oven, and thank the Lord as if the whole meal had come down like manna from heaven, whereas one little pair of hands had, like magic, produced the whole menu. When I am called upon for a grace, here is what I say: "Heavenly Father and Mother, make us thankful for all the blessings of this life, and make us ever mindful of the patient hands that oft in weariness spread our tables and prepare our daily food. For Humanity's sake, Amen."

GLEN COVE, *September 13*.

Last week Dudley Miller[1] spent a day with me. We drove over to the Danas. Before going, he saw some rhymes which I had written last March for the birthday of Katy Blake,[2] a very sweet girl, who had called and given me some flowers. Unbeknown to me, Dudley read them to Dana, who told him they were worthy a corner in the *Sun*, asked for them, and sure enough out they came the other day in cold type with my name in full attached to them! Of course it was my mothering this doggerel that caused it to find favor with this fun-loving journalist. One has simply to read the lines to see this. Here they are:

---

[1] Grandson of Gerrit Smith.
[2] Katherine D. Blake, daughter of Lillie Devereux Blake, later principal of a girls' public school in New York.

Some wise men hold that Katy did
Evolute from the first man's rib;
Others tell us Katy didn't,
That, in fact, she was never in 't.

But if we judge from Katy's grace,
The sweetness of her youthful face,
And from her many virtues blended,
It's clear from angels she's descended.

NEW YORK, *September 27.*

Anna Hierta-Retzius,[1] with her husband, Professor Retzius from Sweden, where they hold a very distinguished position in the fields of science and reform, called on me this afternoon. They have been traveling extensively in this country, studying the Indians and visiting the Exhibition. They are both charming and well-informed liberals. When the full emancipation of the noble Swedish women comes—and from what the Retziuses tell me it is coming in the near future—the victory will be largely due to the cultivated and enthusiastic woman who so interested me to-day. I do not know when a European woman has so won my affection; at least not since I bade good-by to the Bright group and to Baroness Gripenberg, of Helsingfors.

---

[1] Mrs. Stanton had received this letter from Mme. Hierta-Retzius: "In coming to America from Sweden, it has been one of my greatest wishes to meet you, dear Madam, whose name is sacred to all workers for women's rights in the whole world. I have been in correspondence with your son, Mr. Theodore Stanton, and am an old friend of Miss Fredericka Bremer and Jenny Lind, and of the dear Baroness Gripenberg. Having founded the first society for women's rights in Scandinavia, I am an old worker for woman and therefore a very old admirer of you, Madam."

NEW YORK, *October 6.*

Caroline M. Severance called to-day. She is now living in California and says the woman suffrage cause is making slow but sure progress there. "I'm going in for the hundred," she said, smiling, "so as to vote before I die." [1]

NEW YORK, *October 16.*

Mrs. Russell Sage and Annie Nathan Meyer lunched with us. We had some very lively conversation on Cornell and coeducation, on Barnard College and segregation, and on the comparative merits of these two systems for girls. Mrs. Meyer was the soul of the effort which resulted in the foundation of Barnard College, and speaks with much authority on all matters pertaining to the education of women. I stood up stoutly for coeducation, as the best peculiarity of our American system of popular instruction, and closed my defense with these words: "All the friends of a better humanity should strive never to let us depart from this method; yea, even more, they should spread it wider and plant it deeper in our popular life." School suffrage, full woman suffrage, and all the other questions pertaining to the rights of women were taken up. As Mrs. Sage has just been converted to woman suffrage—perhaps I may claim the credit for this—she was much interested in the conversation, and took a fair part therein, though, "as a newcomer," she said modestly, "perhaps I had better listen." She tells me that she is drawing

---

[1] This she accomplished when woman suffrage was established in California in 1911.

Mr. Sage in the right direction and is building successfully on the foundation which I have laid for her there. He is preparing, at my suggestion, for *Demarest's Monthly*, his views on woman suffrage. They will be favorable. Men and women of the conservative stamp of the Sages can aid us greatly at this stage of our movement, even if they do not open their purses quite as widely as some of the hasty ones would like. Though of course money makes reforms go round, as well as the proverbial mare, still a good reform will win in the end without cash.

NEW YORK, *October 18.*

Have finished *The Heavenly Twins*. It is a wonderful book in many respects, and well illustrates the danger of the empty, vapid lives so many women in easy circumstances are doomed to lead. When our demands invade the field of the popular romance, they have got a hold on public attention that cannot be shaken off. Sarah Grand must be a New Woman. Anyway, her book is full of them.

NEW YORK, *November 12.*

My birthday. I am seventy-eight. Susan dined with us. She has been here for the past week to get me to write a plan of work for the New York campaign, and to get ready for the constitutional convention to be held in this state next May. We also prepared some resolutions for the Brooklyn convention. This plan of work and the resolutions will be printed as leaflets and other names signed to them,

II.—20

so that it will not be known that they are my composition. I have been doing this sort of thing for half a century. My old friend Moses Coit Tyler says I am the Samuel Adams[1] of our movement. As he is an authority on the subject and the period, I cannot question what he says! A half dozen articles—one of them for the *North American Review*—have been written by me during this month. I keep in good physical condition because I act rationally. Every pleasant day I take a drive in the park, and indulge in short naps thrown in between my reading and writing. I mingle good novels with other reading. The half dozen letters—there are sometimes more—which I write daily are disposed of at intervals during the day. A half hour before retiring for the night, I play a few games of backgammon, which requires no mental strain.

NEW YORK, *November 21.*

I have just had a long call from Mary Foster Fordham,[2] of England, daughter of Walter Foster, M.P.

---

[1] "It was not Samuel Adams that Samuel Adams cared to put and to keep before the public—it was the ideas of Samuel Adams. Accordingly, of all American writers for the newspapers between the years 1754 and 1776, he was perhaps the most vigilant, the most industrious, the most effective, and also the least identified. Ever ready to efface himself in what he did, he realized that the innumerable productions of his pen would make their way to a far wider range of readers, and would be all the more influential, if they seemed to be the work, not of one writer, but of many. Therefore, he almost never published anything under his own name, but under a multitude of titular disguises which no man has yet been able to number."—Moses Coit Tyler, *The Literary History of the American Revolution*, II, 8–9.

[2] Mrs. Fordham, referring to the visit, writes: "I well remember the meeting, which occurred on my honeymoon, and the strong and charming personality of Elizabeth Cady Stanton has ever remained fresh in my memory."

She is full of enthusiasm about the suffrage. She was delighted at the news from Colorado, where woman suffrage has just been carried by six thousand majority. "What a pity we cannot Colorado our English men," she exclaimed. Now we have full suffrage in two states. My soul rejoices. But how slowly the world moves.

NEW YORK, *December 22.*

This afternoon we had our annual Pilgrim Mothers' Dinner. Lillie Devereux Blake presided and opened the speechmaking with an excellent toast to "Our Forgotten Foremothers." I came next with "Christmas, 1620–1893, Contrasted." My account of Christmas on the *Mayflower* was mainly a fancy sketch mixed with historical facts. But everybody accepted it as genuine history. A young lady came up to me at the close of the dinner and asked me where she could see "the posthumous family papers" of the Brewsters. And I told her I feared only in the arches of my brain.

NEW YORK, *December 23.*

I spoke to-day before an audience made up wholly of women members of Doctor Adler's congregation. At the close they asked many questions, some of them quite amusing, and several of them old objections to woman suffrage which we answered forty years ago. One of the questions was this: "Has woman the physical strength to exercise the elective franchise?" My answer seemed to please, especially the matrons: "If we can carry babies weighing thirty pounds from day to day, I think we can drop a little piece of paper into a ballot-box." I never forget that we are sowing winter wheat, which the coming spring will see sprout and which other hands than ours will reap and enjoy. "There shall be an handful of corn in the earth upon the top of the mountains; the fruit thereof shall shake like Lebanon."

1894

LOCHLAND,

GENEVA, NEW YORK, *April 12*.

I have been here at Julius' delightful home for the past two weeks. I wrote a speech for Nannie[1] to deliver at the county convention at Canandaigua. It was her first appearance on the woman suffrage platform, and I am told she did well. Her theme was taxation, and I made the argument as strong as I knew how. Susan has been spending two days with us, and I gave the final touches to the woman's rights article for the encyclopedia.[2]

NEW YORK, *May 3*.

The more social side of the suffrage campaign is at Sherry's, where we had a crowded meeting to-day. Several clergymen, as well as myself, spoke. I lunched a day or two ago at Charles A. Dana's, where suffrage was the table talk. I dined later with Mrs. Sanders, wife of the well-known Methodist preacher. Suffrage was the chief topic discussed. I have met Dr. Mary

---

[1] Anne Fitzhugh Miller, daughter of Elizabeth Smith Miller. The 1894 Suffrage Campaign was in flood. Early in March an entry in the Diary says: "I have been busy writing articles and speeches for the Washington and New York conventions. In May the Constitutional Convention begins its sittings at Albany, and we hope to get the word "male" out of Art. 2, Sec. 1 of the New York State Constitution. Our women are busy all over the state circulating petitions and suffrage literature and holding meetings far and near."

[2] "Women's Rights," signed by Mrs. Stanton and Miss Anthony, in *Johnson's Universal Cyclopedia* (New York, 1895).

Putnam Jacobi several times of late. She is one of
the leaders in this new agitation. In the midst of
it all I was invited the other afternoon to speak at
the Misses Ely's girls' school on Riverside Drive.
This is a good sign, as the children of many fashionable people attend this institution. I was diplomatic
in what I said, but managed to run into my remarks
a lot of heresies. The girls kept their big young eyes
on me all the time, and I could perceive that their
brains were working behind their white unwrinkled
foreheads. Would that I could talk thus to all the
girls of the land. We reach the women too late with
the new gospel, and then it requires great labor to
plant the seed. I seem to thrive on all this excitement—this going and coming, this speaking and
feasting. How it does rejoice my heart to witness
this stirring up.

NEW YORK, *May 8.*

Hattie arrived from England the middle of last
month. She came to spend three weeks with *me*,
but as the metropolis is at white heat on the suffrage
question, she was immediately pressed into the service
and has been speaking every day, so we have scarcely
seen each other. She took time to go up to Vassar
and take her second degree. Last night she spoke
at the great suffrage mass meeting held in Cooper
Institute Hall, where were congregated some two thousand people. There is no end to the parlor meetings.
I have spoken at some of them. As a number of
women have organized to oppose the movement—
think of such narrowness of vision!—and are circu-

lating a counter petition, holding meetings, etc., the agitation has been much increased and the excitement intensified. The fashionable women are about equally divided between the two camps. The newspapers are full of the subject—more for than against. The politicians are in a quandary, of course. They don't know which way the cat is going to jump. But any-one who reads the history of the past can tell how she is going to jump *eventually*, and that is the interesting thing about the jumping.

NEW YORK, *May 12.*

Frank Carpenter[1] called the other evening and stayed until after midnight. It was twenty years since we had met, and we had pages of old times to talk over. He said he had been much impressed with the Cooper Institute meeting, and had decided to paint a historic picture of that occasion, with me as the central figure. In his enthusiasm he exclaimed: "Woman suffrage is surely coming to stay, and I should like to leave such a painting behind, as every-thing pertaining to the movement will be interesting some day. Will you believe it? When I was busy at the White House on my 'President Lincoln Signing the Emancipation Proclamation,' there were those who said I was losing my time, so hard it is for con-temporaries to grasp the full bearing of what is hap-pening under their eyes." So the next day, he took me down to Rockwood's, the photographer, in Broad-way, to have my picture taken in various attitudes. We had a very merry time with the two, both of whom

---

[1] Francis Bicknell Carpenter, portrait painter.

are comic at moments. "Quick, George, catch that expression," the artist would shout, and the photographer would jump about as if on springs.

THOMASTON, LONG ISLAND, *May 29*.

I have just finished reading Mrs. Humphry Ward's *Marcella*, an interesting character study. I have much enjoyed the socialistic tendency of the book. When novels begin to take up a kindly consideration of the sociological and industrial problems, we may look for the dawn of a new day of human equality.

THOMASTON, *July 4*.

For the past month we have had strikes on the railroads running through Chicago. Never before have we had so great a one. A Mr. Debs seems to have inaugurated the movement. The strikers make many blunders. But as labor is never half paid, and those who do the hard work of the world are half clothed, half fed, and poorly sheltered, while those who neither toil nor spin enjoy all the good things of life, it is natural for the masses to occasionally ask why we have these extremes of riches and poverty. There must be something rotten in Denmark. My sympathies are with those who build our railroads, bridges, the mighty ships that plough the deep, our cathedrals, colleges, and palace homes, who raise our grains, vegetables, and fruits, and bring all we eat to our doors. Yes, the present conditions are not just and equal.[1]

---

[1] Late in August occurs this entry: "We have been watching with interest the aftermath of last month's lamentable strike. Well, these things must needs be until all the human race enjoy alike the fruits of their

THOMASTON, *August 17.*

The Constitutional Convention at Albany, after a long and earnest debate, has decided, 97 to 58, not to submit to the vote of the men of the State of New York the question of woman suffrage. This was a cavalier way of treating a petition signed by over half a million of the most responsible citizens of the commonwealth. The constitution should be so amended as to make it the duty of a constitutional convention to submit to a vote of the people an amendment asked for by such an immense number of intelligent, law-abiding persons. This should not be optional, but compulsory. I feel sad and disappointed at such contemptuous treatment by so ordinary a body of men as that which composed this convention. The members of real ability you could count on the fingers of one hand. It is very humiliating for women of education to have their sacred rights at the mercy of a masculine oligarchy, especially when this oligarchy is made up largely of inferiors. It is with sorrow that we see the heritage left us by the fathers so mismanaged and endangered as it now is. The shameful revelations of official corruption by investigating committees; the strikes, blocking for weeks all travel and commerce; the puerile action, or, rather, inaction

labor. We are perhaps in the midst of the industrial revolution. And see those stupid men in Congress talking against the income tax, one of the most just measures passed in a long time. Well, the time has come for labor to assert its rights. It is good that the working masses should now and then show their power and our dependence. I have just had an article in the *Sun* in which I recommend our friends to join the People's Party. If the Prohibitionists, the Populists, the labor organizations and the women would all unite, we should be in the majority."

of Congress, doing nothing for nine months but drawing its pay, and the apathy of the voters with all this passing before their eyes—in view of this state of things, we women feel that the welfare of ourselves and our children is in very unsafe hands. Especially to be condemned in this discreditable Albany business is the conduct of Joseph H. Choate, president of the Convention, and his premier henchman, Elihu Root. When the women of this state are finally enfranchised, they should not forget these two men, even if posterity shall have forgotten them. Just as when we look back on the men of the South who precipitated the rebellion for slavery—such strong minds as Jefferson Davis, Alexander H. Stephens, Robert E. Lee, J. M. Mason, John Slidell, Chief Justice Taney—it is difficult to believe that they could have held such narrow views and could not see that their opposition to right and justice was as childish as ineffectual; so will appear Choate's and Root's silly course at Albany when the common sense of the future throws its strong, cold light into the past. I have no hope of doing anything in this state if such a man as Choate can go against his own convictions and declarations. Last winter he came out for woman suffrage, and now in the Constitutional Convention he goes against it. It is said he hopes to be the nominee for governor and must secure the liquor vote. Hence his change of front.

> Sigh no more, ladies, sigh no more;
>   Men were deceivers ever;
> One foot in sea, and one on shore;
>   To one thing constant never.

NEW YORK, *October 10.*

I have just written Josephine Shaw Lowell telling her that it is most satisfactory to many of our mutual friends that she has consented to organize and lead the women of this city who are awake to the pressing need of municipal reform. I do not see, I say in answer to her query, that it conflicts in any way with her interest in woman suffrage. "If we cannot yet, unfortunately, express our opinions and exert our influence on public interests at the ballot-box, we can use all the social power we possess, with pen and tongue, to raise the moral standard of the city and state in which we live. To do this conscientiously and earnestly is the sure way to secure our political equality at last."

1895

NEW YORK, *January 10.*

Everybody is talking about *Trilby.* Even Colonel Ingersoll—we spent an evening with them recently—spoke a good deal about it. Some of our clergy praise it without stint, while some, especially those who have not read it, condemn. Howells' *A Traveler from Altruria,* which I have just finished, is a tale of quite a different sort. But I like the style and refinement of thought of all of Howells' fiction. And then I am always drawn towards him with affection because of his open advocacy of our political emancipation. The support of such men is a mighty aid in our uphill struggle.

NEW YORK, *January 20.*

I have been busy for a week past writing a speech and resolutions for the annual woman suffrage convention to be held this year, not in Washington as has been our habit for twenty-seven years, but in a southern city—Atlanta, Georgia. Susan and Mrs. Chapman Catt have been holding meetings extensively throughout the South, and have aroused so much thought and even enthusiasm that it is expected that the Atlanta gathering will also be a great success. My speech is devoted largely to the question of immigration, and I air my present belief in an educated suffrage open to men and women alike. My view ought to be well received in a southern city.

NEW YORK, *February 9.*

Henry George and his wife dined with us this evening, and we had a long talk on the single tax. His position is a strong one, and he knows how to present it clearly and forcibly. I read them parts of a speech which I have just finished for the meeting of the National Council of Women, to be held in Washington in a few days.

NEW YORK, *February 21.*

Taking up the papers to-day, the first word that caught my eye thrilled my very soul. Frederick Douglass is dead! What memories of the long years since he and I first met chased each other, thick and fast, through my mind and held me spellbound. A graduate from the "Southern Institution," he was well fitted to stand before a Boston audience and, with his burning eloquence, portray his sufferings in the land of bondage. He stood there like an African prince, majestic in his wrath, as with wit, satire, and indignation he graphically described the bitterness of slavery and the humiliation of subjection to those who, in all human virtues and powers, were inferior to himself. Thus it was that I first saw Frederick Douglass, and wondered that any mortal man should have ever tried to subjugate a being with such talents, intensified with the love of liberty. Around him sat the great antislavery orators of the day, earnestly watching the effect of his eloquence on that immense audience, that laughed and wept by turns, completely carried away by the wondrous gifts of his pathos and humor. On this occasion, all the other speakers seemed tame after Frederick Douglass. In imitation of the Methodist preachers of the South, he used to deliver a sermon from the text, "Servants, obey your masters," which some of our literary critics pronounced the finest piece of satire in the English language. The last time I visited his home at Anacosta, near Washington, I asked him if he had the written text of that sermon. He answered, "No, not even notes of it." "Could you give it again?" I asked. "No," he replied; "or at least I could not bring back the old feelings even if I tried, the blessing of liberty I have so long enjoyed having almost obliterated the painful memories of my sad early days."

NEW YORK, *March 13.*

Susan came and spent the day with me, and we talked over the woman suffrage situation.[1] She told me that friends of the movement had just settled on her an annuity of $800. Good!

NEW YORK, *March 16.*

Mr. and Mrs. Chapman Catt spent an hour with me to-day talking over the prospects at Albany, where the House has just passed the woman suffrage bill by a vote of 80 to 31. Now if the Senate will do the same we will feel encouraged.

NEW YORK, *April 19.*

A delegation of orthodox Jewish women called on me yesterday to talk over with me the Bible matter.

---

[1] No sooner were the women of New York defeated in the Constitutional Convention Campaign in 1894, than they began an attack on the Legislature to the end that it should submit to the voters a suffrage amendment.

They said that their religion reverences Jewish women, that the wife and mother were considered to hold the most exalted position a human being could fill, that their men thought it would be a desecration of the holy office of women to tax them with public affairs, that Jewish men worship their women, etc., etc. I asked them why, if this were all so, one heard in the synagogue service every week the "I thank thee, O Lord, that I was not born a woman." "That is an interpolation in our service," they replied, "and was not originally there." "But if the church does not approve of it, why is it not expunged?" "It is not meant in an unfriendly spirit, and is not intended to degrade or humiliate women." "But it does, nevertheless. Suppose the service read, 'I thank thee, O Lord, that I was not born a jackass.' Could that be twisted in any way into a compliment to the jackass?" They smiled, and I closed the interview with this general reflection: "Oh no, ladies, the Jews accord us women no more honor than do the Gentiles."

NEW YORK, *April 23.*

Well, the Legislature of this state has done the honorable thing in agreeing to submit a woman suffrage amendment, though of course they knew their action was not final, and so took no real responsibility in the matter. I much fear the next Legislature will not follow their example, because then some responsibility will be incurred.[1] I am told that Choate was

---

[1] The labor which led up to this apparent success was rendered void by a clerical error in the wording of the concurrent resolution, and Mrs. Stanton's fear was fully justified.

actually up at Albany lobbying against the resolution. We will not waste any immortelle wreaths on the graves of Choate and Root!

PETERBORO, *August 10.*

I have bought here and worn a complete outfit of underclothing made by a man. He does the weaving and sewing on a machine, while his wife sells the goods and takes in the money—a perfect reversal of the old order of things, proving again what I have so often preached, *i.e.*, that if we will only leave men and women quite free and to themselves, each will find his or her proper place.

NEW YORK, *November 13.*

Yesterday was my eightieth birthday and the event was widely celebrated. The scene in the Metropolitan Opera House was beautiful. Among those who came was Robert Collyer, who, in the most natural, spontaneous manner, kissed me on my forehead, such a kiss as only babies and grandmothers ever receive, an evanescent holy tribute, love for those supposed to need our protection. Nothing which has happened these past two days, so full of emotion to me, has touched me more deeply. I was particularly pleased with some friendly articles from the pen of Baroness Gripenberg, of Helsingfors, which appeared in the leading Finnish papers, and which I have had translated to me. But nothing caused me more pleasure, perhaps, mixed though it was with regret, than the ballot-box of onyx and silver sent

me by the free women of Utah. It will not open,
and ballots cannot penetrate to the interior. It is
indeed a suggestive gift from the enfranchised of the
far West to a political pariah of New York, and this
beautiful heavy stone is as heavy as our hearts when
we think of our civic degradation. There it stands
on my mantelpiece seemingly saying: "You have
tried for fifty years to enter these sacred precincts,
but may you not be condemned to try for fifty years
to come." I have been affected to tears more than
once during these days of triumph. Knowing myself,
conscious of all my shortcomings, remembering how I
have left undone so many things I should have done,
I often feel myself unworthy these generous praises,
the outpouring of so much love and friendship from
so many unexpected sources. All this I cannot forget.

1896

NEW YORK, *February 1.*

Susan writes to me that when she presented my address[1] to the Judiciary Committee she asked that it be printed. Her request was granted, so my work of December will be repaid.

NEW YORK, *February 9.*

I am just back from Cousin Charley's funeral.[2] The house was flooded with sunshine, and flowers were everywhere; no black anywhere. Cousin Lizzie and all the women of the family, dressed in their usual colors, sat in the parlors conversing quietly with the guests. The coffin was covered with gray cloth, one of Cousin Charley's favorite colors. He was dressed in his habitual drab suit, yellow cravat, and buttonhole bouquet. Felix Adler spoke at the house and said a few farewell words at the cemetery. A fine span of Charley's own horses drew the hearse, and Rolando, his favorite saddle-horse, followed with empty saddle. Verily a new day is dawning when we put aside our gloomy views of death. Maggie has just asked me how I wish my funeral conducted, and I answer that I should like to be in my ordinary dress, no crape or black, no fripperies or fandangoes of any sort, and some common-sense women to con-

---

[1] See *History of Woman Suffrage*, vol. iv, p. 268.
[2] Charles Dudley Miller, of Lochland, Geneva, son-in-law of Gerrit Smith.

duct the services. However, I am not quite ready to go just yet, so that there will be plenty of time to make these arrangements.

NEW YORK, *February 25.*

Felix Adler writes me: "I have repeatedly referred in my lectures to the circumstance that, whereas in the older religions woman sometimes occupied the position of a prophetess and a priestess, the place assigned to her in Christianity is a distinctly subordinate one. The older cults seem to have been wiser in this respect, in that they regarded woman as a vehicle of inspiration and hoped for oracles from her lips. My own feeling is that this view will also be characteristic of the religion of the future." The claim which is so often advanced that woman owes all the advantages she possesses to Christianity is not based on fact.

NEW YORK, *April 24.*

To-day I drove all over the lower part of the city. I had not been down to the Battery in thirty years or more. I found the streets clean and I was surprised at the many fine buildings. I was glad to see that all the ugly telegraph poles were gone. What an improvement that is. I enjoyed very much all the changes.

NEW YORK, *May 16.*

Susan sends me every day the San Francisco *Examiner,* which gives me the news of the progress of the suffrage campaign on the Pacific Slope. I hope with her for a complete victory in another "free state."

I often smile at the obtuseness of people in calling the northern part of our domain "the free states," when one-half of the population of those commonwealths are political pariahs. Thirty-five millions of intelligent law-abiding citizens with no voice in the making of the laws under which they live! And yet these are said to be free states!! Would that another Abraham Lincoln might arise and issue a proclamation of emancipation for the women of the Republic.

NEW YORK, *May 20.*

I am being constantly asked by reporters to talk and write on every imaginable subject. I have just finished for *The Wheelman* a little article touching on these points: Should women ride the bicycle? What should they wear when riding the bicycle? Should they ride on Sunday? My answers to these three questions are as follows: No. 1. If women can ride, God intended they should do so. No. 2. They should wear what they find most convenient and comfortable. No. 3. This is the most serious question of the three, and interests me the most. I believe that if women prefer a run in the open air on Sunday to a prosy sermon in a close church, they should ride by all means. With the soft changing clouds before their eyes, and the balmy air in their lungs, moving among hills, rivers, trees, and flowers, singing with the birds the praises of the Lord in that temple not builded with human hands, but standing eternal under the blue heavens—this worship is far preferable to playing the role of "miserable sinners" in the church service, and listening to that sanctimonious human wail, "Good Lord deliver us."

NEW YORK, *May 22.*

Every evening Bob and I play backgammon. Sometimes I gammon him and then he says it is because he is not feeling well. When he gammons me he boasts of the superiority of the male sex. I tell him he belongs to the boastful sex, and I remind him that the rooster does the crowing while the faithful hen lays the egg. I tell him he should rather do as I did many years ago when I got pulled into a chess contest with Theodore Tilton, who then edited the *Golden Age*, while I edited the *Revolution*. The trial was to be the best out of three games for the championship of the sexes, and the result was to be announced in our respective sheets. Mr. Tilton won the first game, I the second, and he the third and last. So I gave in the *Revolution* a diplomatically worded account of the match and wound up my remarks with this sentence: "I leave it to Mr. Tilton to tell the result." He was gallant enough to leave the matter there!

GENEVA, NEW YORK, *June 3.*

I tell Susan that by the first of October I shall arrive in my reminiscences at the point where I take her up and I ask for some notes covering the period prior to when we first met. "I do think in this earlier part of your life there should be some mysterious sort of undefined references to some faint suffering love affair! If your sisters can glean any facts in that line from your true inwardness nothing could be more agreeable to me than to weave a sentimental chapter entitled, for instance, 'The Romance of Susan B. Anthony's Younger Days.' How all the daily papers would jump at that!''

GENEVA, *June 30.*

We have been here at Lochland for the past month. On the Fourth of July there will be a large meeting in the public hall, and I am down for a ten minutes' speech, and a gentleman fresh from Cuba is to give us some startling information on the condition of that unhappy island. I have long felt that the United States should recognize the Cubans as belligerents.

PETERBORO, *July 20.*

As my eyes are growing dim, many of the guests read to me in turn, and I pay one young lady to do so regularly an hour each day. One of the guests, whose favorite subject is politics, reads me the books which he intends to read for himself. Another, who prefers romance, gives me the new novels which he has chosen for his own delectation, while a third, who considers biography the best kind of a story, has enabled me to share with her the delightful letters of Maria Mitchell. In this way my infirmity is not too much of a bore to them nor to me.[1]

---

[1] This is a striking example of Mrs. Stanton's invariable habit of making the best of the inevitable. What she really felt of this hotch-potch comes out in an entry at the end of this summer: "I have a young woman who reads, as I cannot use my eyes long at a time. I can write without spectacles, but cannot read without them. Failing eyesight is a great loss for me whose chief pleasure is reading. We are just now reading Lecky's *Democracy and Liberty.* It is a very suggestive book. It will be followed

NEW YORK, *October 1.*

Since I got back to town, my chief occupation has been looking over my papers, destroying many and putting the rest in order. As from day to day I have worked alone at this monotonous task, I have felt that perhaps this is the last time I shall ever handle them, and that I should make the work of destruction easier for my children. How we dislike to burn what we once deemed valuable, and yet what a nuisance to those who came after us are bushels of old papers. Well, I have thinned mine out and may try it again should I remain on this planet half a dozen years longer.

NEW YORK, *December 7.*

The faithful are busy planning for the annual convention which is to be held this year, or rather next month, in Des Moines, Iowa. Susan writes: "You must prepare an argument, strong resolutions, and tributes to those of our band who have died during the present year." One would think I were a machine; that all I had to do was to turn a crank and thoughts on any theme would bubble up like water. I replied: "Dear Susan, is it not time that some of our younger coadjutors do the bubbling? The fact is that I am tired bubbling on one subject. Last year I wrote a tribute to dear old John Hutchinson on his seventy-fifth birthday, and to Frederick Douglass and Theodore Weld, who had passed away. In fact I have become

by a novel. I like to sandwich the solid with the light. But I do not like to read two books at the same time. It is a case of 'mixing drinks,' as my menfolk would say, and I believe this is never good."

a sort of spiritual undertaker for the pioneers of the woman suffrage movement. How much longer must I embalm the dead and weave wreaths of immortelles for the living, dwelling on their graces, virtues, and heroic deeds?" By the way, in my little eulogy of Mr. Weld, who was always very happy and virile in his use of English, I forgot to insert these characteristic lines sent me at the time of the founding of the *Revolution:* "All hail Iconoclast! God speed the great revolution, its organ and organists. Smite away! The old dragon's scales fly at every stroke." How like him these words are.

1897

I am happy to learn that the people of Rochester, New York, who would never treat Frederick Douglass as a social equal while he lived amongst them, are now proposing to build him a monument. Of this noble man I have varied memories—sad for all he suffered because of narrow prejudices against his race and insults to his proud nature, pleasant for the tender love and friendship for him entertained by a few broad-minded souls. Suffering myself from the slights cast upon me because of my sex, I loved him as he loved me because of the indignities we both alike endured. When I saw him for the last time, he remarked with that gentle play of humor which was one of the characteristics of his sunny nature, that though I had been denied the rights of an American citizen on account of my sex, and he on account of his color, he felt sure that "we would stand on equal ground with the angels in heaven." "Alas," I answered, "we had better not be too sure of that, for earthly prejudices die hard, and even St. Peter might be influenced against us by some of the 'antis' of color or sex." "Then," he replied, "hand in hand we will go below." As regards the proposed monument, I have but one criticism to make. I sincerely regret it is not to take the form of a schoolhouse for colored children, or a model tenement house for colored families. It always seems to me a great pity to set up useless shafts of stone when humanity is in need of so many ameliorations. But if a statue it must be, perhaps it would be well to follow the suggestion of our common friend, Tilton, who exclaims in a series of beautiful sonnets in honor of Douglass:

> My country, hark to me!
> Let us, in yonder capitol of ours,
> Mould him a statue of enduring brass
> Out of the broken chains of slaves set free!

NEW YORK, *March 12.*

A Washington clergyman named Kent has been preaching a sermon on the "Woman's Bible." It is admirable. I was filled with surprise and gratitude as I read line by line, so fair, so clear, and so appreciative.

NEW YORK, *March 18.*

The country has been quite stirred with the fight between Corbett and Fitzsimmons, in which the latter is triumphant. A strange ambition, to be the champion fighter in the world. What would men say if we women had some such foolish, not to use any other adjective, pastime as this? "This alone shows them unfit to have the vote," we would then hear the Sir Benjamin Backbites say in a tone that would not brook contradiction.

NEW YORK, *March 27.*

I received from Paris this morning a letter from Theodore Tilton in which he says he "was solemnized into a religious frame of mind by reading in a Boston paper your recent essay on Ruth and Boaz," and then he continues: "I have known you for more than forty years in more than forty characters—suffragist, journalist, lecturer, historian, traveler, prophetess, materfamilias, housekeeper, patriot, nurse, baby-tender, cook, milliner, lobbyist, parliamentarian, statistician, legislator, philosopher, tea-pourer, story-teller, satirist, kite-flyer, chess-player—and I know not what else; but I now think that, after all, you shine chiefly as a theologian! Go on, O sacred scribe and commentator! I always find a pious satisfaction in reading everything that comes from your biblical pen! As for yourself, O mother in Israel, I send my humble wish for an interest in your prayers!"

NEW YORK, *April 1.*

I have had all winter a friend read to me. My eyes grow dimmer and dimmer. Oh, what a privation! I say nothing to my children of this great grief, but it is a sore trial, with prospective total blindness!! I will then be able to do nothing but think. However, I can still write without spectacles, though I cannot read my own writing. But my hearing is as good as ever, and I am perfectly well otherwise. As Stevenson says, "No man lives in the external truth, among salts and acids, but in the warm, phantasmagoric chamber of his brain, with the painted windows and the storied walls."

NEW YORK, *April 27.*

From my eyrie on the Boulevard, I have witnessed to-day's celebration of Grant's tomb. I shall have an article in the *Sun* on the point that I have witnessed two somewhat similar events of the century—

the national tributes to Napoleon and General Grant. I was in Paris just as the remains of the Emperor arrived from St. Helena, fifty-six years ago. I have not forgotten the wild enthusiasm of the old soldiers when the body reached the Hôtel des Invalides. Many cried, and I confess tears were brought to my own eyes.

GENEVA, *June 25.*

I have met the new President of Hobart. I am always very circumspect on approaching clergymen, especially as sometimes I find them to be comparatively broad and liberal. There is, I think, such a side to Doctor Jones, due, perhaps, to the fact that after leaving the theological seminary he seems to have hesitated as to whether he was intended for the cloth, for he tells me he spent two years as a topographer in the United States Geological Survey, where he must have learned the geological absurdities of the Book of Genesis, and other things too.

GENEVA, *July 5.*

The Revolutionary Dames celebrated the Fourth in a new hall. I made the speech of the occasion, which they all said was very good. A gentleman read a paper on the American flag. The first one, he informed us, was made out of a sailor's blue coat and a woman's red petticoat and white apron. So the petticoat was in the beginning and waved over the corner-stone of the Republic, while all the men of the thirteen colonies were tied metaphorically to an apron-string.

GENEVA, *August 29.*

I have spoken in public twice here this month.
The first time at a great picnic where were present a
thousand people, I held forth for an hour and a half,
and was heard, I was told, to the utmost limits of the
crowd. The second time it was in the Geneva Sana-
torium. Though my eyes may be failing, my voice
seems to hold its own.

NEW YORK, *November 12.*

I was greatly interested in the election for the mayor
of Greater New York, and had sincerely hoped that
Henry George would be the successful candidate.
But alas! he died suddenly in the midst of the campaign, and we have again fallen into the hands of the
Philistines, with Van Wyck at their head. Such
results weaken the faith of many in democracy. But
they never have that effect on me. The evils which
arise from any other system than democracy are so
much greater in the long run, that I never get blue
over a mistake of the people, especially a mistake
made by the electorate of New York City, where the
conditions for democratic government are the worst
in the world. When immigration ceases and we have
had time to leaven the whole lump—perhaps a century
hence—then, and not till then, will it be fair to judge
American institutions. To-day we are suffering polit-
ically from the evils of European monarchy and mis-
rule transplanted to our shores. This is especially
the case in this city, the great port of entry and the
dumping-ground of the people from the Old World,
most of whom have scarcely one element fitting them

for the exercise of democratic principles. Like Rome, an American citizen is not made in a day, or in six years either. He must be born on our soil, educated in our schools and freed from the home influence which is foreign. Then he becomes one of the best of American citizens.

NEW YORK, *December 2.*

I cannot go on to Washington, as Susan urges[1]— I am really getting too old for such things—nor can I write four papers, as she also desires; but I have made up my mind to prepare two—one for the Congressional hearing—"The Significance and History of the Ballot"—and the other for the Convention— "Our Defeats and Our Triumphs."[2]

NEW YORK, *December 18.*

Moncure D. Conway dined with us this evening. His wife is very ill. She may pass away any day.

---

[1] Miss Anthony's letter, which is pasted in the Diary, reads: "Of course you have not forgotten that we are to celebrate in February at Washington the fiftieth anniversary of the first woman's rights convention, of which you were the prime mover and the soul, young as you were. The summing up of the achievements of women in the past fifty years is a big job, and one you alone are equal to. So don't let anybody or anything divert you from getting your papers written—one for the Judiciary Committee of the House, another for the Suffrage Committee of the Senate, another for the opening of the Jubilee celebration, and yet another for its closing session. Now, my dear, this is positively the last time I am ever going to put you on the rack and torture you to make *the* speech or speeches of your life." The entry in the Diary January 26, 1898, tells its own story: "I have practically finished my two papers [see *History of Woman Suffrage,* vol. iv, p. 316] for the Washington convention next month. Susan is urging me to be present in person. But I shall not go, as my eyes grow dimmer and dimmer and my legs weaker and weaker. My brain seems as strong as ever."

[2] See *History of Woman Suffrage,* vol. iv, p. 292.

He is very, very sad.   She sent him to us to be cheered up.   After the meal he became very entertaining and said many interesting things.   The conversation turning on women poets, I mentioned the fact that my friend Moses Coit Tyler once told me that the first professional poet of New England was a woman—Anne Bradstreet—whereupon Mr. Conway, who knew her work very well, quoted these spirited lines from her pen, which refer to Queen Elizabeth:

> She hath wiped off the aspersion of her sex,
> That women wisdom lack to play the Rex.
> Now say, have women worth, or have they none?
> Or had they some, but with our Queen is 't gone?
> Nay, masculines, you have thus taxed us long;
> But she, though dead, will vindicate our wrong.
> Let such as say our sex is void of reason,
> Know 'tis a slander now, but once was treason.

NEW YORK, *December 24.*

The Woman's Bible [1] and my reminiscences [2] are now in print, and I am as much relieved as if I had given birth to twins.

---

[1] Before the end of the first year the first part had gone through three American and two English editions, 20,000 copies having been called for. The first American edition of the second part was 10,000 copies.

[2] *Eighty Years and More.* An English edition was also brought out. The book was well received by the critics on both sides of the Atlantic.

1898

NEW YORK, *January 1.*

I have just written to Mr. Godkin, thanking him for a friendly review, which has appeared in the *Nation,* of my book, *Eighty Years and More.* The comments are very fair in the main, though there are two statements which are misleading to the readers of that excellent periodical and unjust to me. I am accused of saying that "the State has nothing to do with either marriage or divorce." I tell him that on careful reading he will not find such a sentiment in any of my writings, speeches, addresses before legislatures, in the proceedings of our women's rights conventions, or in the chapter entitled, "Views on Marriage and Divorce," found in this last book of mine. All alike show that I have not only recognized the wisdom of having laws that govern the marriage relation, but have advocated that these laws, in so far as they relate to the entering into the contract, be made more restrictive. For instance, to my mind, the contracting parties should be over eighteen years of age, and they should not take this important step without the consent of their parents. Any person of common sense must see the necessity of laws regulating the duties of parents to their children and to each other, laws governing the rights of property, inheritance, support, alimony, etc., all of which are important for the welfare of the State as well as the family. I advocate absolute individual sovereignty only in the matter of separation, when the parties find themselves wholly incompatible and antagonistic. Here they should have completely free choice. But if they ask for a divorce in order to marry again, then the State may reassert itself. I have always favored more liberal laws than unhappy husbands and wives enjoy in the State of New York. "This is the extent of my heresy on the question of marriage and divorce," I write to Mr. Godkin. "Having been, by example and precept, true to one relation over fifty years, I consider myself a law-abiding citizen who has paid due respect to the State, and so have a right to speak on this subject, if not with authority, at least with freedom." In all of which I think I may say without conceit that I show more sense than St. Mark in the opening verses of his tenth chapter, where I feel sure he misreports the words of Jesus.

NEW YORK, *January 10.*

The critics and the reading public are all taken up with a novel entitled *Quo Vadis?* by a Polish writer, Sienkiewicz. The plot is laid in the time of Nero. The burning of Rome and the awful scenes in the amphitheater when the wild beasts are let loose on the Christians afford the talented author an opportunity to produce some terrible and graphic word-painting. I understand that this powerful book was practically unknown outside of the writer's own country until brought out here, and that it is not yet known in England and France. But this is not the first time that a European literary masterpiece has received its first foreign recognition in the United States. We owe the discovery in this instance to the cultivated tastes and curiosity of the secretary of our legation at St. Petersburg, a good example of the excellent habit of our State Department in sending literary men abroad.

New York, *February 15.*

I have just finished Mrs. Humphry Ward's *Helbeck of Bannisdale,* and I find it a great novel. Most people criticize it and say they do not see what the author intends to illustrate. I do see. She draws a woman free from all religious superstitions, true, honest, honorable, governed by common sense and not by blind faith, whose self-assertion and logic baffle all the Jesuits and priests, whose love side comes in contact with a man dominated by unreason and bigotry. We see the battle with its tragic end— wrong pushing to the wall right, as it often does in this world, because of the dislike of the gentler souls to give pain.

New York, *March 2.*

Apropos of *The Woman's Bible,* Mrs. Josephine K. Henry writes me as follows from Kentucky:

Women are such strange creatures. They seem to love the hand that smites. A colored servant, while cleaning my room this morning, said to me: "Miss Josephine, I believe de Bible with my whole heart. De Bible says, 'Whom de Lord loves, He chaseth'; and de Lord has been a-chasin' me up hill and down dale for these forty years. I knows de Bible is true." This negro woman is a reflex of her sex, having the same lack of self-respect and using the same logic.

New York, *April 7.*

I met yesterday the Rev. John W. Chadwick, and this is what he said: "The criticism I should make upon your Bible is that it is much too obsequious to that venerable book. What else can you expect from a book written so long ago and reflecting such social conditions? But we cannot do much better now than 'Give her of the fruit of her hands and let her own works praise her in the gates.'"

NEW YORK, *April 15.*

The whole country is deeply stirred over the Cuban situation. I hope we will recognize the Cubans as belligerents.

NEW YORK, *May 13.*

We are at war with Spain. Though I hate war *per se,* I am glad that it has come in this instance. I would like to see Spain and Turkey swept from the face of the earth. They are a disgrace to the civilization of the nineteenth century. Spain's history in her colonies is one long record of crime.

WASHINGTON, CONNECTICUT, *June 30.*

A farmer's daughter, Lucy Nettleton, reads to me two hours every day. We have been deep in Lecky's *European Morals* and *Rationalism,* and we are now in the midst of Gibbon's chapters on *Christianity,* which have always been brought up against him by the over-pious. It seems to me he makes out a very strong case, though of course I cannot verify his authorities. But as Gibbon was past master in Latin and Latin authorities, we must assume that his strictures are based on solid facts. Anyway, it is well to have "the other side," especially as English literature is teeming with the Church presentation. There are six churches here within a radius of two miles, and the chief business of the inhabitants, especially the female half, seems to be to "raise" church debts by eating ice cream and cake and drinking lemonade.

WASHINGTON, *July 4*.

Our guns are firing and bells ringing over the war news this morning. It is now plain that we shall drive that brutal Spain out of all her islands, though it pains my heart to perceive the loss will be heavy among the flower of our young manhood. But he who puts his hand to the plow and turns back is not fit for the kingdom of heaven.[1]

NEW YORK, *September 25*.

It is those with "push" who have the rougher time, and it is generally these last that get the so-called honors of life. My father is an example of this. Though a distinguished lawyer and judge, he was exceedingly modest and apt to keep himself in the background. On entering a room and being introduced to several persons, he would blush like a girl and display embarrassment in every movement and word. He felt at home and at his ease in the court room and in his own family, but nowhere else. When such men or women attain success, it is due to pure

---

[1] On October 30th she makes this entry in regard to some friends: "They are all on the rampage against the war and Roosevelt. I am in favor of both."

personal merit. But he would have attained still higher honors if he had been more self-asserting.

NEW YORK, *October 6.*

I hear of failing health among my sisters. I suppose we will all soon go to the "land of pure delight, where saints immortal reign." Well, I must confess that I am in no hurry to go there. Life has been, and still is, very sweet to me, and there are many things I desire to do before I take final leave of this plant.

NEW YORK, *December 21.*

I had a chat recently with Florence Kelley[1] and I found we agreed exactly about the war. Among other sensible things which she said on this subject were these: "It is most extraordinary how melodramatic the good people do get over this episode of our history. Although my young brother underwent some acute hardships with his battery, they do not seem to me to compare with the strain or effort made for even a little amelioration of our social conditions. That long, steady, disappointing effort which we have all to make for civil improvements has none of the charm and excitement of war. But how infinitely more vital it is! I think this brother stated the just attitude as to the war when he wrote to a friend who was begging him not to go with the battery: 'I understand that there is, down below Tampa, a nuisance

---

[1] Florence Kelley, general secretary of the National Consumers' League. Author of *Some Ethical Gains Through Legislation* and *Modern Industry in Relation to the Family.*

which must be abated at once. When it is abated, I'll come home and talk it over with you.'"

NEW YORK, *December 27*.

Frank Sanborn called the other day. He spoke very nicely of my book *Eighty Years and More*. Among other things he said: "I was especially interested in what you write of your experiences in England among the Quakers, for I have just finished a *Life* of my old friend Pliny Earle, who, like you, saw much of those elder Gurneys, Frys, Peases, *et al*. It is evident that the handsome, lively, and witty Quakeresses amused themselves with the handsome young American, under which treatment he winced a little. He visited at Upton, Plaistow, Dublin, etc., just as you did. Your impressions correspond with his. From all these things I draw the conclusions that those early Quakers were a fine body of men and women." And they certainly were, and so are many of their descendants whom I saw in my later visits to England.

1899

New York, *January 25.*

I have been somewhat seriously indisposed of late. So a faith-curist gave me a treatment two nights ago. She placed her hands on my hands and knees alternately, and prayed aloud, suggesting to the Lord that I was a worthy child, etc. The next morning I did not see nor did I skip about. The faith-curist said: "The patient must have faith or the work cannot be accomplished." Then I sent for Dr. Caroline Cabot, who plied me with beef tea, glycerine and whisky. I inhaled pine steam and took two kinds of pills in quick succession during all my waking hours. Finally she ordered a very hot bath. To-day I am as agile as a grasshopper. Who would believe that I am a homeopathist!

New York, *February 4.*

As my eyes grow dimmer[1] from day to day, my intellectual vision grows clearer. But I have written Susan not to lay out any more work for me, but to

---

[1] It was about this time that my mother consulted a famous oculist, Dr. D. B. St. John Roosa. I was with her. She accepted his diagnosis of cataract without a word. When we were seated in our carriage I laid my hand on hers. She said, as if to herself, "And both eyes." She never referred to the matter again, but in her Diary on May 26, 1899, there is this entry: "The papers are full of things about the 80th birthday of Queen Victoria. I learn from my English friends that she has a cataract on her eye, which the surgeons wish to remove. But she says nay. I suppose she feels just as I do—that so long as one can see fairly well, it is better to wait."—H. S. B.

call on our younger coadjutors to write the letters to senators and congressmen. Say to them, I write, that "it requires no courage now to talk suffrage; they should demand equality everywhere—*hoc opus, hic labor, est.*" So many of our followers think they do enough if they sing suffrage, which now calls down no ridicule or persecution. But the battle is not wholly fought until we stand equal in the church, the world of work, and have an equal code of morals for both sexes. Suffrage achieved in some places, we have thrown down the outposts to the land of liberty that lies still beyond. Now for new women, new measures, and the birthday of a new Republic. There are many phases of our question which have not yet been sufficiently studied, many strongholds of the enemy yet to be taken. We have battered away at the old ship of state until she is riddled through and through. This has been the work of half a century, one whole generation of earnest men and women. Now the younger apostles should do the same in the church and society.

NEW YORK, *April 12.*

John Martin, a Fabian from London, dined with us this evening, and we had a long talk on socialism. He tells me he was a member of the executive committee from 1894 to 1899, wrote two or three Fabian tracts, and came to this country to lecture for the Fabians. I like the Fabian way of working, and, in principle, prefer it to the more revolutionary system of the French socialists, though I recognize the fact that things cannot go on in the same way under different conditions, in other lands and among dissimilar races.

NEW YORK, *May 10.*

I have been very much annoyed with the criticisms passed in some quarters on my letter[1] to the Grand Rapids convention. It appears that it was considered by the dainty ones as "Too savage." The longer I live, the more I am struck with the stupidity of people in not doing the right thing at the right time. Our younger coadjutors seem to be too satisfied with painting in the brightest colors the successes of the woman movement, while leaving in the background the long line of wrongs which we still deplore. A rose-water campaign for a discourtesy might do, but when the vast majority of us are deprived of all of our civil and political rights, the struggle must be a fierce one. What Nathan the Prophet said to David, when arraigning him for the greatest crime of his life, we should say to those who have defrauded us directly or indirectly: "Thou art the man!"

NEW YORK, *June 16.*

My article on "Trailing Skirts and No Pockets" appeared to-day. Imagine our beloved lords of creation rushing to and fro in the busy marts of trade, with their hands behind them holding up their trousers to prevent the "bottoms" from trailing in the mud

---

[1] On April 10th the Diary had this entry: "I have sent a letter to the annual suffrage convention. Susan is to read it. Among other things, I say: 'Every man who is not for us in this prolonged struggle for liberty is responsible for the present degradation of the mothers of the race.'" (See *History of Woman Suffrage*, vol. iv, p. 337.)

and dust, and with no pockets for purse or bunch of keys. What a picture this would be! Women with trains always make me think of peacocks, slowly strutting around the barn-yard. If a woman has a nicely shaped foot and a well fitting boot, it is a much prettier sight than yards of silk filled with microbes. It is an old saying that no man should marry a "trail," which in the time of my childhood meant a woman who trailed her dress through the gutters. It was looked upon as a term of reproach, about equivalent to that of being an untidy woman.

PEEKSKILL, *July 27.*

This morning brought us the sad news of the sudden death of Col. Robert G. Ingersoll. No other loss, outside of my own family, could have filled me with such sorrow. The future historian will rank him as one of the heroes of the nineteenth century.

GENEVA, *August 20.*

I have been reading Eugene Lawrence's *Jews and Their Persecutors.* I have always been deeply impressed with the misery of that people in all nations and ages. The Dreyfus trial, which began early this month at Rennes, France, is in line with these same outrages so long inflicted on this unfortunate race. Theodore writes me from Rennes that he has been very much struck by the excellent conduct and straightforwardness of the prisoner, which are in strong contrast with the tergiversations of the generals and the court. This whole affair will ever be considered a terrible blot on the French sense of justice. I wonder the man ever lived through the cruelties and the tortures of five years.

NEW YORK, *September 30.*

During the past two days we have had a celebration in honor of Admiral Dewey and his ship, the *Olympia*. The city is bedecked with flags, and the hotels are crowded to bursting. Our landlord covered the top of the house with seats for his lessees and their guests, so that we saw well and at our ease the naval pageant in the Hudson. Naturally the topic to the fore just now is "expansion." I am strongly in favor of this new departure in our foreign policy. What would this continent have been if we had left it to the Indians? I have no sympathy with all the pessimistic twaddle about the Philippines.

NEW YORK, *October 3.*

I will take "The Basis of Representation" as the subject for my speech before the Congressional Committee.[1] A national law providing that voters only should count in establishing the basis of representation would check the movement for disfranchising the colored people, and might give an impulse to the enfranchisement of women in different states.

NEW YORK, *October 30.*

As the day for the State election approaches, the corruption in both parties becomes more and more the topic of all those who speak out impartially. If good men would take more interest in the government,

---

[1] See *History of Woman Suffrage*, vol. iv, p. 376.

of the state and city, and manifest a conscientious duty for the public weal, such low characters as Croker and Platt would not wield the power they do. While some men manifest indifference to good government and a large class never vote at all, we need not wonder at the present base condition of our politics. We ought to apply to these non-voters that excellent New Zealand law which requires a citizen who fails to vote to give an adequate excuse or else he may not vote again at a subsequent election. I learn from Mr. Hugh H. Lusk, of that country, that this law has worked like a charm. He tells me that 80 per cent of those enrolled vote.

NEW YORK, *November 8.*

Grace Greenwood called to-day and is as bright as ever. Speaking of my coming birthday, she sat down at my writing-desk, and while I was conversing with others, dashed off these lines, which I found on my table after she left:

TWO ELIZABETHS

A great and good Elizabeth,
    Was Hungary's royal saint,
For whom rare miracles were wrought,
    That pious poets paint.
She fought with nature and her heart
    For many weary years,
Resigning ease and joy and love
    For penances and tears.

Once from excessive prayers and fasts,
    Sorrows and scourging sore,
She was about to faint and sink
    Upon her chapel's floor,

When lo! the water that she craved
Was by some power divine
Changed on her trembling, pallid lips,
To good old Tokay Wine.

She prayed and wept herself to death,
This hapless saint, Elizabeth.

Another great Elizabeth,
I sing, in greater times,
Who merits better tributes, far,
Than these my halting rhymes.
Her life a noble poem is
In cantos eighty-four—
A record of long warfare waged,
And victories galore—

Not hers her own pure flesh to scourge,
But folly, vice and wrong;
At peace with Nature, loving love,
Home comfort, mirth and song.
She faints not, though the way seems drear
And hard, and far the goal.
'Tis we who sink, and need the cheer
The good wine to her soul—
Her earnest, royal soul.

Still loving life, not fearing death,
God save our Queen Elizabeth!

GRACE GREENWOOD.

NEW YORK, *November 10.*

The death of Jacob Bright is announced in this morning's papers. I am deeply affected by the sad news. He was the great champion of woman suffrage in the House of Commons, and he it was who carried through the Married Women's Property Bill in 1882. I saw much of him during my visits to England, and I always admired his broad-mindedness, his simplicity, and his earnestness in the cause of woman. In this last measure he was more consistent and perspicacious than his better known brother John. Not a little of his firmness in our behalf was probably due to the influence of his able wife, a woman of superior parts. It is worthy of note, by the way, that the whole Bright family in all its branches, men as well as women, young and old, have, with the one single exception of the Right Honorable John, ever stood shoulder to shoulder for woman suffrage, and have thus been a power in England in this movement.

New York, *November 12.*

Among other greetings received to-day was a warm telegram from my dear Susan, and a resolution of "respect and gratitude" from the Federation of Women's Clubs. But I think nothing pleased me more than receiving a Chicago paper containing an interview with Mrs. Russell Sage, in which she prophesies that at the time of the next constitutional convention in 1914, there will be a general uprising of the women of the Empire State in a demand, which cannot be denied by that future body, for suffrage. I am inclined to believe that the prophesy will come true. *Qui vivra verra.*

New York, *November 15.*

The editor of one of the daily papers has just asked me to send him a few lines in reply to the question, "What would make you more thankful than you are?" Here is what I sent him:

Having just celebrated my eighty-fourth birthday, I should be most thankful for the power to roll back the wheels in the horologe of time at least thirty years, in order to enjoy the generation in which liberty, justice and equality will everywhere be vouchsafed to the mothers of the race. I would fain linger on this planet a while longer, to work six days in the week for the emancipation of woman and read the rich and racy columns of our metropolitan journals on Sunday. Who, in fact, would not gladly live at least a part of one's life again, avoiding past blunders and improving lost opportunities, so that the heroes of one's generation might say, "Well done, thou good and faithful servant."[1]

NEW YORK, *December 3.*

Susan writes asking me to put on paper what I think ought to be done by our national association at its next annual meeting. So I have replied as follows:

1. A resolution should be passed in favor of establishing a new government in Hawaii. It is a disgrace to the civilization of the nineteenth century to make that island a male oligarchy.

2. We should protest in clarion tones against the proposal by railroad kings to turn women out of all the positions which they hold in the North Western Railroad, especially as it is generally admitted that they have given faithful service.

3. We should discuss and pass a resolution against the proposition of the Knights of Labor to remove women from all factories and industries which take them from home. If these gentlemen propose to provide every woman with a strong right arm on which she may lean until she reaches the other side of Jordan; a robust generous man pledged to feed, clothe and shelter the woman and her children to the end of life; a husband or a brother sure not to die or default on the way—why then this proposal might be worthy

---

[1] The birthday season seemed always to mean optimism. Here is the entry one year: "I do enjoy life more and more every hour, and am truly thankful that I have so few annoyances and so few pains and aches to rob me of the satisfaction." And here is another: "This is my birthday. Well, I am glad I was born. I feel that I have done something to make the world better, especially to render it a more endurable sphere for woman."

of woman's consideration. But as long as she is often forced to
be the breadwinner for herself, husband, and children, it would
be suicidal for her to retire to the privacy of home and with folded
hands wait for the salvation of the Lord. There is an immense
amount of sentimental nonsense talked about the isolated home.
This is evident when we see what it really means for the mass of
the human family. For Deacon Jones, a millionaire surrounded
with every luxury, no material change may be desirable. But
for a poor farmer with wife and child in the solitude of a prairie
home, a co-operative household with society would be inestimable
blessing. Woman's work can never be properly organized in the
isolated home. One woman cannot fill all the duties required
as housekeeper, cook, laundress, nurse, and educator of her children. Therefore we should oppose all sly moves to chain woman
in the home.

4. To my mind, our Association cannot be too broad. Suffrage
involves every basic principle of republican government, all our
social, civil, religious, educational, and political rights. It is
therefore germane to our platform to discuss every invidious distinction of sex in the college, home, trades, and professions, in
literature, sacred and profane, in the canon as well as in the civil
law. At the inauguration of our movement, we numbered in
our Declaration of Rights eighteen grievances covering the whole
range of human experience. On none of these did we talk with
bated breath. Note the radical claims we made, and think how
the world responded. Colleges were built for women, and many
of the older male colleges opened their doors to our sex. Laws
were modified in our favor. The professions were thrown open to
us. In short, in response to our radicalism, the bulwarks of the
enemy fell as never since. At that time you gave on many occasions a radical lecture on social purity. I was responsible for an
equally advanced one on marriage and divorce. Lucretia Mott
was not less outspoken on theological questions. But at present
our association has so narrowed its platform for reasons of policy
and propriety that our conventions have ceased to point the way.

5. Our national convention should always be held in Washington, where we could examine intelligently the bills before Congress
which nearly or remotely affect the women of the nation. We
should have a sort of Woman's Congress, if we can afford it, which
should sit at the federal capital for a longer or a shorter period
every year.

NEW YORK, *December 15.*

During the past weeks I have enjoyed these works among others: Andrew D. White's *A History of the Warfare of Science with Theology,* read for the second time; Boswell's *Life of Johnson,* which is pleasant and profitable; Cross's *George Eliot's Life,* whose editing does not wholly please me; *Rev. Amos Barton;* Matthew Arnold's *Essays in Criticism,* both series; Bacon's *Essays;* Herbert Spencer's *Education;* Irving's *Oliver Goldsmith;* Higginson's *Cheerful Yesterdays;* Ingersoll's *Great Speeches,* full of telling passages; Sallie Holley's *Reminiscences;* Ralph Waldo Trine's *In Tune with the Infinite;* Hughes's *Tom Brown at Oxford;* several of the novels of Charlotte Brontë, Thackeray, George Eliot, and Cabot Lodge's *Life of Washington.* The heroic struggles of George Washington show at what a great price we secured our liberty as a nation, and after reading such a book as this last one, I feel more than ever the immense debt we owe posterity to maintain what our revolutionary heroes achieved for us.

II.—23

1900

NEW YORK, *February 16.*

I learn by the papers and by reports from those present that the convention at Washington passed off exceedingly well. One of the amusing features of the proceedings was the presence, for the first time, before Congress, of the anti-suffragists, who begged to be left in their chains. They were supported by a masculine advocate who acted as a sort of "steering-committee" and who helped them plead for a continuance of their political degradation. Cardinal Gibbons, representing the Catholic Church, and Lyman Abbott,[1] representing the Protestants, are both actively engaged against the exercise of the right of suffrage by women. Really, such men should be ashamed of themselves, and they will be, or their descendants for them, when the day of liberty, justice and equality for woman comes, as it surely will in the not distant future.

---

[1] In a later entry Mrs. Stanton says: "I am told that Isabella Beecher Hooker has an article in one of the Hartford papers scarifying Lyman Abbott. Just think of his trotting all the way to Boston and facing the women of Massachusetts before the legislature of that state in order to denounce them for demanding their right to self-government! I have written to Mrs. Hooker congratulating her, asking for her bull, and closing with these words: 'What a man to occupy the pulpit of Henry Ward Beecher, one of our noblest champions.' When I perceive what Cardinal Gibbons, Lyman Abbott, Bishop Doane, and all their like are saying and doing to degrade woman, I can't find language strong enough to express my indignation."

NEW YORK, *March 12.*

In this month's *North American Review* I have an article on divorce.[1] Several papers have commented on it, and yesterday the Rev. Minot Savage preached a very fine sermon on the subject. In a country where marriage is so easy, divorce must be easy too.

NEW YORK, *April 12.*

Rev. Antoinette Brown Blackwell and her daughter lunched with us a short time ago. She believes firmly in immortality, and speaks with cheering confidence on that very fascinating but foggy subject. "You may be sure we shall meet in heaven," she said in parting. "I don't object," I answered. A few days later we had at dinner Mr. and Mrs. St. John Gaffney. His wife, who was Fannie Humphreys before her marriage, is "one of us." He is bitterly opposed to the Transvaal war, "one of the blackest of the many disgraces that stain the history of England. It is a blot that will never rub out." I could not work myself up to this state of indignation, although I am of that sex which England has always treated about as shamefully as my friend thinks she is now treating the stolid Boers. The fact is that in this South African affair my sympathies have all along been with the British, for it seems to me that they will plant a better civilization there.

NEW YORK, *May 21.*

I have an article in the *Sun* against the proposed subway under the Boulevard, as I understand it will

---

[1] "Are Homogeneous Divorce Laws in All the States Desirable?"

destroy for miles beautiful turf and trees, young elms that require long years to reach maturity. Men as a general rule have very little reverence for trees. Some masculine vandal cut down to no purpose one of the giant trees of California which was four hundred feet high. I saw this with my own eyes when I was on the Pacific Slope years ago. In order to provide temporary seats for the Dewey parade, men cut down beautiful horsechestnuts on Riverside Drive. It will be remembered that even the immortal Washington, through this male passion for chopping, did not spare the famous cherry tree.

NEW YORK, *May 23.*

I am told that the women in their clubs are wild over progressive euchre parties, where they gamble and drink cocktails. I ask myself if the young mothers who participate in these vices are aware of the fact that they are making gamblers and drunkards of the next generation? During the nine months of prenatal life, they are stamping every thought and feeling of their minds on the plastic beings to whom they are giving life and immortality.

NEW YORK, *June 14.*

Helen Bright Clark, daughter of John Bright, called on me with her husband, and we had a pleasant chat of over an hour. They are traveling extensively in this country. "Woman suffrage seems to be almost at a standstill in England," they said, "and we do not appear to know what to do to wake it up. Our women are not sleeping, but our male supporters,

especially those in Parliament from whom we expected
so much, are dead or discouraged." "My impression of the movement in Great Britain," I answered,
"obtained on the spot, was that you are all too afraid
of overstepping the conventionalities. Don't mind
the Mrs. Grundys, political or social, and do something, especially something that will attract attention
to the cause. The average Englishman has never
heard of woman suffrage." "I think you are right,"
they both said in chorus.

WEST HAMPTON BEACH,

LONG ISLAND, *July 28.*

We have been spending a delightful month here
at the seashore. The women are remarkably frivolous, and seem to know nothing of the vital questions
of the hour nor of the progressive steps made by their
own sex in the last fifty years. One lady asked me
what I meant by a "woman's paper." One evening
I gave them a well-attended lecture on the great
changes which have taken place in woman's position
during the last half century, and I distributed twenty
dollars' worth of "literature." So I trust a few seeds
were sown which may bring forth fruit in the various
localities to which these ladies return at the end of
the season. What can be done to strike these dull
minds and awaken them to the deep significance of
our agitation? Something sensational should be done,
like Miss Burr's march on the capitols. Once set a
woman to thinking, and she thinks faster and often
better than a man. But she has been kept under so

long, that she must be given the necessary momentum, and then how she will go!

NEW YORK, *September 16.*

I have been busy writing various articles, especially one entitled "A Remarkable Household." This household consisted of five rich women who paid heavy taxes, seven others who were well developed physically, but were less favored with worldly goods, and one little man of African descent whose head was the size of an apple, who had but one eye, who was lame, and whose only earthly possessions were his wages. Any one of these women could have thrown him over the wall. Yet, on the Tuesday following first Monday of each November, this little man did the voting for these twelve big women. He had a voice in the making of the laws of this Republic, while the twelve women had not a word to say in all this!

NEW YORK, *October 10.*

Is there any reason why women should take an interest in the pending election? Neither the orators in their speeches nor the party platforms mention our existence. These same politicians appear to be very anxious as to the status of the people in our newly acquired territory, but express no sympathy for the fifteen million women who might vote at this election if permitted to do so. Bryan and Roosevelt alike are flying in all directions talking with tears in their eyes, against the wrongs of various classes of men, but neither has a word to say on the emanci-

pation of women and the tyranny of the ages in respect
to us!

NEW YORK, *October 17.*

We had a pleasant surprise this evening in the
sudden appearance of Moncure D. Conway, who has
just returned from Paris. He dined with us. Our
conversation was on the pending presidential election, and especially on the question of Imperialism.
I found him very much depressed over the wars in
South Africa and the Philippines. "I had hoped,"
he said, "that long ere this, England and America, the
leading liberal nations of the globe, would have risen
to the moral altitude of settling all disputes by arbitration and not by war."

NEW YORK, *November 12.*

My eighty-fifth birthday. I have received telegrams and letters of congratulation from hosts of
friends in every part of the country. But these last
days have been shadowed by toothache. What a
nuisance teeth are, and yet what a blessing. Mine
have done good service for these long years. I asked
the dentist to-day if he could patch me up for five
years longer, as I wished to live as long as my maternal
grandmother did, and thus maintain the family reputation for longevity. While in the chair, I told Doctor
Carr that if I had my life to live over again, I would
marry a dentist that I might have some one on the
watch-tower all the time to look after my molars,
cuspids and bicuspids. It has been a very serious
task to take myself, seven children and, worst of all,

my husband, to these trying dental operations during more than half a century. The last named, who should have been our chief prop on all such occasions, used to declare that he could not summon up courage to have a tooth out unless I was there to laugh at him.

NEW YORK, *December 3.*

This morning the Woman Suffrage Bazaar opens at the Madison Square Garden. I had thought of going, but have been persuaded not to do so. I seldom go to crowded places, and always have pure air coming into my apartments, waking or sleeping. I am writing articles, long and short, all the time. Last week I had something in seven different papers. The December number of the *North American Review*[1] contains an article of mine, and so does the *Cosmopolitan*. In a word, I am always busy, which is perhaps the chief reason why I am always well.

---
[1] "Progress of the American Woman."

1901

NEW YORK, *February 12.*

We have celebrated Lincoln's birthday by reading aloud extracts from his writings, and recalling the principal acts of his checkered career. I have never forgotten the only time I ever saw him. It was during a private call on him in Washington in the early part of the Civil War. He was then not antislavery enough for me, an old Garrisonian abolitionist. So I went to the White House prejudiced, and came away in much the same state. But I see now the wisdom of his course, leading public opinion slowly but surely up to the final blow for freedom, and to-day, in my mind's eye, I enjoy that visit more than when I actually made it. My conscience pricks me now when I recall how I worked and prayed in 1864 for the defeat of Lincoln's re-election, and now I perceive what a grave misfortune it was that he was not left to reconstruct the South according to what would surely have been a better and wiser plan than that pushed through by the Radicals with whom I then stood. So when his birthday comes round each year I celebrate it somewhat in sackcloth and ashes.

NEW YORK, *February 22.*

This is Washington's Birthday. I think it probable, by the way, that the little hatchet which Mrs. Carrie Nation is just now using so effectively among the rum-shops of Kansas is the same one with which Washington cut down the famous cherry tree; for it is as much talked about. The fact is that it is high time women started up somewhere to revenge the wrongs of their husbands, fathers, brothers, and sons, on those wicked rum-sellers, by emptying the vile whisky bottles and barrels into the streets. I wish we had ten thousand "Madame Nations," smashing the gilded mirrors and ornaments in the haunts of vice in every state of the Union.

NEW YORK, *February 25*.

We had a long call last night from a member of the House of Commons. He says that England is in a very depressed condition owing to the war and the death of the Queen; that neither King Edward nor his son have any physical or mental stamina; that the national debt is beyond all bounds, and that hundreds of families are mourning their loved ones lost in "this insensate Boer adventure." Altogether, dear old England was never before in so sad a plight, if all this is true.

NEW YORK, *April 29*.

Carrie Chapman Catt [1] lunched with me the other day. We suffragists are all rejoicing over a bill which has just passed the Legislature giving to tax-paying women the right to vote on municipal improvements in this state. But if men recognize the justice of granting to women a voice in what affects their purse,

---

[1] At another point in the Diary Mrs. Catt is referred to as—"a good speaker, fine looking and a woman of rare common sense and executive ability."

why not also in those things which touch their moral and spiritual interests? Oh, the shortcomings and inconsistency of the average human being, especially when this human being is a man trying to manage women's affairs!

NEW YORK, *May 1*.

Prince Kropotkin was to have called to-day, but he writes me from the Hotel Gerard that he was attacked with the grippe in Chicago, and has had a relapse which has uspet all his New York plans. He is confined to his room and sails for Europe to-morrow, I believe. He sends me his Memoirs. A grand man who has suffered much for his principles.

NEW YORK, *June 3*.

Ida Husted Harper dined with me this evening. She has done with her pen and through the press a splendid work for our cause.

NEW YORK, *June 5*.

I have been very busy the last three months rewriting my reminiscences for a new edition, and preparing my speeches, essays, and miscellaneous articles for publication in book form. In looking over what I have written during the past sixty years, I am surprised with the excellence of the chirography and the ability of the composition, if I may be permitted even in the secrecy of my Diary to throw bouquets at myself.

NEW YORK, *June 8*.

The suffrage convention began at Minneapolis on May 30th, and lasted a week. It was very largely attended, and was one of the most enthusiastic ever held. But perhaps what is a more significant sign is the fact that the New York *Sun* gave us a column every day during the sittings, the first metroplitan daily that ever did us such a good service. Susan wanted me to go to the convention, but I replied I thought she and I had earned the right to sit in our rocking-chairs and think and write. But it occurred to me later that that would be purgatory for Susan!

WARDENCLYFFE, L. I., *July 12.*

We are down here on the Sound for the summer. Nikola Tesla has his laboratory near us. He said to me the other day: "It is possible to telegraph to all parts of the earth without wires." Think of it! Where will the wonders of science end?

WARDENCLYFFE, *August 25.*

We are reading the *Life of William Lloyd Garrison*, by his children, a most interesting biography to me, for I knew personally so many of the actors whom these four volumes bring on the scene. They are a mine of information to American reformers, and bring out clearly the character and personality of the noblest man I ever knew. We have finished Tolstoy's *Resurrection*. It is the saddest of novels. I see that the Russian Church has just excommunicated him. But little will he care for that, if we may judge from his writings. Marion Crawford's *In the Palace of the King* is in strong contrast to Tolstoy's novel—ending to every reader's satisfaction. We are reading *Ten-*

nyson's Life, by his son. We are sandwiching in between these various books a good deal of Mark Twain, whose fun is only equaled by his morals.

NEW YORK, *October 10.*

A note received to-day from ex-Speaker Reed reminds me of how often he has spoken out openly for woman suffrage. The first time I saw him, if I am not mistaken, was in January, 1882, when I was in Washington for our annual convention. Our effort to secure a special committee on woman suffrage, which had often failed, was finally successful, due largely to Mr. Reed, who was at that time a simple Representative from Maine and had not yet become a national figure. In 1884, his name stood at the head of the House minority report in favor of a 16th amendment granting the suffrage to women. He once said to me: "When the eleventh hour strikes, we will all flock in clamorous for pennies!"

NEW YORK, *October 20.*

I met recently Kate Stephens,[1] and the conversation coming on to life and death, she quoted some Greek author who said: "Not to be born is the best thing of all; but when one has been born, to go as quickly as possible thither whence one has come is much the second best thing." I told Professor Stephens that I did not at all agree with the first part of this statement, though I would accept the second part if it referred to a person wasting away on a bed of sick-

[1] Professor of Greek at the University of Kansas (1878–85).

ness. "To go as quickly as possible thither whence one has come" is the way I should like to die when the time comes.

NEW YORK, *November 6.*

The election passed off most triumphantly and Seth Low has been chosen mayor of New York. We trust that Croker and Tammany are buried too deep ever to be resurrected again. The women of the city took a very active part in the campaign and were the means of raising nearly $40,000 for election expenses.

NEW YORK, *November 12.*

I am eighty-six years old to-day. The first thing to arrive was a cablegram from England, followed by letters and presents from all parts of the country. My parlor looks like a flower garden. Fanny Garrison Villard sent me twelve magnificent chrysanthemums, some of them measuring nineteen inches in diameter, and a year's subscription to the *Evening Post,* of which her son Oswald is one of the editors, and which in a day or two will celebrate its centennial. Mrs. Villard tells me that Alexander Hamilton was one of the founders of the *Post.* I reminded her of that fine remark of his, which I have so often quoted in the crusade for woman's elevation: "Give a man a right over my subsistence and he has a power over my whole being."

NEW YORK, *December 5.*

Theodore writes me from Paris about a pleasant call he made recently on Maeterlinck, who lives not far from him in a queer old house in the quaint Rue

Raynouard. I remember the street very well, having gone up there once when I was last in Paris to see the site where Franklin lived when he was American Minister to France during our Revolution. Theodore says he was charmed with "the modest, plain, gentle ways of this big, sturdy Belgian or rather Flemish writer." His letter came while I was reading Maeterlinck's last book—*Wisdom and Destiny*—and marking this passage, which seems to me so true: "However clear, advanced, and independent may be our conception of duty, justice, and truth, it will naturally never be so clear, advanced, and independent as it will be some years or centuries later. We would do well, therefore, to go as promptly as possible to the extreme point of what we see or hope for." This would be a good rule for reformers to follow and always bear in mind.

NEW YORK, *December 22.*

Adelaide Johnson has just dined with us and told us of a haunted house in which she lives, staying bravely alone there at night, seeing visions and hearing strange sounds. Her narrative gave us "creeps" up the back as if we had been reading "The Fall of the House of Usher," or some other Poe creation. I do not ridicule these stories, for in my own life I have had several marvelous experiences. But I attribute all these strange phenomena to some natural laws which we do not understand and may never understand.

1902

NEW YORK, *January 5.*

The Grimm brothers were trained by their mother to write their delightful fairy tales; yet nobody can tell me anything about this mother, a remarkable example of the German custom of sinking the woman entirely in the man, one of the weak characteristics of that powerful race. Julius says she was traveling once in Bavaria, when a German father, wife, and half a dozen children came into the compartment of the train. While the father sat all the time comfortably reading, the weary mother devoted her every minute exclusively to the little ones. At a station she even got out and brought her husband a glass of water! This was too much for Cousin Lizzie; so when he, at the next station, left the train "in order to stretch my legs a little," as he complacently said, she remonstrated with the wife at not putting some of the burden of the care of the children on her selfish spouse. Whereupon, the mother answered in a surprised tone, "Why, we cannot do too much for him, he is the father of all these children!"

NEW YORK, *February 10.*

We have just finished reading a little volume by Annie Nathan Meyer, which tells the history of the persecution to which women were subjected in this country in their early efforts to secure an education, and to gain admittance to the trades and professions. I feel sure the men of America will feel ashamed some day when they look back and see how hard they made it for women to get an equal place in this world.

NEW YORK, *February 20.*

Anna Garlin Spencer called to-day. I found her as ever most suggestive. When I expressed some impatience that so many people seemed indifferent to the suffrage cause, she said she often thought we should not blame the lukewarm too severely as we were really asking them to turn back to things which had been discussed and decided long ago. Political enfranchisement, she quite rightly urged, occupied the best thought of America at the time of the Revolution. And again, after the Civil War. Mrs. Spencer carried me with her when she argued that now when the nation had turned away from the discussion of the mechanics of government to the more humanitarian consideration of what government could accomplish, there was naturally some impatience with those who proclaimed with insistence that the mechanics must be taken up again. Logically, our enfranchisement ought to have occurred in 1776, or at least in Reconstruction days. And that was what I urged in the sixties. Our movement is belated, and like all things too long postponed now gets on everybody's nerves.

NEW YORK, *February 24.*

Though I could not be present at the recent woman suffrage convention at Washington, I sent a paper on

"Educated Suffrage," which was read by the Rev.
Olympia Brown.   Kate Gordon, the corresponding
secretary of our association, writes me: "Your able
paper was read to us and was appreciated by all
present."   My own impression is that this document
is the best thing I have written this past winter.   I
hold that it is quite as important for a man to be able
to read and write the English language intelligently,
in order to vote, as it is that he be twenty-one years
of age.   The growth of the mind should mean as
much in citizenship as the growth of the body; perhaps even more.

NEW YORK, *March 21.*

To-day's papers announce the death of Judge Noah
Davis at the age of eighty-three.   I had thought him
at least as old as I am, for he looked so the last time I
saw him.   When we met he did not seem to nourish
any ill-will towards me for the rather ungloved manner
in which I handled him in the *North American Review*
some years ago.[1]   As we parted, he remarked pleasantly, referring to this article, "Well, as Pittacus
once said, 'forgiveness is better than revenge.'"   And
I replied with, "Pray you now, forget and forgive."
To-day, while this able jurist lies dead only a short
distance away, I find a soothing pleasure in recalling
how gentle our last words on this earth were.

NEW YORK, *April 14.*

In a few days we are expecting Miss Anthony to
make us a visit.   She has had a very remarkable

---

[1] See *ante*, June 28, 1884.

dream. The physician ordered her from Philadelphia to Atlantic City for her health. While in the latter place, she had a very vivid dream one night. She thought she was being burnt alive in one of the hotels, and when she arose in the morning, told her niece what she had dreamed. "We must pack at once and go back to Philadelphia," she said. This was done, and the next day the hotel in which they had been, ten other hotels and miles of the boardwalk were destroyed by fire.

NEW YORK, *June 2.*

A Finnish lady, just arrived from Helsingfors, called to-day and gave me the latest news of my old friend Baroness Gripenberg, who is one of the leaders of the woman's movement in that far-off and radical land. She is president of the Finnish Woman's Association and is the author of several books, among them being *Six Months in the United States*, a one-volume account of her visit to this country in 1888, when we crossed the ocean together. Baroness Gripenberg has been taking great interest in the revival of home industries and was sent recently by the Finnish government to study this question in several foreign countries. She has always had a strong affection for me as I for her and has often expressed regret in her letters that I cannot follow her work, "because," as she once said to me, "I am so far away and it is all told in a language which nobody reads." [1]

---

[1] "Your mother's letters used to be such treasures to me," Baroness Gripenberg wrote in 1906, "that I carried them with me to my friends and read them to them. What your mother was to me, I can never explain; I owe her so much as to my whole development. I could not agree with

WARDENCLYFFE, *August 1.*

Somebody has said: "*A morning* of ardor and of
hope; *a day* of clouds and storms; *an evening* of gloom
closed in by premature darkness—such is the melancholy sum of what the biography of Men of Letters
almost uniformly presents." I don't know how it is
with men of letters, but with me it is not so. The
designation of the "morning" and the "day," I will
accept, but so far my "evening" has had no "gloom"
worth speaking of, and much less any "premature
darkness," for of course the author of these reflections
refers to spiritual things.

NEW YORK, *October 1.*

I am expecting to meet this month or next two very
distinguished Englishmen, pronounced woman suffragists, who are coming over to America to attend
the ceremonies in connection with the inauguration
of the new Chamber of Commerce building. I refer
to Sir Albert Rollit and Mr. F. Faithfull Begg. The
first, though a member of the Conservative party,
is very radical in many directions. He calls himself
a "progressive and independent Conservative." His
second wife is the Duchess of Sutherland, which takes
me right back to the 1840 World's Convention. I
met him in London during my 1890-91 sojourn in
England, when he had charge of the Women's Fran-

---

her on the religious question, but the difference in our views on this point
did not alter in any way my personal feelings for her. Among the happiest
experiences of my life is my having had the honor to know her. So long
as I live and work, I shall feel her influence, the inspiration of her personality and her teaching. I infinitely regret that I could not go to America
again whilst she was living, and that my work had to be carried on in a
language and a country which were unknown to her."

chise bill in the House of Commons and made a strong fight for the measure. He once wrote me: "On April 28, 1892, my motion for the second reading of the bill was defeated only by a narrow majority, and I believe it would have been carried but for a speech by Mr. Gladstone." What a marplot Gladstone has been in English public life. Sir Albert was presented with a memorial of thanks, signed by many hundreds of the supporters of the measure, for his services to our cause. I was reading to-day in Sir Richard Temple's *Life in Parliament,* these lines, which I think quite true, referring to this matter: "He [Sir Albert Rollit] discharged his task with remarkable ability, tact, and skill. Never has that cause been better advocated than by him. The debate disclosed much warm support, but also much of insuperable opposition, Mr. Gladstone being included among the opponents." So this M. P. also evidently lays much of the blame for defeat at the door of Gladstone. Mr. Begg is much the same sort of man, mingling politics and stock-broking, and is especially interesting to me because his mother was a sister of Emily Faithfull. I have always felt that Mr. Begg's ten years' sojourn in New Zealand, though this happened before the women got the vote there, did much to broaden this big-minded man.

NEW YORK, *October 17.*

On Sunday, October 12th, a long article of mine on the divorce question appeared in one of the New York papers. Three days later came this postcard from a Chicago lady whom I do not know: "To-day's

American has a half-page that should be framed, or, better still, writ large or megaphoned everywhere. How many hearts to-day will thrill in response and how many heads will begin to think. It is by a G. O. W. God bless her! So say we all of us." [1]

Letter to Theodore Roosevelt

NEW YORK, *October 25, 1902.*

DEAR SIR,—As you are the first President of the United States who has ever given a public opinion in favor of woman suffrage, and when Governor of New York State, recommended the measure in a message to the Legislature, the members of the different suffrage associations in the United States urge you to advocate, in your coming message to Congress, an amendment to the National Constitution for the enfranchisement of American women, now denied their most sacred right as citizens of a Republic.

In the beginning of our nation, the fathers declared that "no just government can be founded without the consent of the governed," and that "taxation without representation is tyranny." Both of these grand declarations are denied in the present position of woman, who constitutes one-half of the people. If "political

---

[1] This was the last entry in the Diary. But Mrs. Stanton was active with her pen on her favorite themes to the very end. During the closing week of her life she was engaged in preparing documents and a letter to President Roosevelt urging the claims of woman suffrage. The very last letter she wrote was addressed to Mr. Roosevelt, and was dictated to her secretary on October 25th, twenty-four hours before her death. This letter to the President and the documents were to have been revised and signed on Monday. The drafts were found inserted loosely between the last pages of the Diary. The letter is given above as it was left.

power inheres in the people"—and women are surely people—then there is crying need for an amendment to the National Constitution, making these fundamental principles verities.

In a speech made by you at Fitchburg, on Labor Day, you say that you are "in favor of an amendment to the Constitution of the United States, conferring additional power upon the Federal Government to deal with corporations." To control and restrain giant monopolies for the best interests of all the people is of vast import, but of far vaster importance is the establishment and protection of the rights and liberties of one-half the citizens of the United States. Surely there is no greater monopoly than that of all men in denying to all women a voice in the laws they are compelled to obey.

Abraham Lincoln immortalized himself by the emancipation of four million Southern slaves. Speaking for my suffrage coadjutors, we now desire that you, Mr. President, who are already celebrated for so many honorable deeds and worthy utterances, immortalize yourself by bringing about the complete emancipation of thirty-six million women.

With best wishes for your continued honorable career and re-election as President of the United States.

ELIZABETH CADY STANTON.

THE END